framed

framed

LESBIANS, FEMINISTS, AND MEDIA CULTURE

Judith Mayne

University of Minnesota Press / Minneapolis London

For information on the copyright and original publication of particular essays, see page 213.

Unless otherwise noted, all images are from the author's private collection.

Published by the University of Minnesota Press
111 Third Avenue South, Suite 290
Minneapolis, MN 55401-2520
http://www.upress.umn.edu

Library of Congress Cataloging-in-Publication Data

Mayne, Judith.
Framed : lesbians, feminists, and media culture / Judith Mayne.
p. cm.
Includes bibliographical references and index.
ISBN 0-8166-3456-4 (acid-free paper) — ISBN 0-8166-3457-2
(pbk. : acid-free paper)
1. Women in motion pictures. 2. Feminism and motion pictures. 3. Feminist film criticism. 4. Lesbianism in motion pictures. 5. Women on television.
I. Title.
PN1995.9.W6 M359 2000
791.43'652042–dc21

00-008440

Printed in the United States of America on acid-free paper
The University of Minnesota is an equal-opportunity educator and employer.

11 10 09 08 07 06 05 04 03 02 01 00 10 9 8 7 6 5 4 3 2 1

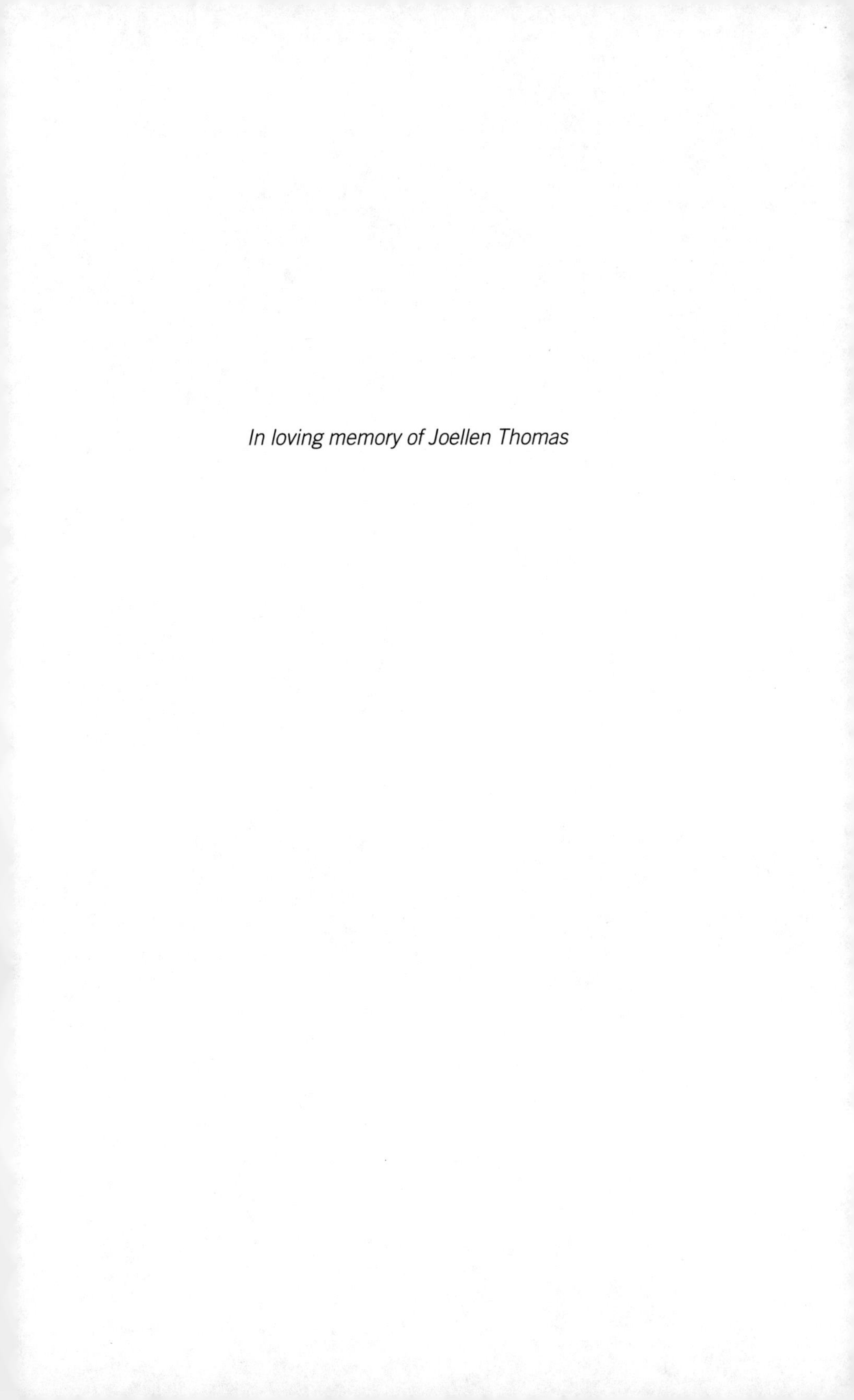

In loving memory of Joellen Thomas

Contents

Acknowledgments ix

Introduction xi

I. Cherchez la Femme Fatale

1. Marlene Dietrich, *The Blue Angel,* and Female Performance 3
2. Female Criminality and Servitude in Claude Chabrol's *La Cérémonie* 23
3. Inversion and Lesbian Plots in Henri-Georges Clouzot's *Les Diaboliques* 41

II. In and Out: Feminism in Mass Culture

4. Walking the *Tightrope* of Feminism and Male Desire 67
5. *L.A. Law* and Prime-Time Feminism 79
6. Fear of Falling 103
7. Caged and Framed: The Women-in-Prison Film 115

III. Lesbian Looks

8. A Parallax View of Lesbian Authorship 149
9. Julie Zando's Primal Scenes 161
10. Girl Talk 179
11. Su Friedrich's Swimming Lessons 193

Permissions 213

Index 215

Acknowledgments

I thank Joellen Thomas, for her wit, her courage, and her friendship. Other friends and colleagues have provided various forms of support and encouragement for which I am grateful; thanks to John Bush, Teresa de Lauretis, Gwendolyn Foster, Su Friedrich, Laura George, Mitchell Greenberg, Stephen Heath, Bill Horrigan, Lucretia Knapp, Linda Mizejewski, A. J. Nania, Yvonne Rainer, B. Ruby Rich, Jennifer Terry, Marie-Claire Vallois, and Julie Zando. For institutional support, I am grateful to the College of Humanities, the Department of French and Italian, and the Department of Women's Studies at the Ohio State University. I owe an enormous debt to the staff members at the BIFI (Bibliothèque du Film) and the Bibliothèque de la littérature policière in Paris. For research assistance, I am grateful to Jodi Lastman, Nancy Mortell, and Melanie Sklarz, and for technical assistance, to Todd Post. A special thanks to Terry Moore.

Introduction

The essays collected in this volume span approximately fifteen years of my involvement in the field of feminist film studies. I call this field feminist film studies rather than feminist film theory because I am less interested in claiming theory for its own sake than in incorporating theoretical inquiry into studies of individual films. Feminist film theory has generally been understood as having to do not just with theory in the large sense—that is, an understanding of how knowledge is produced, how critical assumptions are made, and how specific texts fit into larger patterns of meaning—but with a very particular kind of theory, shaped by the intersection of psychoanalysis, Marxism, and semiotics (especially psychoanalysis), as well as by a particular time, the mid-1970s. My own exposure to what were then new theoretical models coincided with my own graduate education, as well as my discovery of the cinema as an object of study. Film studies became a kind of testing ground for the insights of these new theories, which might be described in shorthand as theories of the subject. For film offered both a semiotically and culturally rich form and a relatively young art form that attracted the attentions of those seeking to rethink our understandings of representation.

In the past twenty years, theoretical trends have come and gone, and theory "wars" have provoked heated discussions of a kind that can only seem dramatic in academia. In feminist film studies, feminist film theory remains resolutely associated not only with theories of the subject but especially with psychoanalysis. I do not think there are too many fields that continue to debate and reflect on a single essay, Laura Mulvey's 1975 "Visual Pleasure and Narrative Cinema." Mulvey's essay set the psychoanalytic terms of analysis—the male gaze, defined by Oedipal crises, and the nature of visual pleasure, relying as it does on the objectification of the female body—which have remained stubbornly in place, even as they have been contested and redefined. It is not my purpose here to go over, once again, the strengths and limitations of Mulvey's argument or of the relevance of psychoanalysis to film studies. Rather, I would like to introduce this volume of essays by reflecting on some of the questions that feminist work on film and related areas, like television and popular culture, has raised about the very nature of theory.

As a graduate student in French in the early 1970s, I was introduced to film studies at the same time as I was introduced to semiotics, structuralism, and poststructuralism. The theorist and critic whom I remember as most influential at the time was Roland Barthes, and his work, which only tangentially related to film studies, was nonetheless taken up in the analysis of film by people like Raymond Bellour, Thierry Kuntzel, and Stephen Heath. Phrases like "pratique signifiante" (signifying practice) or "le degré zéro de l'écriture" (zero degree writing) or "le pluriel limité" (limited plurality) rolled off the tongue and made writing and representation, criticism and theory more dynamic and palpable to me than my admittedly limited exposure to theory and criticism had before. Theory was, in short, seductive, and it promised the possibility of seeing in a new way.

Poststructuralism has become the shorthand term for the ways in which the theoretical inquiries of the 1970s have been distilled into a diverse critical methodology that examines the manifestations of the subject in representation, presumably while questioning both the overarching claims and the self-aggrandizing aspects of theory. In this sometimes vaguely defined (and often confusing) poststructuralist universe, psychoanalysis may be more or less important, but it functions more often as a perspective, not as a theoretical model in its own right. This does not seem to be the case in film studies, and especially in feminist film theory, where psychoanalysis remains omnipresent as theory and method. One of the standard criticisms of the allegiance to psychoanalysis is that it promotes a master theory, a monolithic paradigm. But as much as poststructuralism has criticized theories that propose grand explanations of everything, the tendency toward overarching, monolithic pronouncements may well be a function of theory itself.

Batya Weinbaum has a wonderful anecdote about her own attraction to Marxism. On a trip to Latin America, Weinbaum is having a conversation with a male Marxist, during which they move to a balcony and watch the political turmoil going on in the streets below them. "I was scared," she writes. "But the fellow next to me on the balcony was an economist. He was also a Marxist. And he remained calm. I decided to return to the states, study economics, and become a Marxist in the hopes that I, too, could learn to stand calmly overlooking chaotic situations" (1983, 9). Weinbaum may be describing Marxism specifically, but I believe her anecdote can stand for the ways in which virtually all theoretical discourses function, on some level, as a way of providing a position of mastery, however mediated or problematized. While there are many reasons why Marxism is no longer the preoccupation it once was, theories of the political remain, sometimes considered totally of a piece with psychoanalysis, and sometimes defined in relationship to other factors. Witness the extent to which contemporary film studies, feminist or otherwise, still insists on subversion, on the radical potential of a given film (or more commonly in the past several years, on the radical uses to which audiences may put a given film or television show). Some work may well be subversive, or politically radical, but I suspect that this is as much a desire to adhere to some standard of mastery, of effectiveness, of relevance, as anything else.

When I look back on my own discovery of contemporary theory (and with my own privileged hindsight), I also see that desire for relevance, that desire to ensure that the analysis of film meant something. But I also see a passion that had far less to do with Marxism or psychoanalysis than with the sheer joy and pleasure of analyzing film closely, of seeing it literally transformed once one began to look at the choices involved in a single scene, at the beauty of how individual pieces of celluloid were transformed in the editing process. My interest, then as now, is not in theory as an autonomous area of inquiry but, rather, in how the acts of looking and seeing are transformed when one looks differently. To be sure, what I saw was shaped by the theoretical context of the time—Classical film creates a passive subject! Shot reverse shot objectifies the woman! Discontinuous editing decenters the subject!—but of utmost importance was learning how to see. Thus, what seems to me most important in those years of theoretical hypothesis and grand claims about Oedipal scenarios and castration anxiety is not the theory but the practice, and specifically, the practice of textual analysis.

The practice of textual analysis promised to bring film from the darkened corners of passively consumed fantasy into the bright light of active spectator involvement, through strategies of defamiliarization and so-called materialist analysis—materialist in the most literal sense of the term. The analytic tool of choice was a Steenbeck editing table, where individual scenes were clocked, frames counted, dialogue transcribed. Textual analysis took Roland Barthes's *S/Z* as a model, trying to create for film that patient, exhaustive breakdown of the text into its components, so as better to analyze how they delayed, deferred, or otherwise prolonged the Oedipal patterns of crisis and resolution. Yes, there was a sense that you knew from the outset what you were going to find. But there was also a sense of discovery, a sense of seeing in a way you had not seen before, a sense of finding what exceeded theoretical truisms.

Part of what made textual analysis so exciting at the time was the radical transformation it allowed of the film object. Now that cable television, laser discs, and DVDs, not to mention videotapes, make film much more accessible, textual analysis has lost some of its power and mystique. Raymond Bellour, who was perhaps the most articulate practitioner of textual analysis, describes the film text as "le texte introuvable," the "unattainable text," and many of the methods deployed in 1970s film theory were, paradoxically, intricate modes of analysis that often seemed to affirm, rather than challenge, that very unattainability. While the availability of new technologies would seem to have made the unattainable text attainable, a new unattainable text has taken its place—the audience. Particularly as influenced by cultural studies and the attempt to contextualize the individual text, contemporary film studies retain a fascination with what is most difficult to pin down, to grasp, to theorize in a way that does justice to the complexity of the object.

Yet what connects the two seemingly opposed points of reference (the individual film text, the audience) is spectatorship. The preoccupation with spectatorship—with how the cinema speaks to desires and fantasies, whether by analysis of the "implied spectator" in an individual film's construction, or of the various exhibition practices that shaped how audiences would view films, or of interviews with audiences about their viewing practices—has been constant in film studies of the past three decades. Psychoanalysis has been central to these inquiries, although not always in a positive sense. In the 1970s, theories of spectatorship tended to adapt a psychoanalytic model, and the emergence of feminist film theory both followed that model and suggested the problems with it, particularly insofar as the female spectator was concerned. More recently, approaches to spectatorship have proposed other possibilities, especially having to do with reception.

Laura Mulvey's analysis of the classical Hollywood cinema may rely on psychoanalysis, but her categories of the male gaze and the female object of the gaze make sense without psychoanalysis. Psychoanalytic critics may then argue that Mulvey's argument is lost without an understanding of the unconscious, but given how the unconscious itself in many psychoanalytically inspired works functions as one more object to be explained and mastered, one could argue that this is no great loss. Put another way, then, it is not always clear where textual analysis ends and the psychoanalytic begins, in the sense that many of the categories of cinematic textual analysis are very much defined by psychoanalytic film theory.

Constance Penley, in her introduction to a collection of classic feminist film theory, praises the authors in the collection for taking film theory on its own terms, which means taking psychoanalysis on its own terms. Penley stresses that none of the authors adopts the "what if?" approach to psychoanalysis, including, as she says, "most commonly: What if we could hold on to the notion of the unconscious and dream-work, and just forget about castration and the Oedipus complex?" (1988, 2). The withering description that follows makes clear the status of psychoanalysis as a theory-not-to-be-contradicted, at least at the time of the book's publication in 1988: "These 'what if's' are no more than the signs marking the well-worn dissident paths of a reductive biologism, sociologism, or mysticism of the feminine. . . . The essays in this volume have rejected such alternatives inasmuch as they represent merely another version of the easily accepted . . . or the already known" (2).

To be sure, Penley is defending psychoanalysis at a time when feminist film theorists were engaged in not always polite debate about its uses. But what I find particularly striking in Penley's account is the unexamined premise that what film theory had adopted was some pure definition of psychoanalysis. Isn't film theory already a "what if" about psychoanalysis, namely, what if psychoanalysis were adapted to read films, not people? What if psychoanalysis became not a medical practice but a cultural one? What if psychoanalysis became a self-sufficient method for understanding artistic production? I'm not objecting to the "what if's," far from it, but I am wondering why psychoanalysis seems to demand either loyalty or rejection, and why it continues in film theory to be the theoretical standard against which all others are measured. I am not by any means a psychoanalytic critic or theorist, but neither am I willing to dismiss all that psychoanalysis has offered film theory. "What if's" not withstanding, I am more interested in how certain insights of psychoanalysis offer perspectives, not absolute certainties. At the same time, it is worthwhile noting just how much critical vocabulary is indebted to psychoanalysis, and how extensively the very possibility of cinematic textual analysis is indebted to a certain understanding of psychoanalysis.

I refer to psychoanalysis in particular because it has had such a privileged theoretical position in film studies. It may well be that feminist film theory has been so influenced by psychoanalysis because of the nature of film theory; in other words, that the *feminist* in feminist film theory has been more defined by film theory than by related fields of feminist inquiry. The intersection of feminism and psychoanalysis exists outside of the boundaries of film studies, but nonetheless feminist film theory has been far more influenced by psychoanalysis than other areas of feminist analysis. It is useful, then, to imagine feminist film studies as drawing on the resistances to psychoanalysis that have characterized other feminist projects, not in order to refute them or to claim the superiority of feminist film theory but to situate and resituate a conversation that draws on the particular qualities of the cinema as well as the ways in which cinema exists in relationship to other objects and other practices. Central to virtually all feminist theory and criticism is the engagement with contradiction, whether between the status of women as agents and as victims, or in the terms that Teresa de Lauretis uses in her book *Alice Doesn't: Feminism, Semiotics, Cinema* (a work, not coincidentally, that draws on film theory and psychoanalysis as well as semiotics and anthropology) between woman as image—that is, as object for the male subject—and women as historically defined subjects. Linda Gordon describes feminist method as "liminal," as opening up a space between the competing demands of domination and resistance, of evidence and interpretation: "My sense of a liminal method is . . . a condition of being constantly pulled, usually off balance, sometimes teetering wildly, almost always tense. The tension cannot be released. Indeed, the very desire to find a way to relax the tension is a temptation that must be avoided" (1986, 22). The tension to which Gordon refers is made possible only when theory retains its sense of hypotheses and perspectives, not of absolutes or models to be imposed.

Many of the essays in the present volume are not only about women in the cinema but about lesbianism in the cinema and in television. Queer theory and gay/lesbian studies have challenged feminist film theory not only for its reliance on psychoanalysis, which has been a source of contention from the earliest years of the field, but also and especially for its narrow definition of sexual difference. Yet many of the issues that have been central in the articulation of lesbian questions vis-à-vis feminist film theory are not unfamiliar; they echo questions about female spectatorship that have been posed throughout the history of feminist film studies. For instance, at the beginning of *Vampires and Violets,* the first book devoted entirely to an analysis of lesbians and film, Andrea Weiss observes that her study follows from a contradiction: "The relationship of lesbians to the cinema has always been complex. . . . it resembles a love-hate affair which involves anticipation, seduction, pleasure, disappointment, rage, and betrayal" (1992, 4).

The love-hate affair suggested here is not unlike claims that have been made for female spectatorship. It is as if the examination of lesbian spectatorship involves considering lesbians as female spectators, but as female spectators with a difference. If lesbians have a long history of a love for the movies—despite the failure of the movies to reciprocate—then it comes as no surprise that much of the work in lesbian film studies focuses on examining this apparent paradox. Just as this paradox underlies the concept of lesbian spectatorship, so too does the notion of lesbian spectatorship itself inflect the various components of lesbian film studies: film history, theory, reception, and artistic representation. This does not mean that lesbians respond in a particular way to the cinema, or that there is a universal "lesbian viewer," but rather that in significant ways lesbian culture, lesbian communities, and lesbian identities have been shaped by the ways in which films are watched, imagined, and understood.

The reception of *Fried Green Tomatoes* (1991), for instance, suggests that lesbian viewing involves much more than a simple identification with (or rejection of) cinematic images, or—to use the language of feminist film theory—more than a choice between invisibility or co-optation by Oedipal desire. *Fried Green Tomatoes* is one of many recent films that simultaneously opens up and closes down lesbian possibilities. *Fried Green Tomatoes* appropriates the codes and conventions of Hollywood romance to visualize the relationship between Ruth and Idgie, from longing gazes exchanged meaningfully to the contrasting styles of butch and femme, not to mention scenes so loaded with lesbian symbolism (the beehive in particular) they seem to burst with it. *Fried Green Tomatoes* was extremely popular among lesbian audiences, but this popularity was definitely of a love-hate variety. The decision of GLAAD (Gay and Lesbian Alliance Against Defamation) to award the film a prize for best lesbian content may have been a strategic decision to try to foreground the invisible visibility of lesbians not only on screen but also in the audience (Pryor 1992). But many lesbians were as taken aback by the award as those legions of heterosexual viewers supposedly unaware that they had even been exposed to lesbian content. Perhaps the GLAAD award brought attention to the paradox of lesbian visibility (there and not there at the same time), but it is a mistake to assume that lesbian audiences who flocked to *Fried Green Tomatoes* did so because they confused the experience of watching *Fried Green Tomatoes* with that of identifying the film as "lesbian."

Lesbian spectatorship vis-à-vis *Fried Green Tomatoes* is not confined to "finding the lesbians" in the film or insisting that the only way the film makes sense is in lesbian terms, even though those strategies are a part of lesbian film culture. Rather, lesbian spectatorship is concerned with that space between visibility and invisibility. There is something liminal about the experience of watching *Fried Green Tomatoes,* knowing that others will be oblivious to what is totally obvious to you. This flirtation with lesbianism is matched, in a very peculiar way, by the film's insistence on a racist narrative, in the sense that the film presents a supposedly enlightened antiracist character in a decidedly racist way. Bell hooks identifies correctly the racist dynamic central to the film, but her opposition between the "progressive" quality of the film for white lesbians and its backlash racist narrative is off the mark: "In *Fried Green Tomatoes,* we may be transgressing a boundary about how lesbianism is pictured, but the images of black people in that film fit every sort of stereotype. . . . the film was simply a modern plantation story with a white-lesbian twist" (quoted in Jones 1992). The GLAAD award notwithstanding, the popularity of the film does not mean it is "progressive," and in any case if lesbian spectatorship is to be a useful concept, it cannot be reduced to a checklist of what films are "progressive" and what films aren't. Far from being progressive on one front and reactionary on another, the film marginalizes lesbianism and African Americans in similar ways, particularly by recycling old plots (the "plantation" film, the "female friendship" film) (Holmlund 1994; Vickers 1994).

Lesbian film studies are defined, theoretically, at a curious intersection between feminist film theory and queer theory. While the genesis of queer theory is complex, much of the work in queer film theory appears to be a response, explicit or not, to feminist film theory. For queer film theory insists on the wide range of responses to the cinema that are not reducible to the paradigm of sexual difference. However, as many lesbian commentators on feminist film theory have noted the extent to which *sexual difference* really means heterosexuality, so have lesbian commentators on queer theory noted how often *queer* really means gay male. While it is important to examine the limitations that theoretical perspectives create, it is equally important to historicize the ways in which questions are asked of the cinema. In this context, it is useful to consider an article titled "The Sapphic Cinema," which appeared in 1960 in *The Ladder,* the journal of the Daughters of Bilitis. *The Ladder* holds an important place in North American lesbian history for it was one of the first magazines written by, for, and about lesbians (see Soares 1998). Author LauraJean Ermayne notes that "in sober point of fact," few films can qualify as "little more than lesbian*oid*—only semi-sapphic in content—for *The Well of Loneliness* and the real butchnik pix in biliti-scope and sapphonic sound are still among the 'shapes' of things to come" (5). Ermayne then goes on to list twelve films, a "pitiful little list of films with at least a tinge of interest for the Uranian" (5). The films are *The Adventures of King Pausole* (Germany, 1933; directed by Alexis Granowsky); *Children of Loneliness* (United States, 1937; directed by Richard C. Kahn); *The Children's Hour* (United States, 1961; directed by William Wyler); *Escape to Yesterday* (France, 1935, aka *La Bandéra*; directed by Julien Duvivier); *Mädchen in Uniform* (Germany, 1931; directed by Leontine Sagan); *No Exit* (France, 1954; directed by Jacqueline Audry); *Open City* (Italy, 1946; directed by Roberto Rossellini); *Pit of Loneliness* (aka *Olivia*; France, 1950, directed by Jacqueline Audry); *Time of Desire* (Sweden, 1957; directed by Egil Holmsen); *Törst* (Sweden, 1949; directed by Ingmar Bergman); *Turnabout* (United States, 1940; directed by Hal Roach) (Ermayne 1960, 5–8).

Ermayne devotes special attention to the twelfth film, *Club des femmes* (France, 1936; directed by Jacques Deval), as a film that not only has a lesbian plot or a lesbian character but that is actually motivated by lesbian desire. Some of these films continue to appear on lists of "lesbians in the movies," such as *The Children's Hour* and *Open City,* and some of the films are still praised today as landmarks in lesbian representation (*Mädchen in Uniform* and *Olivia*). Unfortunately, many of the films on Ermayne's list are inaccessible or accessible only with great difficulty today.

Ermayne's exploration of the "sapphic cinema" is quite interesting for another reason. At the beginning of the essay, Ermayne compares her lesbian cinematic exploration to the work done by Forrest J. Ackerman in classifying and categorizing science fiction cinema. The comparison thus suggests that the lesbian perspective is every bit as valid as any other generic perspective in looking at motion pictures. But there is more, for LauraJean Ermayne was the pen name of Forrest J. Ackerman! Whatever one might think of Ackerman's lesbian impersonation, the Daughters of Bilitis welcomed him as an "honorary lesbian" (Matthesen 1995, 5). It is common to relegate *The Ladder* to a distant and quaint lesbian past, whereas the magazine may well have been far more queer, in today's lexicon, than is usually assumed to be the case. Ermayne's/Ackerman's explorations of the sapphic cinema are witty, provocative, and astute. "LauraJean Ermayne" may well be a man impersonating a lesbian, thus challenging any essentialist notions of lesbian spectatorship. At the same time, this impersonation enhances the validity of a lesbian perspective by insisting on what one might call, in homage to Ermayne, a "bilitoscopic" approach to the cinema.

Ermayne's sapphic cinema foregrounds lesbians' love-hate relationship to the movies. Ermayne bemoans the absence of interesting, exciting, tantalizing images, yet she takes enormous pleasure in making lists, teasing out the implications of what is there, cataloging possibilities. The sapphic cinema, as Ermayne defines it, is only secondarily a function of the films themselves; more aptly put, lesbian spectatorship is defined in the act of cataloging, of pastiche and recombination, and in the simultaneous work of "decoding" (an addendum to Ermayne's essay by Z. Newell describes a secondary character in one film as "obviously a lesbian" [1960, 9]). The preponderance of European "art film" titles perhaps suggests the white, middle-class aspirations for which *The Ladder* has been criticized; no B movies appear on Ermayne's list, for instance. This preference for European films reflects a desire to see not just lesbianism on screen but particular configurations of lesbianism that conform to ideologies of class and race and that offered the legitimacy of high art. At the same time, Ermayne is working with what was available at the time, what could be seen and appropriated by lesbian audiences.

The apparently simple and mundane activity of making lists of preferred lesbian films is informed by a theoretical perspective. Ermayne is drawn to the European art film; contemporary lists of preferred lesbian films (which are, now as in *The Ladder* in the 1960s, a common feature of lesbian magazines) gravitate toward classic Hollywood films (especially those featuring Garbo or Dietrich) and independent films by lesbian directors. Ermayne suggests the very possibility of lesbian spectatorship, and in doing so her perspective is informed by a variety of conscious and unconscious choices. If, from a contemporary perspective, there is something arcane about Ermayne's choices, it isn't because we somehow now possess theoretical tools to distance ourselves from the unenlightened past. Rather, the process of theoretical engagement is ongoing, partial, and necessarily self-reflective. If Ermayne's list suggests a desire for a particular aesthetic of lesbianism, then contemporary lists suggest a desire to find that erased presence in mainstream culture, while simultaneously inventing new languages of visibility. *Visibility* is a problematic term, and just as feminist film theory inspired by psychoanalysis insisted on questioning what is meant by the term *woman*, so contemporary inquiries into lesbian representation ask similar questions of the term *lesbian*. Questioning "visibility" is not the same as rejecting it. Following Linda Gordon's affirmation of a "liminal method," the point instead is to situate and understand, historically and theoretically, the desire to simultaneously affirm visibility and question it. And thirty years from now, someone may well look back at contemporary lists of lesbians and the movies and wonder at the choices, perhaps finding quaint the continuing preoccupation with Hollywood, or the fascination with Garbo and Dietrich, or the desire to make such lists in the first place.

All of the essays collected here are examinations of individual texts, and they reflect my own interest in reading the contradictory ways in which film and mass culture represent women, lesbians, and feminism. Part I, "Cherchez la Femme Fatale," includes three essays that focus on different manifestations of the transgressive woman. "Marlene Dietrich, *The Blue Angel*, and Female Performance," originally published in 1989, examines how, in the film by Josef von Sternberg that made Dietrich an international star, Dietrich's modes of performance change as she becomes more and more defined in relationship to Herr Rath, the schoolteacher who falls in love with her. "Female Criminality and Servitude in Claude Chabrol's *La Cérémonie*" explores the ways in which the murderous women in this film are defined as "potentially" lesbian, as well as how the film draws on one of the most famous criminal cases in French history, the Papin sisters' murder of their employers in 1933. "Inversion and Lesbian Plots in Henri-Georges Clouzot's *Les Diaboliques*" examines how the trope of inversion inflects Clouzot's adaptation of the novel by Pierre Boileau and Thomas Narcejac, as well as how the presumably heterosexual intrigue of the film is undercut by lesbian desire.

In Part II, "In and Out: Feminism in Mass Culture," I am concerned with feminist approaches *to* mass culture, but also and especially with how feminism is a part of mass culture. My assumption here is that feminism often appears in unexpected places. This should not be surprising, since both feminism and mass culture are attempts to respond to some of the same cultural preoccupations. In chapter 4, "Walking the *Tightrope* of Feminism and Male Desire" (originally published in 1987), I look at how, in what is perhaps the most self-reflexive Clint Eastwood film ever made, feminism and sexual violence are evoked in relationship to male heterosexuality. In chapter 5, "*L.A. Law* and Prime-Time Feminism" (first published in 1988), I look at the first season of the popular television series in terms of its very frequent engagement with feminist issues and sexual politics. In an epilogue to the essay, I look at what has become a famous moment in a later season of *L.A. Law,* when CJ and Abby, two women lawyers, kissed. Chapter 6, "Fear of Falling" (originally published in 1995) focuses on the world of ice skating, specifically through the spectacle of Tonya Harding and Nancy Kerrigan, and I suggest that the fall is one of the most important elements of the popularization of the sport. Chapter 7, "Caged and Framed: The Women-in-Prison Film" is a study of how race and lesbianism intersect in one of the most interesting film genres of all time.

Many of the essays in the book are concerned with lesbian representation, and in Part III, "Lesbian Looks," I examine the works of four contemporary independent film and video makers whose works offer beautiful and complex explorations of the stakes of lesbian representation. Chapter 8, "A Parallax View of Lesbian Authorship" (originally published in 1991), focuses on Midi Onodera's very controversial film *Ten Cents a Dance (Parallax).* In chapter 9, "Julie Zando's Primal Scenes" (originally published in 1993), I look at how the videos of Zando engage with psychoanalysis in relationship to storytelling and lesbian desire. Chantal Akerman's moving coming-of-age film, *Portrait d'une jeune fille de la fin des années 60 à Bruxelles,* is the subject of chapter 10, "Girl Talk." Finally, in chapter 11, "Su Friedrich's Swimming Lessons," I look at how, in Friedrich's haunting and complex meditations on desire, the family, and growing up, lesbianism is seen as possibility and potential.

Whether writing about relatively "classical" films (in Part I), about mass culture (in Part II), or about representations of lesbianism in experimental and independent film (Part III), I've attempted in all these essays to do justice to the complexity of the works themselves. The title of this collection, *Framed,* refers, of course, to the standard and stereotypical ways in which women have been imagined in classical Hollywood cinema and in feminist readings of it—framed by male desire, framed by the plot, framed by the conventions of Hollywood. At the same time, representation is impossible without some kind of frame, conceptual, formal, or otherwise, and so is any kind of theoretical or critical reflection. *Framed,* then, refers simultaneously to the limitations and to the possibilities of film and mass culture, and equally to the limitations and possibilities of theory and criticism. Framing embodies the contradictory impulses that I think are central to feminist critical practice.

Works Cited

Barthes, Roland. 1970. *S/Z*. Paris: Editions du Seuil.
Bellour, Raymond. 1975. "The Unattainable Text." *Screen* 16, no. 3: 19–28.
De Lauretis, Teresa. 1984. *Alice Doesn't: Feminism, Semiotics, Cinema.* Bloomington: Indiana University Press.
Ermayne, LauraJean. 1960. "The Sapphic Cinema." *The Ladder* 47: 5–9.
Gordon, Linda. 1986. "What's New in Women's History." In *Feminist Studies/Critical Studies,* ed. Teresa de Lauretis. Bloomington: Indiana University Press, 20–30.
Holmlund, Chris. 1994. "Cruisin' for a Bruisin': Hollywood's Deadly (Lesbian) Dolls." *Cinema Journal* 34, no. 1: 31–51.
Jones, Lisa. 1992. "Rebel without a Pause (Interview with bell hooks)." *Village Voice Literary Supplement,* October: 30.
Matthesen, Elise. 1995. "Vampires and Aliens: Pam Keesey and Eleanor Arnason." *Lavender Lifestyles,* 24 November, 2–6.
Mulvey, Laura. 1975. "Visual Pleasure and Narrative Cinema." *Screen* 16, no. 3: 6–18.
Newell, Z. 1960. "Addendum—*The Goddess.*" *The Ladder* 47: 9.
Penley, Constance, ed. 1988. *Feminism and Film Theory.* New York: Routledge.
Pryor, Kelli. 1992. "Women in Love: Hollywood Has It Both Ways with *Fried Green Tomatoes.*" *Entertainment Weekly,* 28 February, 6–7.
Soares, Manuela. 1998. "The Purloined *Ladder*: Its Place in Lesbian History." In *Gay and Lesbian Literature since World War II: History and Memory,* ed. Sonya L. Jones. Binghamton, N.Y.: Harrington Park Press, 27–48.
Vickers, Lu. 1994. "Excuse Me, Did We See the Same Movie? *Fried Green Tomatoes.*" *Jump Cut* 39: 25–30.
Weinbaum, Batya. 1983. *Pictures of Patriarchy.* Boston: South End Press.
Weiss, Andrea. 1992. *Vampires and Violets: Lesbians in the Cinema.* London: Jonathan Cape.

I

Cherchez la Femme Fatale

1. Marlene Dietrich, *The Blue Angel*, and Female Performance

In recent years, feminist critics of the classical narrative cinema have attempted to rethink and reformulate the widely held view that the seductive pleasures of the cinema are rooted in voyeurism and fetishism, and structured by the polarities of the active, male look versus the passive, female object. It has been pointed out frequently enough that Laura Mulvey's famous formulation of the man as "bearer of the look" and woman its object assumes a male spectator (1975, 11). Accordingly, increasing attention has been devoted to the vantage point of the female spectator, and to the ways in which a consideration of female spectatorship might then complicate, problematize, or otherwise put into question cinematic seduction understood as the regime of rigid gender polarity and heterosexual desire. Analysis of female spectatorship raises questions concerning how the cinematic apparatus addresses the sexual differentiation of spectators, and how spectators respond to films in ways that may well be unauthorized but nonetheless meaningful, in terms other than those prescribed by the institutions of narrative cinema.

A promising direction for such explorations of the multiplicity of spectator positions, as opposed to the monolithic position of the spectator implied by the scenario of castration anxiety, is the analysis of stars—of actors and actresses and the myths generated about them (Britton 1983, 1984; Dyer 1979; Hansen 1986; *Wide Angle* 1985). Recent studies of stars and the phenomenon of stardom have suggested the insufficiency of a number of critical and theoretical models in film studies. However different they may be in other ways, both traditional studies of the film auteur and more recent psychoanalytically based theories of the cinematic apparatus, for instance, share a definition of the cinema as reducible to a single, homogeneous entity, be it the film director or the apparatus. Analysis of stars has emphasized, by contrast, the shifting and sometimes contradictory levels at work in the creation of a "star image," challenging the definition of actors as mere vehicles for a director's vision, and challenging as well the notion of the "ideal spectator" as constructed and contained by the institutions of the cinema. Examination of the appeal of stars offers the possibility, then, of an understanding of cinematic seduction attuned to the contradictory movements of desire, and to scenarios of pleasure that exceed narrative formulas—whether the formula in question is the naive articulation of an author's vision or the more complex (but equally reductive) reenactment of castration anxiety.

Richard Dyer states that

> star images function crucially in relation to contradictions within and between ideologies, which they seek variously to manage or resolve. In exceptional cases, it has been argued that certain stars, far from managing contradictions, either expose them or embody an alternative or oppositional ideological position (itself usually contradictory) to dominant ideology. (1979, 38)

Along those lines, Andrew Britton's study of Katharine Hepburn begins with the following affirmation: "The significance of the great female stars of the Hollywood cinema for feminist cultural studies lies in the contradictions they generate within narrative structures which are committed overall to the reaffirmation of bourgeois-patriarchal norms" (1984, 1).

Marlene Dietrich is a particularly appropriate example of the difficulties and complexities of a feminist reading of the female star.[1] Her sexual ambiguity has been noted more than once, in the sense both of her androgynous beauty, underscored by her appearances in drag, and of her transgression of heterosexual boundaries (for instance, the famous scene in *Morocco* where Dietrich kisses a female member of the audience) [(Bell-Metereau 1985, 103–10]). Moreover, Dietrich's presence on screen virtually always implies a detachment, a sense of cool irony, even though her film roles often lead to an affirmation of sacrificial love and devotion. The myth of Dietrich as it has developed both on and off screen is without question full of contradictions. Her relationship with director Josef Von Sternberg remains the most famous example of the myth of the Hollywood director as Svengali, the actress as Trilby. Little in Dietrich's career leads us to believe that theirs was a collaboration of equals, even though it was Dietrich who emerged the more successful when their collaboration ended. Dietrich was also reputed to be an extremely difficult star who demanded control over her image, particularly later in her film career. Alfred Hitchcock, who worked with her in *Stage Fright* (1950) said: "Miss Dietrich is a professional. A professional actress, a professional dress designer, a professional cameraman" (quoted in Walker 1984, 174). Similarly, the image of Dietrich that circulated through the popular press, and fan magazines in particular, focused constantly on the glamour queen who was really a hausfrau and a devoted mother, suggesting her contradictory status as an image, one that required regulation by recourse to stereotypical myths of woman-as-mother.

Central to many recent analyses of the female star is the notion of resistance, a subtle undermining of the very notion of woman-as-object-of-spectacle, with attendant implications for the film spectator for whom such ironic detachment may well be the basis for another kind of cinematic pleasure.[2] The notion of resistance is certainly a useful reminder that patriarchal discourse is neither a monolithic system nor a totally successful one in its objectification of the female body. However, the concept of resistance, if it is indeed useful in understanding the female star in relationship to female spectatorship, requires further elaboration. If a female character "resists" the power and authority of the male gaze, that resistance may well be nothing more than a temporary distraction, a brief interlude that serves to reinforce the conquest of the female body. Thus, using that resistance to read a film against the grain may be somewhat self-defeating. In other words, and as many critics have suggested, resistance may be a function of the classical cinema, and not an exception in absolute contradiction with narrative and visual momentum.[3]

Dietrich is often described as an example of a resisting image, and it has been suggested that many of her films are riven with contradictions.[4] *Blonde Venus* (1932) has received particular attention in this context, for the image of Dietrich as the title character Helen Faraday strains credibility. She is presented as a sexually enticing performer and as a mother who returns to the stage only to save her husband's life. That the film never manages successfully to integrate these two roles into a convincing whole has been taken as suggestive of a critique of women's position in patriarchy (Kaplan 1983, 49–59; Nichols 1981; Wood 1978). In a more general way, Dietrich has been cited as an example of an "exceptional" female star who consistently gets away with a return of the look—with, that is, an ironic commentary on the mechanics of performance and particularly on the sexual politics of the look. Dietrich's performance numbers are virtually always marked by a tone that ranges anywhere from subtle mockery to downright sarcasm. As a result of this attitude, so firmly identified with the Dietrich persona, even those performances that seem to entail a cutting-down-to-size of the Dietrich legend (such as *Destry Rides Again* [1939]) are never quite successful. For if one could argue that Dietrich's ironic presence is contained and thus recuperated by the narrative structures of individual films, one might argue as well that her cool detachment has its own kind of recuperative value.

The Blue Angel (1930) marks the first collaboration between Josef Von Sternberg and Marlene Dietrich, a collaboration that is credited with having brought Dietrich international stardom. She portrays Lola Lola, a seductive nightclub singer who embodies many of the characteristics that would become central to the myth of Marlene Dietrich: she is self-absorbed, disdainful of men, inexplicably mysterious, and above all, unquestionably and irresistibly desirable. Thus *The Blue Angel* deserves particular attention not only as a central text in the creation of the Dietrich persona but also as its founding myth. For Lola Lola is not unlike the actress to whom Von Sternberg was attracted, as he tells us in his autobiography, certainly for her face and her figure, but primarily for her "cold disdain" and "indifference" (1965, 231). *The Blue Angel* serves, then, as an appropriate vantage point from which to consider Marlene Dietrich and the phenomenon of resistance as constituting a seductive appeal of the cinema in its own right.

The story of *The Blue Angel* is well-known. A professor is humiliated and degraded by his fatal attraction to the cabaret performer Lola Lola. Every description, even a rudimentary plot summary, however simple and straightforward, is also a reading. Numerous accounts of *The Blue Angel* begin with an apparently innocent summary of the film. John Baxter describes the film:

> Emmanuel Rath, professor of English at a provincial high school, pursues a group of his pupils to a sleazy night club called "The Blue Angel," is infatuated with the cabaret singer Lola, gives up his career to marry her, and becomes a stooge in the troupe. Years later, the combination of Lola taking a new lover and his appearance on stage in the town where he once taught drives Rath insane, and he runs to his old school room, dying with his arms around the desk that was a symbol of his standing. (1971, 70)

The significant terms in Baxter's description are Rath's *infatuation,* and the fact that he *gives up* his career, while Lola later *takes* a new lover. For such terms assume that Rath is an innocent creature who is corrupted by

Marlene Dietrich as Lola Lola in *The Blue Angel.*

Lola. This reading may well be encouraged and authorized by the film, but it is just that—a reading. Similar readings are evident in the ways other critics describe significant details or the overall tone of the film. Alexander Walker says of Lola that she "regards the spectacle her victim is making of himself coolly and egoistically" (1984, 59). Donald Spoto describes the tone of "social and moral meanness" in the film that is located—"of course"—in the person of Lola Lola (1985, 26). What is assumed, then, about *The Blue Angel* is that however complex or ambiguous the film may be in other ways, it nonetheless tells a straightforward story of a man who is humiliated by a woman.

That there may be something askew in such descriptions of the film is suggested pointedly by Angela Carter: "[Rath's] marriage to Lola-Lola looks less like the surrender to a fatal passion than a grab at the chance of a lifelong meal ticket. How anybody has ever been able to see this film as the tragedy of an upright citizen of Toytown ruined by the baleful influences of a floozy is quite beyond me." Carter's reading of *The Blue Angel* takes as its point of departure another point of view, that of Lola herself, whom she describes as the "attractive, unimaginative cabaret singer, who marries a boring old fart in a fit of weakness, lives to regret it but is too soft-hearted to actually throw him out until his sulks, tantrums and idleness become intolerable" (1985, 122). This is a point of view that insists as well on the position of a *female* spectator, for whom *The Blue Angel* is another film entirely from the one described by Baxter, Walker, and Spoto.

While there is by now an impressive tradition in feminist criticism of reading "against the grain," Carter's remarks suggest to me much more than a counterreading of the film. I would argue, rather, that *The Blue Angel* is structured by a tension between different modes of performance, and that the image of Marlene Dietrich that emerges in this film cannot be reduced to the simple duality of the male look versus the female object of the look. Nor would I argue, as some critics have, that Dietrich subverts that duality by "returning the look"—a dubious subversion in any case, since such a return of the gaze affirms the duality and defines the female gaze as a reactive intervention.[5] If Dietrich has a resistant function at all, it is in articulating a mode of performance that is appealing and seductive precisely because it has a marginal place within the phallocentric logic of the gaze.

Professor Rath is a teacher whose authority over his male students is compromised by their fascination with Lola Lola. They look at photographs of her during class, and Rath discovers that even his prized pupil has pictures of this wanton female. Thus Herr Rath's first visit to the Blue Angel, the seedy nightclub where Lola performs, is motivated by a desire to affirm his authority by preventing the students from frequenting the club. This first journey to the Blue Angel is one fraught with obstacles, suggesting the enormous psychic and social distance between his world and that of the cabaret. With its excessive movements, its seeming disorder and anarchy, its proliferation of bodies and smoke and grotesque symbols of lust, the nightclub seems a far cry from the orderly and authoritarian universe of the professor's classroom.

Professor Rath's teaching skills are based on intimidation and mimicry. When a student recites Hamlet's soliloquy, he stumbles on "that is the question," unable to pronounce properly the *th* sound. Indeed, mimicry is something of a problem for Professor Rath, for his student's inability, or refusal, to perfect an English sound both reflects his own failure to impart an image of perfection and assures his position of authority. Likewise within the Blue Angel, mimicry is everywhere on display. Lola herself is a parody of certain images of female decadence and sexual attraction, recalling nineteenth-century femmes fatales as well as Wedekind's Lulu and Berlin cabarets of the 1920s (Baxter 1971, 68–69; Weinberg 1967, 84–85). She is a pastiche, a collection of allusions, exemplifying Roland Barthes's suggestion that "beauty cannot assert itself save in the form of a citation" (1974, 33).

Within the nightclub, though, mimicry has no pretense of authority. The first image that we see of the interior of the Blue Angel presents a spectacle that is in every way opposed to the spectacle of Rath's classroom, where there is clear demarcation of the boundaries between performer and onlookers, teacher and students. Lola is onstage, singing, surrounded by other women in the performing troupe onstage with her. Lola drinks from another woman's glass and casually wipes her mouth

Lola Lola onstage with the other performers at the Blue Angel.

with a piece of her costume. Scenery is changed in full view of the audience; the mechanics of performance are just as much part of the spectacle as the finished product. Lola is a curious object of attention, for distraction seems to be a fundamental principle of the cabaret: waiters shout orders over her song, and the stage is so full of women and stage props that it is difficult to center one's attention on her. Indeed, the close-up, the centering device par excellence in the cinema, is rarely used in the film, and during the first scenes in the Blue Angel, what few close-ups there are, are used for what seem initially to be quite inappropriate objects. A cardboard cherub, part of the stage scenery, is seen in close-up, foreshadowing the role that Rath will soon acquire; another close-up shows a very large woman who rolls her eyes in a mockery of sexual seduction. The close-up is used, in other words, to foreground and caricature performer and onlooker alike.

Most strikingly, of course, the cabaret is populated by women, of all shapes and sizes, both onstage and in the audience. In Rath's classroom, a female chorus is heard when Rath opens the windows while his class writes a composition. But whereas Rath can shut out those female voices at will simply by closing the window, the image of Lola, secretly circulating among his students, is not so easily contained. The female voice and the female body that are presented in such a fragmented way in the cabaret come together with a vengeance in the classroom. Lola sings off-key and she parades around in a variety of silly costumes, all of which parody the conventions of femininity, from the half-skirt that covers only Lola's front to the cutaway skirt that reveals her underwear and garters; from the excess of frilly stereotypes to the combination of male and female attire. And the female chorus remains, now a chorus most vehemently of the flesh as well as the voice.

The women who surround Lola onstage have from the outset an ambivalent status. It has been suggested that Von Sternberg surrounded Lola with "horses" to better accentuate her charms (Kyrou 1967, 194). The women onstage are of different shapes and sizes, but they are all plump. Donald Spoto remarks that Lola herself is plump, "but she's surrounded by so many who are downright fat that we don't notice" (26). Interestingly enough, however, there is little within the film to mark this differentiation between Lola and the "horses." To be sure, she is the featured performer, but when another woman carries on her song while Lola changes clothes, or when extremely heavy women are seen onstage, there is nothing in the reaction of the audience within the film to suggest that these women are somehow less attractive for their abundance of flesh. Put another way, there is more connection between the women of the Blue Angel than there is opposition, a connection defined by the open mockery and satire of the objectification of the female body. There is no hierarchy in the club comparable, say, to that of the classroom. The first glimpse that we have of the nightclub is remarkably suggestive of the carnivalesque mode famously described by Mikhail Bakhtin (1984): an abundance of flesh, a mockery of established conventions of taste and art, and a preoccupation with the body, and in particular with the lower regions of the body (emphasized by virtually all of Dietrich's costumes).

If I envision the female bodies onstage as something other than so many props to set off Lola, it is to suggest that there is more to *The Blue Angel* than the story of Professor Rath's fatal discovery of his libido. There is another downfall in *The Blue Angel* that may not have quite the dramatic contours of the professor's humiliation but that is crucial to a reading of performance in the film. This downfall is the disintegration of the carnivalesque world of the cabaret, a disintegration that is initiated, in narrative terms, by the scrutiny of the professor. For however much he appears to lose virtually every sense of bourgeois reason once he has become "contaminated" by the sheer erotic energy of Lola and her surroundings, Professor Rath nonetheless continues to exercise supreme narrative authority. The activation of his desires provides the necessary complications and oppositions to make a story.

However confused the professor is when he ventures into this alien world, his presence does initiate a significant change. When Rath first enters the nightclub, he becomes entangled in a fishnet and is suddenly caught unaware by a spotlight that the women turn on members of their audience. Rath may well be befuddled by suddenly being thrust into the limelight, but his position as a spectator within the film soon neutralizes the frenzied excesses of the performance initially associated with the Blue Angel. For if the professor is flung into the recesses of his own desires, a parallel reversal occurs in Lola. The professor makes a second visit to the nightclub, ostensibly to return Lola's underwear, which a student had mischievously placed in the professor's pocket. Kiepert (the manager of the performing troupe) and the proprietor of the club have arranged a rendezvous between Lola and a customer. Lola refuses the advances of the customer, and Rath creates a disturbance by insisting that the man leave Lola alone. Suddenly, it becomes clear that Lola has a desire for bourgeois respectability that is just as repressed as Rath's sexual desires. For Lola looks somewhat stunned when she says, "Someone fighting over me? That hasn't happened for a long time!"

Parallel to this revelation of another side to Lola is the emergence of a different kind of spectacle, one that provides a sharp contrast to the carnivalesque performance characteristic of the first nightclub scenes. When Kiepert seats Rath in the honored loge in the cabaret during Lola's performance of "Falling in Love Again," a conventional shot-reverse-shot, moving from (male) spectator to (female) performer, isolates the man who is falling in love and the woman who emanates her desirability. To be sure, there are disturbances in this neat symmetry: Lola is still surrounded by women performers, even if she is much more centered than in previous performances, and Rath's schoolboy giggles betray a male spectator who possesses little of the authority that we have come to associate with the subject of the look. Images of the clown—described by Siegfried Kracauer as a "silent witness" in the film (1967, 218)—and a female statue strain the symmetry of the scene but do not upset it. The traces of the carnivalesque atmosphere remain, in other words, but they have been repressed and marginalized.

It could be argued that the principal male subject of *The Blue Angel* is Kiepert, the manager of the performance, the master of ceremonies who stages the encounter between Lola and Rath. That the central struggle in *The Blue Angel* is between Rath and Kiepert becomes increasingly evident, particularly near the conclusion, when it is Kiepert who humiliates Rath onstage: the final performance number of the film, when Kiepert puts Rath in the role of student and orders him to crow, is a parody of Rath's teaching techniques. The scene suggests that mimicry has come full circle in the film. However, there is an enormous difference between the parody that concludes the film and leads to Rath's death, and the parody that characterizes the nightclub earlier in the film. Among the women, and between the women and the audience, there is little of the deadly humiliation that emerges when a spectacle is created from the power struggle between two men. And it is precisely that struggle that affirms a principle of male sovereignty.

The role of Guste, a secondary female character, is significant in this respect. When we first see the cabaret, Guste is one of many women onstage. She is the performer who continues Lola's song while Lola changes clothes, and she later scolds Rath mockingly when she discovers him holding Lola's underwear. Only when Rath comes to the Blue Angel with the intention of proposing marriage to Lola is Guste revealed to be Kiepert's wife. From that point on, she becomes a cliché, a nagging wife. Previously, Guste was associated with the ebullient and straightforward sexuality of the women in the cabaret; once Rath proposes, and once bourgeois order is imposed, she becomes nothing more than the stereotype of a conventional wife. The shift in representation of Guste thus reflects the changing mode of performance in the film, but with an interesting twist. Guste does not become the object of the male gaze in any typical sense, but her transformation in the film is determined by an equally phallocentric principle of narrative representation. Initially defined in terms of her identity as part of the community of women who appear onstage, Guste is suddenly removed from the world of performance proper. She then acquires a narrative function only by virtue of her relationship to Kiepert. Her heterosexual identity, and her connection to the manager of the performance, becomes visible only when the opposing worlds of Rath and Lola intersect.

After the marriage of Rath and Lola, the performances change even more drastically, for Lola performs virtually solo. Gone is the group of women sitting onstage, with the suggestions of the erasure of boundaries between spectator and performer; instead, Lola appears in the foreground of the image, accompanied by an orchestra or by a group of chorines—the visual equivalent of the chorus of voices heard early in the film in Rath's classroom. In Lola's final number, a rendition of "Falling in Love Again" that functions as an ironic commentary on Rath's final return to the schoolroom, she is isolated in a medium close-up, with virtually no background material. Lola's performance is now a mirror image of what Rath attempted to impose on his classroom, for she has become a perfectly containable image of a tart, a man-eater, a seductress and destroyer of men. To be sure, Lola is from the outset a superb mimic of the conventions of sexual desire, but her mode of imitation is playful and irreducible to the clichés of seductress that are produced in the course of the film. What *The Blue Angel* demonstrates, then, is the creation of an image of woman to the measure of male fantasy.

If Rath's attraction to Lola is fatal, then so too is Lola's attraction to Rath. Lola may emerge at the conclusion of the film as a conventional vamp, but the price paid for her victory—if indeed it can be called a victory—is her representability within the confines of patriarchal discourse. What *The Blue Angel* traces in the reciprocal seductions of the male bourgeois and the female performer is the transformation of one kind of performance into another: the transformation of a world of transgressed boundaries between spectator and performer, male and female, thin and fat, into woman defined, purely and simply, as object of the male gaze. In this sense, I would agree with Laura Mulvey's assertion that Von Sternberg produces the "ultimate fetish, taking it to the point where the powerful look of the male protagonist (characteristic of traditional narrative film) is broken in favour of the image in direct erotic rapport with the spectator" (14). However, what makes *The Blue Angel* interesting in these terms is not simply the fact of that "direct erotic rapport," but the way in which it is produced and manufactured during the course of the film.

What *The Blue Angel* offers, then, is the exposition of two conflicting modes of performance, and two conflicting modes of subjectivity—one a dissolution of the boundaries between self and other, the other an affirmation of them. But two questions remain as to the position of this carnivalesque mode of performance. The first is a narrative question: is this mode of performance evoked as a fleetingly glimpsed other world, as the embodiment of everything the professor fears and loathes? Is this carnival of female bodies and voices nothing more than the projection of male desire, the reverse image of the idealized woman? Or, rather, does *The Blue Angel* suggest another point of view, a position other than that of Rath or Kiepert or the presumably eager fetishist in the audience? The second, related question concerns the implications of a feminist reading of performance in terms that reach beyond this particular film. As Mary Russo puts it, "In what sense can women really produce or make spectacles out of themselves?" (1986, 217).

Gender identification in the cinema does not mean that female viewers identify automatically with women and male viewers with men. While *The Blue Angel* seems to insist on spectatorship as a complex and contradictory entity, it is presented in the film as a male-centered entity, where issues of pleasure and humiliation, activity and passivity, looking and being looked at, are posed from a uniquely male vantage point. Indeed, Peter Baxter's reading of *The Blue Angel* suggests quite convincingly that "around the sight of the female organ, and the threat of castration, the whole network of the fragmented and partially evident text spreads out" (1978, 23). Such a reading may expose the repressed fantasy of the text, but begins—as any reading must—with a vantage point, a narrative position, within the text. If *The Blue Angel* focuses so obsessively on a male point of view, how do the conflicting modes of performance acquire a separate point of view of their own?

The Blue Angel articulates male desire through a series of stages, from a group of schoolboys who gape and gaze at photographs of Lola Lola, to the professor's foray into the cabaret where he himself becomes a spectator of Lola's charms. For all its obsession with Lola's fatal powers of attraction to men, however, *The Blue Angel* introduces Lola not through the eyes of men but through the reaction of a woman. The film opens on a crowded village street. A woman worker opens the metal grill of a shop window and throws a bucket of water on the window. Displayed in the window is a poster of Lola Lola, her hips thrust forward in the provocative pose for which Dietrich is famous, with a cherub clinging to her leg. The woman proceeds to clean the window, seemingly impervious to what lies behind it. When she catches sight of Lola's legs, however, she pauses and imitates Lola's pose.

The first male response we see to Lola Lola is the reaction of the young men in Professor Rath's class who ogle photographs of her and blow on the feathers affixed to them in imitation of her costume. That these responses to the images of Lola are to be the narrative and symbolic matrix of the film is suggested from the way in which they are represented, and the difference between those actions and the actions that open the film. For the photographs are kept from the view of the film spectator until Professor Rath later discovers them in the notebooks of his prized pupil. The narrative strategies of delay and secrecy are thus marshaled in relationship to the male look and the female object of the look. In contrast, the image of the cleaning woman briefly imitating Lola's pose is flat, obvious, and transparent: there is no mystery here, and nothing worthy of narrative density or complexity. The surface separating the image of Lola from the cleaning woman, the shop window streaked with water, suggests some distance. But the gesture of imitation that this surface inspires pales in comparison with the ogling eyes and the pursed lips of the schoolboys who energetically blow the feathers concealing Lola's crotch. The female spectator thus identified in *The Blue Angel* is characterized by what Mary Ann Doane calls her "inability to fetishize" (1982, 80).

The cleaning woman suggests the two interrelated ways in which the relationship of women to the screen image has been defined in contemporary film theory. On the one hand, the female spectator is identified with the object of the male gaze; hence the position of the female spectator is a negative position, that is, one defined only by her absence. Female spectatorship defined in this way is predicated on the assumption of the cinema as the acting out of male desire; the dilemma, as Sylvia Bovenschen puts it, is that "woman could either betray her sex and identify with the masculine point of view, or, in a state of accepted passivity, she could be masochistic/narcissistic and identify with the object of the masculine representation" (1977, 127). On the other hand, female spectatorship has been defined as emanating from the role of women as consumers, hence the function of film as a "living display window" (Eckert 1978, 4). These two aspects of female spectatorship are in no way contradictory; indeed, the one functions as the visible support for the other. For what else do women consume, if not images of themselves made to the measure of male desire? And if the movie screen is in fact a display window, then the idealized figure reflected back to the female spectator is part of a fantasy in which she plays a role only as object and as consumer—never as subject.

The resulting role assigned to the female spectator is precisely what we see in the opening of *The Blue Angel*—mimicry. Mimicry is, as Luce Irigaray reminds us, the path "historically assigned to the feminine" (1985, 76). For the cleaning woman, consuming the image and identifying with it are one and the same process: they allow a momentary break in a routine, but one that the film will not pursue in any systematic way. But what, then, of the female spectator watching *The Blue Angel*? Recent discussions of female spectatorship have moved away from the denial of female spectatorship implicit in the polarities of the active male look versus the passive female image and have emphasized the multiple positions of identification and desire implicit in female spectatorship. As Teresa de Lauretis points out,

> The analogy that links identification-with-the-look to masculinity and identification-with-the-image to femininity breaks down precisely when we think of a spectator alternating between the two. Neither can be abandoned for the other, even for a moment; no image can be identified, or identified with, apart from the look that inscribes it as image, and vice versa. If the female subject were indeed related to the film in this manner, its division would be irreparable, unsuturable; no identification or meaning would be possible. (1984, 143)

Given the importance of mimicry in *The Blue Angel,* from the male student's inability (or refusal) to mimic his teacher's English sounds, to the profusion of parody and imitation that contributes both to the creation of the figure of Lola Lola and to the mode of performance associated with the nightclub, it would be mistaken to consider it as nothing more than the reified and objectified relationship of woman to the image. For what this film opens up is another space, another definition of mimicry: the playful, ironic imitation of the conventions of femininity and masculinity.

A risk encountered in the work of those who have used Bakhtin's explorations—indeed, a risk present in Bakhtin's own work—is the assumption that the mode of carnival is by very definition radical, posited from outside the dominant order rather than from within it, or at the very least posited as the discourse of those who are excluded from power and from dominant discourse. Such enthusiastic celebration of the carnival obscures the extent to which the carnival may exist as a safety valve, as a controlled eruption that guarantees the maintenance of the existing order (Stallybrass and White 1986).

In feminist terms, flirtation with the carnivalesque is equally risky. Equating the carnivalesque with female resistance to the patriarchal order may be a celebration of precisely those qualities that define women as irrelevant in patriarchal terms. Hence Juliet Mitchell, for instance, responds to the notion of the carnival as "the area of the feminine":

> I don't think so. It is just what the patriarchal universe defines as the feminine, the intuitive, the religious, the mystical, the playful, all those things that have been assigned to women—the heterogeneous, the notion that women's sexuality is much more one of a whole body, not so genital, not so phallic. It is not that the carnival cannot be disruptive of the law; but it disrupts only within the terms of that law. (1984, 291)

The risk, then, is ascribing a resistant function to an element that may function quite well within the logic of patriarchal discourse. While I agree that conflating the feminine with any of a number of murky regions, from the carnival to the pre-Oedipal, is a potentially conservative gesture, it is equally problematic, not to mention conservative, to define discourse as so dominated by a single, overarching structure that there are only either/or propositions—either one is within dominant discourse and therefore recuperated, or outside of discourse and therefore incoherent. A figure like Dietrich is both contained by patriarchal representation and resistant to it; this "both/and" rather than "either/or" constitutes the very possibility of a feminist reading of performance.

If *The Blue Angel* has a special place in the mythology of Marlene Dietrich, it is in part because the film articulates a narrative and visual structure that would be associated with Dietrich for virtually all of her career. As I have suggested, there are competing levels to that structure, so that it is not so much incorrect as incomplete to describe Dietrich uniquely in terms of her image as a femme fatale—that is, uniquely in terms of her status as object of the (male) look. The conflicting modes of performance represented in *The Blue Angel* suggest conflicting narratives and conflicting points of view. While it is tempting to label these narratives as "male" and "female," that temptation is better resisted, even though the difference established by the film at the outset between the cleaning woman and the boys in Rath's classroom suggests that there are indeed two distinct ways of looking at an image of the female body, two distinct desires—mimicry and possession. However, that difference is undone by the film, for what separates the conflicting modes of performance are radically different conceptions of address and of representation: a carnivalesque mode of performance where dualities are broken down, and a hierarchical mode of performance where they are reasserted most forcefully. To be sure, the space that links the cleaning woman to the carnivalesque performance of the nightclub is closed down in the film, swept away by the momentum of a conflict and collision of desires the most appropriate representation of which is the final rendition of Lola singing "Falling in Love Again." But *The Blue Angel* is but one chapter in another narrative, another story, which is the myth of Marlene Dietrich.

Indeed, the Dietrich image is fashioned precisely on the kind of structure articulated in *The Blue Angel*: the representation of a woman's body and of female performance as contained by certain stereotypes of the femme fatale and yet resistant to them. If *resistance* is, then, an appropriate word to describe the Dietrich image, it is not because Dietrich returns the male look but, rather, because that process of resistance is fully a part of the narrative and visual imageries that comprise the Dietrich persona. Feminist critics have perhaps accepted too blithely the proposition that cinematic discourse is fully and totally under the sway of patriarchal dominion. Sylvia Bovenschen reminds us that "an element of female resistance, if only a passive one, has always contributed to artistic production" (125). Dietrich embodies that element of female resistance with a vengeance.

Discussions of Dietrich, whether as a femme fatale or as resisting presence, tend to concentrate on the seven films made with Josef Von Sternberg. While these films may well be the most stunning demonstrations of the Dietrich persona, they form nonetheless only one part of her career. Dietrich continued to play the part of the sexually attractive woman long beyond the age when other actresses would have been relegated to the euphemistic category of character roles. As Mary Russo suggests, the aging female body is a particularly strong point of displacement in theories of the carnival, and in Dietrich's later films this remarkable actress functions consistently to "destabilize idealizations of female beauty" and to "realign the mechanisms of desire" (Russo 1986, 221).

Witness for the Prosecution (1958) is a particularly appropriate conclusion to this discussion of Dietrich and performance. Based on Agatha Christie's play, Billy Wilder's film version becomes among other things a retelling of *The Blue Angel.* Dietrich plays the role of Christine Vole, the wife of a man who has been convicted of murdering an older, wealthy woman. In flashback, Leonard Vole (played by Tyrone Power) tells of how he and Christine met in Germany immediately after World War II. Christine worked in a nightclub called The Blue Lantern, and a poster outside the club is virtually identical to the one seen in *The Blue Angel.* The spectacle inside the club is a quotation of the earlier film, but with some significant changes. Christine stands on a small stage, singing, playing her accordion (!), and wearing a man's jacket and pants (thus evoking many other Dietrich films in which she is dressed in male attire). The crowded club is populated only by men, and two men are designated in close-ups: Leonard and another man, a worker, who operates the spotlight. A riot breaks out and the police are called when the men, eager to see those legs advertised in the poster outside the club, rip Christine's pant leg. Leonard avoids the police, returns later, and begins a relationship with Christine. The Blue Angel that is evoked here is, perhaps not surprisingly, a particularly sanitized version of the first glimpse of the nightclub that is offered in the 1930 film. Here, there is certainly none of the topsy-turvy, frenetic performance that characterizes the cabaret but, rather, an image that corresponds to what is produced at the conclusion of Von Sternberg's film. For in this nightclub, Dietrich is unquestionably the object of the male look, suggested not only by the uniquely male audience, and by Leonard's designation as a privileged spectator, but also by the man with the spotlight. In *The Blue Angel,* we recall, it is the women onstage who turn the spotlight on the members of the audience.

Light has an important function in *Witness for the Prosecution* as a revelation of truth. Leonard Vole is presented initially in the film as innocent, particularly when Sir Wilfred (played by Charles Laughton), the lawyer who defends him, gives him a somewhat eccentric truth test: Sir Wilfred positions his monocle in such a way that sunlight shines directly and uncomfortably in his potential client's eyes. Leonard blinks only momentarily and then continues to speak, unflinchingly. By contrast, when Sir Wilfred applies the same test to Christine Vole, she fails miserably: quite uncomfortably, she shields her eyes from the light, moves to the window and closes the curtain. Christine "fails" the truth test, although she also refuses to play. That is, she refuses to play by their rules—"their" being a curious collection of men, certainly, but also the

English. ("What hypocrites you are in this country," Christine says when a lawyer suggests that Leonard was like a son or a nephew to the murdered woman.) What is revealed in *Witness for the Prosecution* is that Christine and Leonard are both playing parts, but unexpected parts: Leonard's facade of innocence and naïveté conceals a heartless, selfish murderer, whereas Christine's cool, icy exterior conceals a woman who is desperately in love with her husband and wants to save him at any cost, even though she knows he is guilty.

Christine Vole puts on a masterful performance, then, but the disruptive effects of that performance are quickly displaced at the conclusion of the film, when Christine's expert performance is revealed to be motivated by a single cause: her pathetic devotion to a man who couldn't care less for her. And yet this trick ending, quite apart from questions of effectiveness, needs to be seen in relationship to another revelation in the film. Christine's trump card is her disguise as a lower-class woman who presents Sir Wilfred with a set of letters ostensibly written by Christine, which establish definitively her perjurious testimony. Whether one guesses that this is Dietrich at this point or is surprised by the revelation at the end of the film seems to me entirely beside the point. For this grotesque female figure is the other side of Christine Vole, the other side of the Dietrich persona: her bulky flesh, her dress, her affected accent, her scarred face—all suggest the female mimicry characteristic of performance in *The Blue Angel.*

Witness for the Prosecution may present a version of the cabaret that represses virtually every sign of the carnivalesque performance in *The Blue Angel,* but the association between Dietrich and that other mode of performance erupts elsewhere, in the adoption of the disguise. The emergence of Dietrich in disguise speaks her affinity with another female body, with another kind of performance, in which mimicry and impersonation threaten to upset that theater of patriarchal law and order, the courtroom. The threat is dispelled in the narrative resolution of *Witness for the Prosecution,* as it is at the conclusion of *The Blue Angel.* But for those not so readily seduced by the dominant visual and narrative momentum of the classical cinema, Marlene Dietrich powerfully embodies the possibility of other desires and other modes of performance.

Notes

1. In his introduction to the study of Katharine Hepburn's star image, Britton says: "With the exception of Sternberg's Dietrich, who clearly constitutes a special

case, Katharine Hepburn is the only star of the classical cinema who embodies contradictions (about the nature and status of women) in a way which not only resists their satisfactory resolution in a stable, affirmable ideological coherence, but which also continually threatens to produce an *oppositional* coherence which is registered by the films as a serious ideological threat" (1984, 1).

2. E. Ann Kaplan says that "the female spectator may read the masculinized female image as a *resisting* image in a way that no male spectator would suspect" (1983, 50). Annette Kuhn describes how, given the masculine forms of address in mainstream cinema, women may be "peculiarly able to stand at a distance from the ideological operations of dominant cinema, in that the marginal place they occupy in relation to its address may be conducive to the formation of a critical perspective" (1982, 64).

3. Describing the work of theorists such as Raymond Bellour, Thierry Kuntzel, and Stephen Heath, Constance Penley says that "the contradictions and gaps that the feminists had been positivistically ascribing to the attempt to stage a feminine discourse in a patriarchal form or to the specific difficulty that the woman's image entails, were for the male theorists no more than necessary components of the classical film's illusionistic economy" (1984, 377).

4. For example, Julia Lesage writes that Dietrich "is used in Von Sternberg's films to defy patriarchy even though she is reabsorbed into the male plot structure" (cited in Citron et al. 1978, 90).

5. Although Gaylyn Studlar has proposed a theory of cinematic identification based on Gilles Deleuze's reading of masochism as an alternative to the voyeuristic-fetishistic model, she nonetheless describes Dietrich's function in the very terms of the model in question: "The Von Sternberg/Dietrich heroine is the object of male desire, but she is not the passive object of a controlling look. Dietrich looks back. . . . The female subverts the power of the male gaze. . . . Von Sternberg's films emphasize the active aspect of the female's gaze and the passive element in the male's look" (1985, 21–22).

Works Cited

Bakhtin, Mikhail. 1984. *Rabelais and His World.* Trans. Helen Iswolsky. Bloomington: Indiana University Press.

Barthes, Roland. 1974. *S/Z.* Trans. Richard Miller. New York: Hill and Wang.

Baxter, John. 1971. *The Cinema of Josef Von Sternberg.* New York: A. S. Barnes.

Baxter, Peter. 1978. "On the Naked Thighs of Miss Dietrich." *Wide Angle* 2: 18–25.

Bell-Metereau, Rebecca. 1985. *Hollywood Androgyny.* New York: Columbia University Press.

Bovenschen, Sylvia. 1977. "Is There a Feminine Aesthetic?" *New German Critique* 10: 111–37.

Britton, Andrew. 1983. *Cary Grant: Comedy and Male Desire.* Newcastle: Tyneside Cinema.

———. 1984. *Katharine Hepburn: The Thirties and After.* Newcastle: Tyneside Cinema.

Carter, Angela. 1985. *Nothing Sacred.* London: Virago.

Citron, Michelle, et al. 1978. "Women and Film: A Discussion of Feminist Aesthetics." *New German Critique* 13: 83–107.

De Lauretis, Teresa. 1984. *Alice Doesn't: Feminism, Semiotics, Cinema.* Bloomington: Indiana University Press.

Doane, Mary Ann. 1982. "Film and the Masquerade: Theorising the Female Spectator." *Screen* 23: 74–88.

Dyer, Richard. 1979. *Stars.* London: British Film Institute.

Eckert, Charles. 1978. "The Carole Lombard in Macy's Window." *Quarterly Review of Film Studies* 3, no. 1: 1–21.

Hansen, Miriam. 1986. "Pleasure, Ambivalence, Identification: Valentino and Female Spectatorship." *Cinema Journal* 25, no. 4: 6–32.

Irigaray, Luce. 1985. *This Sex Which Is Not One.* Trans. Catherine Porter. Ithaca, N.Y.: Cornell University Press.

Kaplan, E. Ann. 1983. *Women and Film: Both Sides of the Camera.* New York: Methuen.

Kracauer, Siegfried. 1967. *From Caligari to Hitler.* Princeton, N.J.: Princeton University Press.

Kuhn, Annette. 1982. *Women's Pictures.* London: Routledge and Kegan Paul.

Kyrou, Ado. 1967. "Sternberg and the Marlene Myth." In Weinberg 1967, 188–210.

Mitchell, Juliet. 1984. *Women: The Longest Revolution.* New York: Pantheon.

Mulvey, Laura. 1975. "Visual Pleasure and Narrative Cinema." *Screen* 16, no. 3: 6–18.

Nichols, Bill. 1981. *Ideology and the Image.* Bloomington: Indiana University Press.

Penley, Constance. 1984. "'A Certain Refusal of Difference': Feminism and Film Theory." In *Art after Modernism: Rethinking Representation,* ed. Brian Wallis. New York: New Museum of Contemporary Art, 375–89.

Russo, Mary. 1986. "Female Grotesques: Carnival and Theory." In *Feminist Studies/Critical Studies,* ed. Teresa de Lauretis. Bloomington: Indiana University Press, 213–29.

Spoto, Donald. 1985. *Falling in Love Again: Marlene Dietrich.* Boston: Little, Brown.

Stallybrass, Peter, and Allon White. 1986. *The Politics and Poetics of Transgression.* Ithaca, N.Y.: Cornell University Press.

Studlar, Gaylyn. 1985. "Visual Pleasure and the Masochistic Aesthetic." *Journal of Film and Video* 37, no. 2: 5–26.

Von Sternberg, Josef. 1965. *Fun in a Chinese Laundry.* New York: Macmillan.

Walker, Alexander. 1984. *Dietrich.* London: Thames and Hudson.

Weinberg, Herman, ed. 1967. *Josef Von Sternberg: A Critical Study.* New York: E. P. Dutton.

Wide Angle. 1985. Special issue on "Actors and Acting." Volume 4.

Wood, Robin. 1978. "Venus de Marlene." *Film Comment* 14: 58–63.

2. Female Criminality and Servitude in Claude Chabrol's *La Cérémonie*

One critic described Claude Chabrol's 1995 film *La Cérémonie* as a "sinister (and very French) version of *Thelma and Louise*" (Calderon 1996). The film does seem to exemplify what feminist critics have identified as a recent cinematic trend: the-woman-as-killer film, with a variety of subsets based on sexual identity. There is the woman killer who is explicitly lesbian (*Aileen Wuornos: The Selling of a Serial Killer,* 1992), or bisexual (*Basic Instinct,* 1992). Or there is the pair of women killers, one or both of whom is explicitly lesbian (*Butterfly Kiss,* 1995; *Bound,* 1996), probably lesbian (*Heavenly Creatures,* 1994), or not really explicitly identified as lesbian but occupying a position on the lesbian continuum somewhere beyond female friendship (*Thelma and Louise,* 1991). B. Ruby Rich notes that at the very same time that films with "happy lesbian endings" have been increasingly available (*Go Fish,* 1994; *The Incredibly True Adventures of Two Girls in Love,* 1995), this parallel trend has emerged: there is "a renewed interest in true-story movies about pairs of best friends . . . who bond their affections with the spilling of blood and then pay for their crimes." She asks the obvious question: "Lucky coincidence or sinister parallel?" (Rich 1995, xi). Lynda Hart reminds us that criminality and lesbianism have virtually always been associated in the popular and scientific imagination. And so when Hart turns to a film like *Thelma and Louise,* she notes that "the expectation for lesbianism between women who violate the law is so strong that the film works overtime to disavow it" (1994, 75).

To understand what makes *La Cérémonie* particularly French in its contribution to the trend of lesbian-inflected women-as-killer films, we need look no further than the career of the film's director. For Claude

Chabrol has been fascinated by female outlaws and their lesbian tendencies throughout his career. In some of Chabrol's films, such as *Marie-Chantal contre Docteur Kha* (1966) and *Les Biches* (1967), lesbian eroticism is evoked as part of a general atmosphere of deviance, betrayal, and mystery, and one could argue that lesbian desire is presented in fairly predictable ways as part of a male-centered, voyeuristic economy. More interesting, and more complex, are those films that focus on women who have become legendary in French history and culture for their supposedly astonishing crimes. Chabrol does not necessarily strike a blow for lesbian visibility in these films, but he does not adopt the strategy of disavowal noted by Hart, nor does he identify lesbianism in a necessary or simplistic cause-and-effect relationship with criminality. Rather, like virtually every aspect of Chabrol's approach to gender, lesbianism and criminality are presented with great ambivalence. Chabrol's films refuse to designate their heroines as either victims or villains. Instead, the films are marked by a relentless ambiguity—about the crimes, about the women who committed them, and especially about their status as victims, or agents, of their own lives.

Consider his 1978 film *Violette Nozière,* in which Chabrol explores the life of the woman who poisoned her parents in 1930s France and became a cause célèbre, an object of fascination for the general public as well as for French literary figures (Fitère 1975). Her father died, and her mother survived; Nozière later claimed that her father had molested her. The film marks the first collaboration between Chabrol and Isabelle Huppert, an actress noted for her laconic and understated mode of performance. Throughout the film, it is impossible to fix Violette in convenient categories of villain or victim, even when she makes her first remarkable change from an apparently dutiful young daughter (dressed as a girl and devoid of makeup) to a sexual woman (dressed in sleek adult clothes and heavily made-up) who sneaks out of her parents' apartment to look for fun and excitement. The film plays with and evokes the stereotypical duality of virgin and whore but never situates Violette neatly within either category. Violette's sexuality may well seem to be straightforwardly heterosexual, but her encounters with women throughout the film are charged with erotic possibility. Indeed, one could see the concluding scenes of the film, in which Violette shares her jail cell with another female prisoner (played by Bernadette Lafont), as offering a moment of erotic intimacy.

The final moments of the film are noteworthy as well for their ambiguous quality. A close-up of Violette, as she sits in her prison cell awaiting her final sentencing, is accompanied by a male voice-over (the voice is Chabrol's) describing her fate. The voice-over describes how the succession of various political regimes in France made decisions about Violette's life that had less to do with the nature of her crime and more to do with the desire to make of her one kind of example or another. Chabrol's voice is as flat and straightforward as Huppert's apparently detached and distant gaze. This classic example of gender division in the cinema—the voice of the male, the close-up of the female—is evoked here to sustain both the stereotype and its critique, and to open up an ambivalent space where Violette/Huppert and her cinematic creator are suspended in a space beyond the dichotomies of crime and innocence, of virgin and whore.

La Cérémonie is Claude Chabrol's forty-third film in a career that began in 1958 with *Le Beau Serge.* Chabrol is a member of that venerable group, the New Wave of French cinema, the group of critics for *Cahiers du cinéma* who turned to filmmaking and brought an amazing wealth of cinematic history and self-reflexivity to their work. Unlike his more famous compatriots, Jean-Luc Godard and François Truffaut, Chabrol has never been praised for reinventing the cinema. Even the remaining two of the original *Cahiers* group, Eric Rohmer and Jacques Rivette, have been defined by the conventions of "art cinema" throughout their careers. Chabrol is in many ways the odd man out of the New Wave, for his films have remained stubbornly and, some would say disappointingly, conventional. To be sure, Chabrol is still to this day compared to Alfred Hitchcock, but his work has never received the kind of sustained critical attention devoted to others of his generation. My point in this chapter is not to resurrect Chabrol as a reinventor of cinematic form, or to argue, as so many have done in relationship to virtually every French film director since the late 1950s, that his films represent an internal critique of the conventions of classical Hollywood cinema. I do want to argue that Chabrol's work as represented by *La Cérémonie* deserves a place of honor in its ability to create a narrative sustained by the force of female rage. Indeed, *La Cérémonie* is a stunning exploration of one of the most persistent and long-lasting figures of the cinema, classical or otherwise: the femme fatale, the fatal woman, best known in her incarnation in film noir as the beautiful and deadly heroine who seduces and betrays.

At first glance, the two heroines of *La Cérémonie* seem quite far removed from the standard incarnations of the femme fatale. As Sophie, Sandrine Bonnaire is plain and severe; it would require a real stretch to see her as embodying any of the sexual allure or sexual lures so typical of the femme fatale. Fatal she may well be, but femme? Hardly. Yet when Sophie meets Jeanne, the postal worker played by Isabelle Huppert, a peculiar union occurs. True, Jeanne is no typical femme fatale either, although she is certainly closer to the stereotype of the sexually desirable woman than Sophie. Jeanne is quite femme, but her fatal qualities are only revealed in the midst of her developing friendship with Sophie. *La Cérémonie* creates its femmes fatales not by the typical encounter (again, in film noir) between a male hero and a relentlessly attractive and inevitably treacherous woman, but by the encounter between two women.

It is no accident, then, that *La Cérémonie* begins with an encounter between two women, not the two murderers but Sophie and Catherine Lelièvre (played by Jaqueline Bisset), the woman who employs her as a maid. The scene takes place in an anonymous urban setting. We watch Sophie, in a long shot, as she goes toward one café and asks directions of a man who points her toward another café. As Sophie enters the café, we see the back of the head of a woman watching, the woman who will eventually be identified as Catherine Lelièvre. In other words, the scene is mildly deceptive. What appears to be anonymous narration is quickly identified with the point of view of the woman who is about to hire Sophie. While it is almost always a mistake to identify too closely the creation of point of view in the cinema with an overarching point of view in the more abstract sense, there is no question that our first introduction to Sophie Bonhomme—whose last name means literally "good man" or "good guy"—occurs through the perspective of her future employer.

After Sophie sits down with Madame Lelièvre, another apparently straightforward exposition device occurs: shot-reverse-shot, the movement back and forth between the two women in conversation, the one portrayed from the vantage point of the other. Yet here, too, subtle demonstrations of the power of the one over the other are performed. The transition from the shot of the two women to the shot-reverse-shot is motivated by Madame Lelièvre's apparently benign insistence that Sophie join her in a cup of tea (thus introducing a motif, tea, that will have ominous significance later in the film). The dialogue between the two women progresses, again obviously dominated by Madame Lelièvre's description of household duties. Yet something is amiss. When questioned as to whether the isolation of the house might bother her, Sophie provides a peculiar response: "Je ne sais pas" (I don't know). And just moments later, Madame Lelièvre alludes to the art gallery she maintains, thus signaling an appropriate opportunity for Sophie to express, or at least feign, interest in the lives of her employers. Yet a cut to a close-up of Sophie is accompanied by her blunt query as to whether Madame wants to see her references. From this point on, something seems to shift in the transaction, for as if reciting a script that she has prepared, Sophie describes the conditions of her current employment, and she is the one who must bring up the subject of salary.

"I don't know" is the phrase used by Sophie as a kind of bizarre catch-all response to virtually every situation that provokes her discomfort. When she arrives at the house and is shown her room, her employer waits for a stock, polite response as to how charming or comfortable it is and finally asks if the room is suitable. Sophie replies, "I don't know." When shown the library—which as we will later discover represents a forbidden and quite dangerous territory for Sophie—and when asked if everything is clear, she once again replies, "I don't know." And when Monsieur Lelièvre later inquires as to why she doesn't have glasses if she doesn't see well, she replies: "I don't know."

As the film progresses, what Sophie "doesn't know" becomes as clear to the audience as it remains unclear, and unreadable, to the family for whom she works. Like any secret, Sophie's illiteracy, and her desperate attempts to conceal it, has the power to disrupt. And we learn that Sophie has other secrets as well, including her likely, though never "proven," responsibility for her father's death. Some secrets are revealed in *La Cérémonie* and some aren't, and the film is unsettling in its uncovering of some secrets and its apparent disregard for others. The suicide of Monsieur Lelièvre's first wife, for example, is alluded to (by Jeanne, no less) but never really explained, and we are never given a full accounting of what happened between Sophie and her father. Indeed, the power of Chabrol's film lies in its indirection, in its apparently calm yet unsettling portrait of the clash of different social classes with results that are all the more explosive—literally and figuratively—for their apparently subtle exposition.

La Cérémonie is adapted from Ruth Rendell's 1977 novel *A Judgement in Stone.*[1] The novel begins with this sentence: "Eunice Parchman killed the Coverdale family because she could not read or write" (1978, 7). Illiteracy is announced as the very condition, the starting point, of the murder, which is described succinctly and gruesomely in these opening pages of the novel. So much for suspense, at least suspense in the straightforward commitment of a crime. Our attention is drawn in the novel, rather, to the conditions of the crime. Readers familiar with Ruth Rendell's mysteries will recognize the particular affectation of voice, the summoning up of a kind of omniscient wisdom that is both forceful and open to question.

In Rendell's novel, Eunice Parchman has a past, a life that precedes her employment by the Coverdales, the family who hires her. A lifetime of benign neglect is responsible for her illiteracy: "School had taught her one thing–to conceal, by many subterfuges and contrivances, that she could not read or write" (1978, 31). She tends to her mother until she dies and then takes care of her father. Despite the narrator's overarching commentaries on the bleakness of Eunice's world, a certain kind of intelligence is recognized. For Eunice—in direct proportion, it is suggested, to her illiteracy—has "compulsions" that she obeys, such as the sudden desire to walk: "These walks were her education. She saw things one is not taught in school even if one can read. And instincts, not controlled or repressed by reading, instructed her as to what these sights meant or implied" (33). This is how Eunice learns how to blackmail, by observing a woman who collects her mother's pension a year after her death, or a man whom she spies in a homosexual encounter. In a moment of despair and frustration, Eunice kills her father by suffocating him with a pillow. One of her blackmail victims, eager for their financial arrangement to end, convinces Eunice to apply for the job of maid to the Coverdale family, and so she does. The Coverdales are described as prisoners of their own imaginations and projections, particularly insofar as Eunice is concerned.

As in Chabrol's film, we first "see" the maid in Rendell's novel through the eyes of the woman who hires her:

> She saw a placid-looking creature with rather too small a head, pale firm features, brown hair mixed with grey, small steady blue eyes, a massive body that seemed neither to go out nor in, large shapely hands, very clean with short nails, large shapely legs in brown nylon, large feet in somewhat distorted black court shoes. (1978, 14)

Eunice is the ideal servant. The all-encompassing narration of Rendell's novel, with its exposition of the unconscious desires of its characters and the frequent examination of what might have happened otherwise if such and such an event did not occur, explores the inevitable route toward the murder of the family, which occurs both at the beginning and the end of the novel. Slavoj Žižek describes Rendell's narration in relationship to Lacanian psychoanalysis, a connection, as we shall see, that is also relevant to Chabrol's film:

> The story unfolds linearly except that at the very beginning Rendell reveals the final outcome and at every turning point draws our attention to the chance occurrence that seals the fate of all concerned. . . . Far from transforming the flow of events into a fated enchainment, the eruption of the point of view of the final catastrophe renders palpable the radical contingency of the events. (1991, 71)

A fateful encounter occurs when Eunice has one of her "compulsions" to go for a walk and meets Joan Smith, a postmistress whose primary vocation is her membership in a religious fringe group. In the group Joan holds forth at great length about her former life of sin, for she was once a prostitute. The bond between the two women is solidified when Eunice, much to her surprise, discovers that Joan cannot be blackmailed about her past for she welcomes every opportunity to describe it in lurid and patient detail.

The entire novel traces a collision course with the calm authority of a detached observer and an all-knowing intelligence. However supposedly enlightened the Coverdales, they are still masters, projecting their own desires and illusions onto a servant. Daughter Melinda is perhaps the worst offender, for she derides her family's assumption that a servant should eat in the kitchen, but she herself plays the bourgeoise, however unconsciously, when she has needs that require Eunice's dutiful attention. The lethal combination of Joan and Eunice allows the "servants" to turn a critical and deadly reflection back on the "masters."

Chabrol's adaptation of Rendell's novel has some expected contours. The setting is obviously French, although Chabrol chose St. Malo in Brittany in order to be as close to England as possible. The expected name changes occur: the Coverdales become the Lelièvres, Eunice becomes Sophie, Joan becomes Jeanne. As one would expect of the French Hitchcock, suspense is a factor in the film as it is not, at least not in the same way, in the novel, where the murderous conclusion is known from the beginning. Sandrine Bonnaire's Sophie has only a fragmented past, and Jeanne's religious activities are not only far less dramatic than in the novel—they are played for laughs. But the conclusion of the film follows the novel quite closely. Melinda (one of the few characters whose name does not change) discovers that the servant cannot read, and Sophie makes a threat of blackmail, which misfires. The maid is dismissed, and she and her friend in a murderous rage kill all the members of the family as they are watching Mozart's *Don Giovanni* on television, thus offering on two levels the spectacle of class conflict. While the

Lelièvre family watches the opera, Melinda tapes it with a tape recorder she had just received as a birthday gift. The tape recorder is the crucial piece of evidence, although in Rendell's novel another piece of evidence is equally important: Jacqueline Coverdale made notations about the opera in the margins of a printed television guide, which eventually demolishes the fake scenario created by Eunice to cover up her crime. (That it takes investigators a fair amount of time, and it is by chance that they discover the television guide, suggests that the world is not so neatly divided between the literate and the illiterate after all!) In the film as in the novel, the tape recorder transcribes the crime and provides a final spectacular demonstration of Eunice's, and Sophie's, exclusion from a symbolic universe as well as their guilt.

Perhaps the most striking change in Chabrol's film is the transformation of the two female leads from dumpy women in their late forties to women played by two of the best-known female actors in contemporary French cinema, who are younger and flashier than their onscreen counterparts.[2] Now this could be read simply as the "babeification" factor, that is, the perceived need to transform actual or fictive women of a certain age and commonness into gorgeous, alluring stereotypes of film starlets. But these two actresses bring with them not only the babe factor, but also interesting and complex histories that demonstrate how actors, and not just directors, create films. The collaboration between actors and directors is a well-known feature of New Wave cinema; one has only to think of Jean-Pierre Léaud, who literally grew up on screen as Antoine Doinel in the films of François Truffaut; or of Anna Karina, who became an icon of Jean-Luc Godard's inquiry into the politics of desire and representation. Given that Chabrol's films do not perform the kind of radical inquiry into cinematic representation that Godard's work does, the tendency has been to read his collaboration with actors such as Stéphane Audran (his former wife) and later Isabelle Huppert as more along the lines of the Hollywood model exemplified by Josef Von Sternberg and Marlene Dietrich, or, even more relevant, Hitchcock and the various blondes, like Grace Kelly and Tippi Hedren, who became projections of his ambivalence and misogyny (both on and off screen).

A famous anecdote in the history of cinema is relevant here: when Rouben Mamoulian was filming the final scenes of *Queen Christina,* in which Greta Garbo gazes into the distance as the camera moves slowly forward to capture her face in close-up, the director said to Garbo: "I want your face to be a blank sheet of paper. I want the writing to be done by everyone in the audience" (quoted in Milne 1969, 7). Isabelle

Huppert's acting style embodies the "blank sheet of paper" approach, with the most provocative results of that style in her collaborations with Chabrol. More specifically, with Chabrol, Huppert plays the roles of notorious women, legendary femmes fatales in their own rights. After *Violette Nozière* came *Une Affaire de femmes* (*Story of Women,* 1988), based on yet another true story of a woman, who was guillotined in France for having performed abortions during World War II. Huppert's most famous role is also one of her most maligned: her portrayal of Emma Bovary in Chabrol's 1991 adaptation of Flaubert's famous novel. I for one found Huppert's performance one of the few things to like in this film; she plays Emma Bovary not as a readable woman whose downfall can be understood, but as that proverbial blank page on whom are projected the "writings" of the various people in her life as well as of the members of the audience.

What a surprise, then, to see Isabelle Huppert as positively bubbly and ebullient in *La Cérémonie,* at least in relationship to her more familiar screen persona. Huppert is played against type in the film, and more precisely, against the very type elaborated in her work with Chabrol. As Jeanne, she bursts onto the scene in a blaze of color and energy, asking Madame Lelièvre for a ride into town from the train station where she has gone to pick up Sophie (one of many apparently banal, everyday occurrences with fatal consequences in the film). In this, her first film with Chabrol, Sandrine Bonnaire plays the type associated with Huppert—laconic, her face a mask, consistently unreadable. The union that is forged between the two characters in the film is not just a peculiar union of two deeply disturbed women, but also a union of two actors playing both with and against the associations of female stardom. Bonnaire has been associated with somewhat demonic roles, from the hitchhiker who actively alienates virtually everyone she encounters in Agnès Varda's film *Sans toit ni loi* (*Vagabond,* 1985), to the young woman who plots the demise of a man who has seen her involved in a crime in *Monsieur Hire* (1989). In *La Cérémonie,* Bonnaire's incarnation of Sophie draws on the previous roles associated with her screen persona and embodies at the same time the disaffection and marginalized presence associated with Huppert's image.

I've suggested that together Jeanne and Sophie, Huppert and Bonnaire, comprise a femme fatale. It is obvious that the two women complete each other, for Jeanne provides Sophie with both a mirror (note the braids that Sophie wears in apparent imitation of Jeanne) and a way to function in the world. Together they are fatal, certainly, but they

Isabelle Huppert (left) as Jeanne and Sandrine Bonnaire as Sophie in *La Cérémonie.* Courtesy of Photofest.

appear to lack one ingredient so central to the classic femme fatale—sexual allure, that is, the unspeakably powerful ability to lure men into traps they soon regret. Rather, any sexual attraction occurs between the two women. It is quite difficult to assess who lures whom: the post office worker finally given an entry into the bourgeois world she enjoys hating so much, or the illiterate maid who finds a mediator between herself and the world, one whose first act of "translation" is pointing out the best brand of chocolate. This much is clear, however: the shared past of suspected murder without any proof—infanticide for the one (Jeanne's daughter died under mysterious circumstances), patricide for the other—seals a bond between the two women.

Indeed, the scene where the shared past is revealed is one of the most effective in the film. The two women are seen in Jeanne's small apartment, which contrasts with the large country home of Sophie's employers. Sophie has learned from Monsieur Lelièvre that Jeanne was accused of the murder of her own daughter and was found innocent for lack of proof. Sophie presents the information to Jeanne almost gleefully, telling her friend that she knows something about her. But Jeanne immediately replies by telling Sophie that she knows something about her, too, and she displays a newspaper clipping about the suspicious fire that killed Sophie's father. The two women dissolve in giggles as they collapse onto Jeanne's small bed, suggesting perhaps a prelude to a sexual encounter. But no such encounter occurs; rather, the attraction between the two women is suspended, held over the film as a potential event that might well erupt as easily as their laughter. The connection between criminality and lesbian attraction is made forcefully yet indirectly, for the revelation of the respective crimes of the two women functions as a kind of flirtation. The repetition of the phrase "On n'a rien prouvé!" (They didn't prove anything!) suggests that their crimes, like lesbianism in its stereotypical forms, are both there and not there, present and absent at once.[3]

The two main women characters in *La Cérémonie* may well have been transposed from the pages of Ruth Rendell's novel, but they also have an unmistakable historical reference. In 1933, in the small French town of Le Mans, two sisters, Christine and Léa Papin, who worked as maids in the home of the Lancelin family, committed murder. Madame Lancelin and her daughter returned home to find the house in darkness and reprimanded the sisters for having blown a fuse while performing their domestic duties. Christine and Léa, who had been known for their conscientious performance of their duties and for their quiet and meek manners, not only killed their mistress and her daughter; they did so with such vehemence and rage that no one could believe it. The bodies were mutilated, their eyes stabbed out, and blood was everywhere. When the police arrived, the two sisters were found clinging to each other in their attic bedroom (Le Texier 1994).

It is an understatement to say that the Papin sisters inspired a torrent of commentary, theorizing, speculation, and explanation. Newspapers of the day were filled with details of the crime and the trial. Christine was sentenced to death, a sentence later changed to life imprisonment, and Léa was sentenced to ten years of hard labor. Shortly after the completion of the trial, a young psychoanalyst named Jacques Lacan published an essay on the Papin sisters in which he speculated on the significance of female paranoia (1933). Indeed, the female criminal as embodied by the Papin sisters became for twentieth-century Lacanian psychoanalysis what the female hysteric had been for nineteenth-century Freudian psychoanalysis (Dean 1992, esp. chap. 2). Marxists and leftists claimed the sisters as victims of a class system and praised their revolt. Surrealists found the Papin sisters to be a sublime embodiment of the female criminal. Eventually, the Papin sisters inspired various creative works, including, most famously, Jean Genet's play *The Maids* (1954). Simone de Beauvoir wrote about the affair in her memoirs (1962), as did Janet

Flanner (1972).[4] More recently the Papin sisters have undergone feminist rereadings, with Wendy Kesselman's play *My Sister in This House* (1982) and its adaptation in Nancy Meckler's film *Sister, My Sister* (1994).

In his essay on their crime, Lacan alludes briefly, without extensive analysis, to the possible lesbian attachment between the two sisters. After the murders, the two sisters were found in their room, sharing a single bed. While awaiting their trial in prison, Christine, who suffered from hallucinations, claimed that she had been her sister's husband in a former life. Subsequent retellings and reinterpretations of the Papin affair have magnified the lesbian hypothesis, with Lacan's suggestion becoming more pronounced in Genet's play and a central theme in both Kesselman's play and Meckler's film. As Lynda Hart writes of Kesselman's play, the author makes "a very crucial choice that the historical record could not sustain—that the sisters were practicing lesbians." Hart concludes that the "sisters' lesbianism . . . historically and fictively, is culturally constructed" (1989, 142).

In *A Judgement in Stone* Ruth Rendell's narrator also makes a crucial choice in her brief allusion to the Papin affair:

> The relationship between Eunice Parchman and Joan Smith was never of a lesbian nature. They bore no resemblance to the Papin sisters, who, while cook and housemaid to a mother and daughter in Le Mans, murdered their employers in 1933. Eunice had nothing in common with them except that she also was female and a servant. (72)

Notice the peculiar logic that takes place here: we are told that the relationship was not of a lesbian nature, and that the two women are unlike the Papin sisters, whose crimes are described with no mention of or direct allusion to lesbianism. And of course there *is* a striking resemblance to the Papin sisters, if not because of the ghostly and convoluted appearance of lesbianism, then because of the class nature of the crime. There is no better way to suggest a connection than to deny it, particularly in a novel that takes such delight in demonstrating the inevitable move toward a bloody, cataclysmic conclusion. The reader not necessarily inclined to see a "lesbian nature" in Eunice and Joan's relationship has at the very least been given a suggestion to ponder. And a relationship between lesbianism and criminality is made, although incoherently, with no apparent narrative or grammatical reasoning.

There is no direct reference to the Papin affair in *La Cérémonie,* but in keeping with the overall tone of the film there are plenty of indirect references. (And in any case one could argue that a French film does not require direct reference, given how thoroughly the Papin affair is part of the cultural imaginary.) The film is haunted by the specter of motifs and images associated with the Papin murders. Put another way, the film is less concerned with re-creating the Papin affair than with asking how such a horrendous event has retained its hold on the popular imagination.

As I have mentioned, Jacques Lacan was a contemporary commentator on the Papin murders, describing their crime as a "délire à deux," a two-sided delirium rooted in paranoia. Does Lacan find his way into Claude Chabrol's film, as he has found his way into so many aspects of the cinema, at least in its academic contexts? I think so, although not in the way one might expect. It doesn't require too much imagination to see Eunice Parchman and Sophie Bonhomme as embodiments of the imaginary, that realm of misrecognition and narcissism that precedes entry into the symbolic, the world of language, of alienation, of the law. Indeed, illiteracy can be read easily as a kind of enforced imaginary. It is a heavy-handed image, and that may well be precisely the point—that *La Cérémonie* takes Lacan and psychoanalysis not as theoretical truth but as an object, as one of many texts surrounding the Papin affair.

Consider again the key scene, the most explicit yet most indirect suggestion of lesbianism in *La Cérémonie*, where Sophie and Jeanne go to Jeanne's apartment to eat before setting off to do charity work. The reflection that each woman provides the other is as striking as the literal mirror in the room that makes both of them present constantly to each other, and to us. Each not only has a past scandal in common, but also a piece of knowledge. Jeanne's display of a newspaper clipping about Sophie's involvement, or official lack thereof, in the fire that killed her father functions very much like Joan Smith's display of scandalous information in Rendell's novel. As Eunice Parchman was impressed that someone was beyond blackmail, so Sophie has admiration for Jeanne, not only as a would-be criminal, but as a voyeur into her own hypothetical criminal past.

Throughout *La Cérémonie* Sophie and Jeanne function as outbursts in the apparently calm and ordered bourgeois world of the Lelièvre family, and if one wanted to follow the kind of Lacanian logic that has been so dominant in film studies, one could easily read the women—and the film—as tracing the ways in which the imaginary bursts through the symbolic. Once again, the film asks us not so much to apply Lacanian psychoanalysis but to see the film as an example of what one might call "pop Lacanianism." Put another way, the film plays with certain trademark and popularized conceptions of Lacanian psychoanalysis.

When Jeanne first visits the Lelièvre house to deliver a postcard and gets a grand tour, Sophie utters her trademark response, "I don't know," several times in response to questions about the large-screen television set, about a book, about being in the movies. Yet Jeanne seems impervious to Sophie's tic. During this scene, we are given our clearest indication of Jeanne's madness when, introduced to the Lelièvre's bedroom, Jeanne tells the story of how she wanted to be a model but was rejected in favor of a blonde girl, who, she is certain, is Madame Lelièvre. How does she know this? Because, she says, Madame Lelièvre has looked at her in a particular way. There are shades of more than Lacan's commentary on the Papin sisters here, for Jeanne sounds amazingly like Aimée, the subject of Lacan's thesis, which also is a reflection of his fascination with female criminals: Aimée stabbed an actress whom she did not know but on whom she had projected her own desires (Roudinesco 1997, 31–51).[5]

In the later scene in Jeanne's apartment, something quite extraordinary happens. Sophie says "I know" for the first time, in reference to the story she has heard from Monsieur Lelièvre about Jeanne's child. Jeanne gives Sophie a way to say "I know." And from this point on, virtually every time Sophie utters "I don't know," it makes sense: she seems quite literally to be functioning in a more normal, social way. The two women complement each other in a "délire à deux" that alludes both to the Papin affair and to the various discourses—psychoanalytic ones included—that have interpreted and commented on it.

Consider the crucial scene that occurs in the kitchen, Sophie's domain, after she, spurred on by Jeanne to find out gossip about the family, has listened in on the telephone to discover that Melinda is pregnant. In one of many subtle observations on how this liberal bourgeois family has its own set of ceremonies and conventions for separating themselves from the others of the world, Melinda—who is critical of her family for hiring a maid in the first place, furious that Sophie is even called a "maid," angry that she must eat in the kitchen—offers to make tea. But she doesn't know where the teacups are, and she casually expects Sophie to get the sugar. Preceding this tellingly banal incident, Melinda asks Sophie what she would name a child if she were pregnant. "I don't know," replies Sophie, for once her trademark tag line making logical sense. When Sophie tells Jeanne that Melinda is pregnant, and Jeanne asks if there was a scene, once again Sophie's "I don't know" makes literal sense. And right before the murder, when Jeanne cuts the phone line and asks, "Now what shall we do?" Sophie replies, "I don't know."

Of course, it comes as no surprise that given Sophie's exclusion from the world of language there is quite a lot she "doesn't know." But in a curiously paradoxical way, her bond with Jeanne gives her an entry into a world of language. And in the process of that access to a symbolic act, *La Cérémonie* takes us on a whirlwind tour through numerous associations that in turn take us back, directly or indirectly, to the famous murders in Le Mans. The most striking evocation, aside from the murder itself, is what remains to me the most effective and most powerful scene in the entire film: when Sophie's illiteracy is not only made clear, as it has been already, but made clear as a source of humiliation and terror. A note has been left for Sophie by Madame Lelièvre: "Pourriez-vous repasser . . ." (Could you please iron . . .) it begins. In desperation Sophie runs upstairs and takes a book from a drawer in her room, a book that instructs children how to make the association between letters and sounds. Sophie finds the *P* and attempts to follow the instructions in the photograph, making the sound with the gesture that indicates the "explosive" *P*. Explosive, indeed. And what does the note ask of Sophie? That she iron a suit for Madame. The Papin sisters had been scolded for blowing a fuse when doing the family ironing—scolded, that is, indirectly, for in the six years that they worked for the Lancelin family, Madame Lancelin did not speak to the maids; she communicated with them only through writing (in an earlier scene, Madame Lelièvre also mentions with pleasure that she has no need to communicate directly with her maid). As mentioned above, the Papin murders occurred when the mother and daughter returned home to a darkened house, the fuse once again blown. Yet no matter how many signs there are in the film, signs pointing back to the horrible past of the Papin affair, or signs that any filmgoer should know to be obvious (such as when a gun is cleaned, you know that it will soon be used), the conclusion of *La Cérémonie* is shocking, horrible, beyond belief. No matter how many times the story of the Papin sisters has been told and retold, there is something terrifying and surprising about the spectacle of a female servant who turns so brutally on her masters. The title of Chabrol's film refers, of course, to a number of rituals and ceremonies that characterize the lives of the family, as well as to the very ceremony of murder itself, performed here as a kind of ritual reenactment of the Papin sisters' tale. *La cérémonie* is also the word used in France to describe public executions. While Sophie and Jeanne execute the family, Jeanne is also, one could say, executed in her turn. For when Jeanne leaves the Lelièvre house after the murders, her car stalls. A passing automobile hits her car, and Jeanne is killed immediately. The driver of the other car is the priest, who is accompanied by his secretary. (In an earlier scene Jeanne had accused the two of having an affair.) And what of Sophie? In a perverse way she has managed to do the one thing vital to her sense of self: she has prevented the world from knowing that she is illiterate. Her fate remains beyond the final frames of the film: at the end she is left standing alone. But she too is submitted to a public ritual, if not of execution, then of exposure.

I have noted that *La Cérémonie* is typically ambivalent in its evocation of the lesbian attraction between the two women. One critic aptly described the two women as "incipiently lesbian" (Carr 1997). Recall B. Ruby Rich's query—lucky coincidence or sinister parallel?—about the emergence of the cinematic trend of murderous women bonded to each other (1995a, xi). Rich wonders whether "something from the past is calling, some creature from the black lagoon rising once again to the surface to claim our attention, and claim, once again, the badge of utter unacceptability" (1995b, 60). The spectacle of two women who kill is horrifying, and certainly evocative of the pathological associations of lesbian desire, however "incipient." But more horrifying perhaps is the inexorable logic that dictates Sophie's fate. She finally finds someone to talk to, and the result can only be a lethal spectacle that once again enforces her isolation, her simultaneous exclusion from and imprisonment within a language—that of class, of literature, of books, and of tape recorders—that she does not understand.

Notes

1. Chabrol's film is not the first film adaptation of Rendell's novel. That distinction belongs to *The Housekeeper,* a Canadian film made in 1987 by Ousama Rawi and featuring Rita Tushingham as Eunice Coverdale. Rawi's film follows Rendell's novel more closely than does Chabrol's film. Interestingly, Rawi receives a screen credit in Chabrol's film. For while the character of Jeanne in *La Cérémonie* is quite different from Rendell's Joan Smith, Huppert's reincarnation clearly borrows substantially from Rawi's film.

2. Rawi's film portrays Eunice Parchman and Joan Smith as middle-aged women, as does Rendell's novel.

3. Terry Castle's study (1993) of the ghostly presence of lesbianism as a force in the Western literary tradition is enormously relevant here; for a reading of the ghostly lesbian in film, see White 1991.

4. For a comparison of how Lacan, Flanner, and de Beauvoir viewed the Papin affair, see Kamenish 1996; Lane 1993.

5. Chabrol coauthored the screenplay for *La Cérémonie* with Caroline Eliacheff, a psychoanalyst. Chabrol told an interviewer that he was certain that Ruth Rendell's

novel was inspired in part by the Papin sisters, and that Eliacheff pointed out the additional connection between Aimée and Jeanne (Guilloux 1995).

Works Cited

Calderon, Ivan. 1996. "Program Notes for the Puerto Rican International Film Festival." November. http://www.usc.clu.edu/priff/LACEREMONIE.HTM

Carr, Jay. 1997. "Masterful Malevolence." *Boston Globe,* 1 January, 23.

Castle, Terry. 1993. *The Apparitional Lesbian: Female Homosexuality and Modern Culture.* New York: Columbia University Press.

De Beavoir, Simone. 1976 (1962). *The Prime of Life.* Trans. Peter Green. New York: Harper & Row.

Dean, Carolyn J. 1992. *The Self and Its Pleasures: Bataille, Lacan, and the History of the Decentered Subject.* Ithaca, N.Y.: Cornell University Press.

Fitère, Jean-Marie. 1975. *Violette Nozière.* Paris: Presses de la cité.

Flanner, Janet. 1972. *Paris Was Yesterday, 1925–1939.* New York: Viking.

Genet, Jean. 1954. *The Maids.* Trans. Bernard Frechtman. New York: Grove.

Guilloux, Michel. 1995. "Claude Chabrol: À Trop Bouffer de l'Ordre Bourgeois, on Risque l'Indigestion." *L'Humanité,* 30 August: 20.

Hart, Lynda. 1989. "'They Don't Even Look Like Maids Anymore': Wendy Kesselman's *My Sister in This House.*" In *Making a Spectacle,* ed. Lynda Hart. Ann Arbor: University of Michigan Press, 131–46.

———. 1994. *Fatal Women: Lesbian Sexuality and the Mark of Aggression.* Princeton, N.J.: Princeton University Press.

Kamenish, Paula K. 1996. "Naming the Crime: Responses to the Papin Murders from Lacan, Beauvoir, and Flanner." *The Comparatist* 20 (May): 93–109.

Kesselman, Wendy. 1982. *My Sister in This House.* New York: French.

Lacan, Jacques. 1933. "Motifs du Crime Paranoiaque: Le Crime des Soeurs Papin." *Minotaure* 3–4: 25–28.

Lane, Christopher. 1993. "'The Delirium of Interpretation': Writing the Papin Affair." *differences: a journal of feminist cultural studies* 5, no. 2: 24–61.

Le Texier, Robert. 1994. *Les Soeurs Papin.* Paris: Fleuve Noir.

Milne, Tom. 1969. *Rouben Mamoulian.* Bloomington: Indiana University Press.

Rendell, Ruth. 1978. *A Judgement in Stone.* London: Arrow Books, 1978.

Rich, B. Ruby. 1995a. "Introduction to the U. S. Edition." In *Parker and Hume: A Lesbian View,* ed. Julie Glamuzina and Alison J. Laurie. Ithaca, N.Y.: Firebrand Books, i–xi.

———. 1995b. "Lethal Lesbians." *The Village Voice,* 25 April, 60.

Roudinesco, Elisabeth. 1997. *Jacques Lacan.* New York: Columbia University Press.

White, Patricia. 1991. "Female Spectator, Lesbian Specter: *The Haunting.*" In *Inside/Out: Lesbian Theories, Gay Theories,* ed. Diana Fuss. New York and London: Routledge, 142–72.

Žižek, Slavoj. 1991. *Looking Awry: An Introduction to Jacques Lacan through Popular Culture.* Cambridge: MIT Press.

3. Inversion and Lesbian Plots in Henri-Georges Clouzot's *Les Diaboliques*

Does Henri-Georges Clouzot's 1955 film *Les Diaboliques* have a lesbian plot? Approximately halfway through the film, a brief but tantalizing scene suggests both the evocation and the repression of lesbian desire—perhaps not a full-blown plot, but something more than a subplot. Christina (Véra Clouzot) and Nicole (Simone Signoret), the two female leads of the film, are framed in a second-floor window of a school building as they look out toward a swimming pool. The moment is important in that they, and we, assume that the body they have dumped in the swimming pool will soon be discovered. But something else occurs here, a suggestion of another mystery. Nicole wears dark pajamas, in contrast to her blond hair, and in contrast to Christina, who wears light pajamas, which contrast with her dark hair. Behind the two women an unmade bed is visible. Have they spent the night together? Does the visual contrast and symmetry suggest that they have become a couple? Have they plotted to kill the man so that they might be together? Such questions seem to be suspended in the quick movement of the camera across the outside wall of the building to frame the boys in an adjacent window as they perform morning rituals in their communal bathroom. But this apparent movement toward displacement is also odd, for the possibility of some other kind of desire lingers in this framing of one of the classic sites of homoerotic and homosocial desire, the boarding school. We move from a frame of women to one of young boys, and as the mystery of the film continues to become more and more complex, another plot lingers, one that seems both at home and oddly incongruent with the boarding school setting of the film.

Immediately after the word *Fin* appears on the screen at the end of the film, a title is seen, asking spectators not to be "diaboliques" by revealing the secret twist of the film they have just seen. This brilliant marketing strategy was used in advertisements for the film, and to add to the suspense spectators were warned that no one would be seated after the film had begun (Bocquet and Godin 1993, 94). Aside from serving as a precedent for future films with shocking finales—from Alfred Hitchcock's *Psycho* (1960) to Neil Jordan's *The Crying Game* (1992)—this marketing strategy serves as a kind of authorial signature, suggesting that Clouzot, legendary as a controlling director, known for fits of temper and quasi-sadistic behavior on the set, commands his spectators from behind the camera just as surely as the dead man in his film apparently rises from his watery grave. But the secret of the film reaches beyond the murder mystery, and the atmosphere of secrecy surrounding not only the film but also its reception seems perfectly matched to its evocation of lesbianism.

Clouzot's film adapts, freely and compellingly, the first coauthored novel by Pierre Boileau and Thomas Narcejac, *The Woman Who Was No More (Celle qui n'était plus),* published in 1952.[1] Individually, Boileau and Narcejac had been successful mystery novelists. Their collaboration proved to be enormously successful, particularly on film adaptations. On the advice of his wife, Véra (who plays the role of Christina in the film), Clouzot optioned the novel and in so doing beat none other than Alfred Hitchcock to the punch (Bocquet and Godin 1993, 87–88). (A 1958 novel by Boileau and Narcejac, *D'Entre les morts* [Among the Dead], became the basis for Hitchcock's 1958 film *Vertigo.*)

I will be diabolical—it is virtually impossible to discuss this film without being diabolical—and reveal not only the secret twist of Clouzot's film, but also the different but related secret of Boileau and Narcejac's novel. In the film, two women schoolteachers, Christina and Nicole, conspire to kill an abusive man, Michel (Paul Meurisse), the director of the school for boys, who is the husband of one (Christina) and the lover of the other (Nicole). All three live in the school building, and their actions are thus observed by the other schoolteachers and the boys who attend the school. The two women depart for a holiday weekend and lure the man to Nicole's apartment in a small town, where they proceed to drug him and drown him in the bathtub. They return to the school and dump Michel's body in the swimming pool, where they assume it will soon be discovered. The body of the man disappears, however; when the pool is drained on a false pretext, his body is nowhere to be found. His absent presence haunts the film. Signs of him begin to appear in odd ways. His suit is returned from a dry cleaner's; a hotel room has been rented in his name; his face appears as a shadow in a school portrait. Christina, who is fragile and in poor health to begin with, becomes increasingly distraught. She becomes haunted by sounds and the sense of mystery in her apartment. In a return to the symbolic if not literal scene of the crime, Michel emerges from a bathtub at the conclusion of the film, very much alive. Christina is literally frightened to death, and the final twist is revealed: the mistress, Nicole, who appeared to be working in cahoots with Christina, was conspiring all along with Michel in order to drive the wife to her death.

In Boileau and Narcejac's novel, a fishing supplies salesman (Ravinel) and a doctor (Lucienne), his mistress, conspire to kill Ravinel's wife in order to collect a large insurance settlement. Mireille, Ravinel's wife, is drowned in a bathtub in a scenario quite close to that of Clouzot's film, and like Michel in the film, she disappears. Ravinel is fragile, like Christina in the film, and he is driven to despair, madness, and finally suicide as he witnesses the signs of his wife's return from the dead. Ravinel and Lucienne's conspiracy is thus a front, just like that of the two women in Clouzot's film. The secret of *The Woman Who Was No More* is one for which Ravinel has many clues but cannot "see," for it is (to borrow from Terry Castle) even more apparitional than his wife's body (1993). The secret of the novel is lesbianism: the two women were conspiring all along to force Ravinel to the brink of madness and then suicide.

Boileau and Narcejac's novel has not received extensive critical commentary, but those who have commented on the film's literary connection generally read Clouzot's film as yet another example of explicit lesbianism repressed and/or erased in the cinematic adaptation, hence following in a long homophobic tradition of several versions of *Nana* (1926, 1955) in terms of lesbianism, and *The Big Sleep* (1946) and *Crossfire* (1947) in terms of gay male sexuality. Boze Hadleigh, in *The Lavender Screen,* notes that the film was based on a novel "about a murdering lesbian couple" and says that "the film turned them heterosexual, although first-time viewers get the impression that Simone Signoret is Vera Clouzot's butch lover" (1993, 149). Bertrand Philbert (1984) sees the film as backsliding even as compared to Clouzot's earlier film *Quai des Orfèvres* (1947), in which there is a "minor" lesbian character. Noting the transformation of the lesbian couple into Michel (Paul Meurisse) and Nicole (Signoret), Philbert also comments on how the two women in the film can be seen as echoing the two stereotypes of lesbianism usually presented on screen: Signoret's butch lesbian and Clouzot's fragile, hyper-feminine femme. However, says Philbert, "these are but faint traces and the frankness of the book was completely forgotten in the film version." He concludes with an assumption that has characterized many, perhaps most, studies of the cinema vis-à-vis literature: "What literary works could explore, the cinema, at that time, could not, except in exceptional cases" (39).

Clouzot's adaptation of the triangle in the Boileau-Narcejac novel produces effects that cannot so easily be dismissed as a homophobic repression of the plot twist of lesbianism. The result of the change—aside from the most obvious and commercial explanation, that Clouzot wanted to feature his wife in the central role of the film (Bocquet and Godin 1993, 88–90)—is far more screen time devoted to the interactions between two women, not to mention a twist on the original twist ending of the novel. Central to readings of the "erasure" of homosexuality in the film is an assumption not only about the unrepresentability of lesbianism, but also about sources, origins, and the nature of what Philbert calls "frankness." The model of a "frank" literary original from which an inferior, homophobic product emerges (that is, "the novel was better") is as limited in gay/lesbian studies as it is in the study of cinematic adaptation.

And however different they are, the practice of adaptation and the representation of marginal sexualities may well be connected; they certainly are in Clouzot's case, and in ways far more complex than the dismissals of *Les Diaboliques* would suggest. Philbert mentions the "minor" lesbian character in *Quai des Orfèvres,* an adaptation of a mystery novel, *Légitime Défense,* by S. A. Steeman, but he does not mention that this character, Dora, is nowhere to be found in the novel. Her addition to the film turns a rather straightforward tale of marital infidelity and suspicion into a much more complex tale—visually as well as narratively—of heterosexuality and its discontents. Now I do not want to pursue the reverse of the "novel is better" argument by suggesting that any radical change in the cinematic adaptation of a literary source must be seen as necessarily positive, but I do want to argue that the reading of literary sources through the perspective of sexual politics is central to the success of *Les Diaboliques,* to its status as a masterpiece of suspense.

Clouzot had his own "diabolical" stature in the film industry, not only because of his particular directorial practices but also because of the scandal he endured in the purification immediately following World War II and the occupation of France, when *Le Corbeau* (1943) was deemed "anti-French" (Ehrlich 1985, 177–88; Siclier 1981, 236–39). While

Clouzot is exceptional in many ways, he is also fairly emblematic of the status of the film director in post–World War II France, faced with new pressures to reinvent authorship in terms of both France's past and the renewal of interest in American films. It is fairly standard to relegate the 1950s in French cinema to that vast wasteland, the "tradition of quality," with some exceptions, like Jean Cocteau, Robert Bresson, and Jacques Tati—a subject to which I will return. While the so-called tradition of quality did indeed produce its share of clunkers, there was something else going on in popular, commercial French film of the 1950s: a renewed interest in the art of adaptation in ways that far surpass the stereotypical view of the decade.

Now adaptation has been so much a part of the history of French cinema that Marie-Claire Ropars-Wuillemier once declared, somewhat hyperbolically, that cinematic adaptation, insofar as it concerns the development of cinematic language, is primarily a French phenomenon: "Le phénomène, dans son ampleur, fut essentiellment français" (1972, 76). I would argue that alongside the classic division of French filmmakers of the 1950s into the camp of the commercial cinema (Claude Autant-Lara, Jean Delannoy, and virtually any film written by Jean Aurenche and Pierre Bost) and the art cinema (Cocteau, Bresson, Tati), there are other directors, including Clouzot, who approach literary adaptation in order both to re-create the cinema and to break down the boundaries between high art and low art. These adaptations did not really function in the conventional sense of assuring legitimacy for the cinema, for they were concerned with the adaptation of novels that were popular, not a part of the canon of French literature. Prior to *Les Diaboliques,* Clouzot wrote the screenplay for adaptations of popular mysteries by Steeman (*Le Dernier des six,* 1941) and Georges Simenon (*Les Inconnus dans la maison,* 1942), and the first feature film he directed was an adaptation of another Steeman novel, *L'Assassin habite au 21* (1942). Clouzot's approach to adaptation opened up areas of cultural visibility by engaging with literary sources, sometimes deforming them, in order to produce a popular cinema that could also lay claim to cinematic art.

I want to suggest that the term *inversion* offers a way to understand simultaneously the approach to adaptation and the approach to the representation of sexual marginality embodied in *Les Diaboliques.* What might then be called a practice of inversion characterizes the film on several levels. *Inversion* as a term is best known, of course, as an explanation of homosexuality through the "third sex," an explanation that was popular in the early decades of the century and popularized by Havelock

Ellis, whose works were widely available in France. The female invert dressed like a man and desired like a man—that is, desired the woman ostensibly more womanly than herself (Chauncey 1989; Faderman 1991; Newton 1984). While the most famous literary representation of the invert is to be found in Radclyffe Hall's *The Well of Loneliness* (1928), the early decades of the century (especially the 1920s) in France were also home to both a large community of lesbians, some of whom fit the stereotype of the invert, and to a literary preoccupation with the *garçonne,* the eponymous heroine of Victor Margueritte's 1922 novel, who was more boyish than manly but who nonetheless represented a variation of the invert (Roberts 1992). Yet one of the particularities of lesbian life and representation in France is that alongside the female invert, there has also been, throughout the twentieth century, a fascination with the femme figure, with that womanly woman attracted to other women (Marks 1979). Colette is the prime author associated with the feminine lesbian, and the boarding school is the privileged locale for scenes of lesbian passion.

The most obvious and most literal example of inversion in *Les Diaboliques* is the creation of the character of Nicole Horner from the character of Lucienne in the novel. Only the fact that Simone Signoret wears dresses through most of the film saves her character from being a stereotypical representation of the female invert. For Nicole sports the "masculine" swagger, the short hair, and the deep husky voice so typical of the female invert. How did Simone Signoret, icon of hyperheterosexuality and popular symbol in France of the 1950s, make such a believable butch? Signoret's most celebrated roles tended to be as women fatally irresistible to men, as in *Casque d'or* (1951) and *Thérèse Raquin* (1953), films that immediately preceded *Les Diaboliques.* One might say that Signoret's persona is inverted in *Les Diaboliques,* but one could also argue that a hint of inversion was already present in her persona, that it exudes a sexuality so excessive that it is never quite convincingly contained within a heterosexual framework. In *Manèges* (1949), for example, Signoret plays a vicious woman who plots with her mother to get rid of her husband, and the equestrian outfits she sports (the film's central locale is a horse stable) give a hint of what might be behind this desire to get rid of the husband. Susan Hayward describes Signoret's star persona as constructed by "an appeal to both sexes that . . . permits both male and female spectators to undergo an identification that is not straightforwardly gendered with the persona on screen" (1995, 69). But if cross-gender identification is a part of Signoret's appeal, *Les Diaboliques* is a special case for the way that the lesbian aspect of that appeal is foregrounded. Just as *Les Diaboliques* confounds the relationship between the presumably "major" plot of the murder mystery and the "minor" plot of lesbian desire, so the figure of Signoret in the film conjures up both heterosexual and lesbian attraction. And given that popular representations of lesbianism in France have been associated so strongly with both the classic invert and the femme, it is significant that Signoret's Nicole evokes both figures.

The triangle of the Boileau-Narcejac novel is inverted in *Les Diaboliques* so that a story of a heterosexual relationship undermined by a lesbian one becomes not exactly a lesbian relationship undermined by a heterosexual one, but at the very least a story of sexual confusion. *The Woman Who Was No More* follows Ravinel as he attempts to make sense of the peculiar events surrounding the disappearance of the corpse of his wife, Mireille. Ravinel is confronted with many mysteries. He doesn't understand why Lucienne, a doctor who nursed Mireille back to health after a bout with tuberculosis, is his mistress. He doesn't understand why he married Mireille in the first place. In other words, the disappearance of Mireille's body builds on Ravinel's predisposition to what one is tempted to describe as hysteria. In particular, Ravinel is preoccupied with fog, and *The Woman Who Was No More* is a novel in which fog is as important as any single character. Visibility is often low because of the fog; Ravinel can't see clearly in front of him, because of the fog; and most important, Ravinel has been preoccupied since childhood with a game that he calls the "fog game" (le jeu du brouillard), an imaginary crossing over of the forbidden boundary, the "frontière interdite" between life and death (1954, 88).

Throughout the novel, as the vanished body of Mireille poses more and more of a dilemma, Ravinel imagines that she, too, has crossed the boundary line with which he has been so fascinated since childhood: "She had succeeded where he had always failed: she had crossed the mysterious frontier, she was on the other side, invisible, elusive, and it gave her an unfair advantage" (88). Now Mireille has indeed crossed a boundary, but not the one that Ravinel imagines. For all of his preoccupation with boundary crossing, he fails to "read" the clues that are so abundant in the novel. He himself describes Lucienne at every opportunity as anything but womanly. Lucienne has short hair (9), a deep hoarse voice (5); she is "as strong as any man" (30), and Ravinel muses: "Strange how little feminine she was" (57). Ravinel is not even sure how or why they became lovers. Much of Lucienne's butch appearance is explained by the fact that she is a doctor, hence businesslike, straightforward, and strong. But whether Lucienne's profession can explain her peculiar habit of taking Ravinel's blood pressure after sex is another matter!

Two of the most striking images in the novel of Lucienne's butch identity and Ravinel's failure to read it occur in scenes where photographs are remembered or discovered. Ravinel knows nothing of Lucienne's past or her family, with whom she has no contact. The only detail about Lucienne's past that Ravinel can recall is a photograph of a woman: "In her surgery there was a little photograph—at least there had been, but it had disappeared some time ago—the photograph of a very beautiful girl with fair hair and Scandinavian features" (61). Ravinel defers the deciphering of the photograph's meaning: "Later on he would inquire about her. After their marriage" (61).

If Ravinel's impending marriage to Lucienne can serve only as a weak defense against the significance of the photograph, a later scene takes the implications even further. Virtually immersed in the metaphoric fog that inhabits the novel, Ravinel sees the home he shares with Mireille as an alien place that no longer belongs to him. While leafing distractedly through papers, Ravinel comes across photographs of Lucienne and Mireille. This discovery occurs near the conclusion of the novel, and what Ravinel encounters here is something of a primal scene, for these photographs document the beginnings of Lucienne and Mireille's relationship. Ravinel compares the photographs of the two women and notes of Mireille: "How graceful she was, Mireille! Slim as a boy and appealing, with those large candid eyes, which were focused on the camera but which saw farther, infinitely farther, right through the camera and right through him, as though he was standing between her and her future, between her and something she had long been waiting for" (189). Ravinel's syntax reveals what he consciously cannot acknowledge. A description of Lucienne follows immediately, thus taking up the position of the long-awaited object. Lucienne in this photograph is "just as she always was, impersonal, almost stern, her shoulders square, her chin a bit heavy" (189). Ravinel looks for a photograph of himself but discovers that no one thought to take one of him. Rather, all he can find is an official identity photo, old and yellowed. The two women are captured in the desire of seeing and being seen, while Ravinel is captured only as a civilian; the photographs of the two women embody desire, while his embodies institutional identity.

This photographic scene—Ravinel forever banished to the sidelines, whether as the one whose photograph was not taken or as the one who cannot understand the significance of the photographs that were taken—immediately precedes his final breakdown. Ravinel "felt like a person in a dream wandering through a house that had somehow ceased to be his home" (190–91). He now sees himself as the phantom and Mireille as the living creature. A striking choice of words is used to convey Ravinel's sense of the ultimate breakdown of the boundary line between the living and the presumably dead. The English translation tells us that Ravinel and Mireille had "changed places" (191), but the original French is far more provocative: "Les rôles sont intervertis" (177).

While it may be impossible to dissociate the term *inversion* from its homosexual meanings, in a larger and more general sense it suggests a reversal from within, one that respects the original but shifts the terms. The most obvious "inversion" in *Les Diaboliques* is that of the Boileau-Narcejac novel, yet the film's title also suggests a practice of inversion. The working title of the film was *Les Veuves* (The Widows), which was deemed unsellable (Bocquet and Godin 1993, 90). Clouzot then proposed an homage to Jules Barbey d'Aurevilly's 1874 collection of novellas about diabolical women, and in the final film a citation from the preface to Barbey d'Aurevilly's *Les Diaboliques* serves as the introductory title to the film: "Une peinture est toujours assez *morale* quand elle est *tragique* et qu'elle donne *l'horreur des choses qu'elle retrace*" (A portrait is always *moral* when it is *tragic* and shows *the horror of the things it represents* [1973 (1874), 24]). On one level, Clouzot's citation of Barbey d'Aurevilly could be seen as a legitimizing strategy in the sense that in the 1950s in France the allusion to and adaptation of nineteenth-century literary works marked a deliberate effort to recruit France's literary heritage to the reputation of the cinema. It is a peculiar strategy, since it could easily lead French viewers to believe they were about to see an adaptation of Barbey d'Aurevilly's novellas. In addition, Barbey d'Aurevilly is a curious choice if legitimation is desired, for the citation suggests as much a comparison between the two authors—both outcasts—as it does a thematic connection between the novellas and the film. For these two artists were punished for their work; Barbey d'Aurevilly was put on trial after the publication of *Les Diaboliques* (see Petit 1974), and Clouzot was brought before the post–World War II purification committees (and initially banned from the film industry) for what was perceived as the scandalous and anti-French *Le Corbeau*. Finally, in terms of a possible thematic connection between the two works, there is a process of inversion in the citation by Clouzot, not unlike the inversion of Simone Signoret's persona. For in Barbey d'Aurevilly's *Les Diaboliques,* there are tales of hyperheterosexuality behind which lurks the suggestion of lesbianism; in Clouzot's film, there is a tale of possible lesbian attraction behind which lurks hyperheterosexuality.

Throughout *Les Diaboliques* there is that sense of something dangerous that threatens to erupt, with characters constantly looking over their shoulders. Part of what gives Clouzot's film its legendary status as a suspense film is the way an atmosphere of surveillance is established from the outset. This is due in part to the school setting. The film takes place in a private boys' school located in a once-elegant house in the Parisian suburbs. The boys in the film are both sexually curious and very childlike. Yet unlike many examples of the boarding-school genre, where the line between homosociality and homoeroticism is quite thin indeed, the community of boys serves largely to suggest a masculine identity different from either Michel, with his overt sadism, or the two male teachers, whose own adult sexuality seems somewhat dubious. The film both cites and departs from the schoolboy genre, which in French film history is most strikingly embodied in Jean Vigo's 1933 film *Zéro de conduite.* But in *Les Diaboliques* the drama of adolescent and adult sexuality serves largely as a backdrop to the mise-en-scène of heterosexuality and its discontents.

Christina and Nicole are striking embodiments of the contrast between the virgin and the whore, the good girl and the bad girl, the madonna and the slut. The school setting adds another dimension to this contrast by isolating them from other women. Both women have particular pasts that have led them to the school: Christina, a past in Caracas, her marriage to Michel, and her dowry, which led to the purchase of the school; Nicole, a dismissal from a teaching post at another school, which is mentioned twice but never explained. As one has come to expect in a classical narrative film—especially one that relies as heavily as *Les Diaboliques* does on the virgin/whore dichotomy—the women are observed constantly by the other teachers and the students. Yet while these observers watch, they more often than not misunderstand what they see. Very early in the film, the first encounter between Christina and Nicole is observed first by the two male schoolteachers, and then by one of the boys. The schoolteacher remarks on how scandalous it is that the wife (Christina) should comfort the mistress (Nicole), while the child tells his friends that the two women spend all of their time with each other because they drink together. Both observations miss the murder plot in progress. But they develop the contours of what I think is a far more interesting plot—that of the desire between the two women.

Feminist film theory of the past several decades has demonstrated how the woman's gaze in classical film is partial, defective, or otherwise limited, and there is much in the early moments of the film to suggest that *Les Diaboliques* is no different (Doane 1987). Nicole is first seen in the film wearing dark glasses, and her first interaction with Christina is very literally defined by a wounded eye, the black eye that is a result of Michel's assault (an assault that is never seen on camera). And Christina bears, here as throughout the film, a frightened and wide-eyed gaze that is framed constantly by the overpowering presence of others.

Yet within this atmosphere of paranoia and surveillance—within, that is, an atmosphere that requires the woman's sight to be defective—interactions between the two women function according to another logic, one defined less by the observations of others and more by a curious juxtaposition between the rituals of daily life and domesticity, and a camera technique that suggests hovering omniscience. Here, in this "other" logic of the film, is where moments of lesbian desire occur, in a space that is both familiar and strange. The film is evocative of Patricia White's reading of *The Haunting* (1963), which "stage[s] a story of deviant female subjectivity," and in the process of both evoking and repressing lesbianism *Les Diaboliques* provides what White calls a "working definition of lesbianism in the classical cinema" (1991, 153). For like *The Haunting,* it is not a film "about" lesbianism—it is about "something else," and that "something else" summons up and sums up, as White suggests, the specter of lesbianism and the classical cinema. Now there are differences between *Les Diaboliques* and *The Haunting*; while Clouzot's film is a thriller, it is not gothic horror like *The Haunting* is, and most obviously, there is not an overt lesbian character to match Claire Bloom's in *The Haunting.* But there is a lesbian plot.

How, then, does this lesbian plot proceed? The reactions of others—of the two male schoolteachers, of the schoolboys—suggest that something is amiss in the relationship between the two women. The dynamics of attraction between them become increasingly obvious in the film. Christina and Nicole discuss their plot to kill Michel during a break by the school's swimming pool, while Nicole knits. (Admittedly, she is more evocative of Madame Defarge than of a paragon of domesticity!) The scene is framed in an abrupt move from a long shot to a medium close-up, as if to suggest sudden intrusion on an intimate conversation (see Bertin-Maghit 1996). After the two women have hatched their plot to dispose of Michel, they leave for Nicole's home in Niort. (This is an inside joke: Niort is also Clouzot's home town.) The murder plot may be the secret that the two women share, but everything else about their

Véra Clouzot as Christina, Simone Signoret as Nicole, and Paul Meurisse as Michel in *Les Diaboliques.*

activities suggests a secret love affair. Indeed, their arrival at Nicole's home is evocative of a weekend tryst, including worrying what the neighbors will think and trying not to make too much noise. Michel is lured to the apartment under the false premise that Christina has decided to divorce him and has already consulted a lawyer. He drinks the whiskey that Nicole has laced with sedatives, and just as he is about to pass out on the only bed in the apartment, he asks facetiously whose bed he is in, Nicole's or Christina's. Christina, just as facetiously, replies "le nôtre" (ours).

The intimacy between the two women hovers in a space between the rituals of everyday life and the revelation of something more. That "something more" is, on one literal level, the body of Michel and the subsequent plot to get rid of it. But perhaps the something more is . . . something more. I have already mentioned the scene that shows us the two women in pajamas with the unmade bed in the background. If beds play an obvious part in the evocation of a lesbian plot in the film, Christina, for her part, spends a large part of the final moments of the film alone in hers. It is common to describe Nicole as the unrelenting, stronger character and Christina as the weak, fragile one, whose undoing is more and more pronounced as the film progresses. But there is another dimension, and that is the extent to which Christina and Nicole change places even while they continue on the paths required by the "real" intrigue of the film, the murder plot. Nicole is butch, and Christina is a combination of child and femme. Ironically, as Christina becomes more and more ill, spending more and more time in bed, she also appears to acquire, as if by contagion, some of Nicole's qualities.

The most striking example of this exchange of roles occurs in the context of one of Michel's several spectral appearances in the film, when his shadowy presence is seen in a school photograph. As in the Boileau-Narcejac novel, the photographic evidence—and the failure to read it properly—leads to the dénouement of the narrative. As soon as Nicole sees the photograph, she runs to Christina's bedside, seemingly terrified by the implications of this photographic proof. Christina tells Nicole that it is time for her (Nicole) to leave. Their separation echoes uncannily the lesbian plots of many "invert" novels in which the butch is banished so that the femme can lead a normal life (Foster 1985). But another inversion operates here, for typically it is the butch who forces her femme lover to disappear. Christina acquires the role usually assigned to the "true" invert, thus underscoring dramatically and paradoxically the clash between the two plots of the film—the lesbian plot, in which she has an active role, and the murder plot, in which she is about to die.

Something quite bizarre happens at the conclusion of this parting of ways. Nicole tearfully says good-bye, packs her bag, and moves from Christina's room into the hallway. The camera frames Nicole as she enters the hallway. We hear in voice-over a boy who recites the following passage:

> Tremble, m'a-t-elle dit, fille digne de moi;
> Le cruel Dieu des Juifs l'emporte aussi sur toi.
> Je te plains de tomber dans ses mains redoutables. (Racine 1960b, 670)

("Tremble, my daughter, worthy of me," she said;
"The cruel God of the Jews will soon prevail
Over you also, and I mourn that you
Are falling into His relentless hands."[Racine 1960a, 249])

The citation is from Jean Racine's play *Athalie* (Athaliah), which was first performed and published in 1691. The passage occurs early in the play, when Athalie describes a dream in which her mother appeared in order to warn her of the dangers that lie ahead. Are there thematic connections one might make with the film? Perhaps, from the dream in the play to the dreamlike quality of the film at this point, or the pronouncement of death and destruction. And there may well be a connection between Athalie and Nicole, for while it seems far-fetched to suggest a comparison between a biblical queen and a schoolteacher, both women do suffer from greed, and Athalie is often described in the play as masculine.

The citation from *Athalie* is ironic, for the play was written by Racine to be performed by schoolgirls (Racine 1960a, xxv), and the play was often read, well into the twentieth century, by schoolchildren in place of the more famous and renowned *Phèdre* (Phaedra), which was considered by some to be too scandalous.[2] There may not be any plays performed in *Les Diaboliques,* but children's voices are heard throughout the film. Whether reciting English verbs or countries of the world, their voices are a chorus to accompany decisive moments of the murder plot. When, for instance, an inspector visits the school, the boys' voices are heard, and they provide a counterpoint to Christina's growing anxiety about what she fears is their failed plot.

But the voice in this scene, the voice that recites from *Athalie,* is different. There is no classroom and no lesson, as in previous instances of the children's voices. And this is a single boy's voice, not the chanting in unison of an entire class. The voice seems to materialize out of thin air. Not only does this scene stand out as unusual in terms of sound; visually something quite strange happens here as well. As Nicole walks down the hallway, her body quite literally disappears, dissolves, seems to vanish into thin air. A voice materializes out of thin air; a body disappears into thin air. Throughout the film, Clouzot maintains a precarious balance—and therefore a troubling uncanniness—between the codes of film noir and those of horror (Hottell 1996). Strange things happen in the film, but they are grounded in what is visible, whether in the shadows of people and objects, or in what is absent, that is, Michel's body. Here, however, the film moves, quickly, momentarily, and decisively, into a different register—that of the fantastic, certainly, but also and especially that of obvious cinematic manipulation: the voice of a body that isn't there, and the vanishing of a body that is.

This scene is jarring not only stylistically but also in terms of what is spoken. One phrase in particular must have been a striking apparition in a film made less than a decade after the end of World War II: "Le cruel dieu des Juifs" (the cruel God of the Jews). During the German occupation of France, Clouzot worked for Continental Films, the German film production company, and as I've already noted, he was punished after the war for his involvement in *Le Corbeau.* Subsequent assessments of Clouzot's career have generally agreed that *Le Corbeau* was scapegoated, and that Clouzot was no more or less guilty of collaboration than other filmmakers who worked during the Occupation (Ehrlich 1985, chap. 8; Siclier 1981, chap. 15). But Clouzot *was* directly responsible for one of the more flagrant anti-Semitic representations made during the war. He wrote the script for *Les Inconnus dans la maison* (1942), based on a novel by Georges Simenon and directed by Henri Decoin, in which the villain's appearance is clearly evocative of anti-Semitic stereotypes, and in which a courtroom speech (nowhere present in the novel) borrows directly from Vichy propaganda (Ehrlich 1985, 50–52, 209–10). That the word *Jew* appears in a citation from Racine has particular cultural resonance. In *Anti-Semite and Jew,* Jean-Paul Sartre notes a common French anti-Semitic formulation: that Jews are incapable of understanding Racine (1946, 24). It is difficult to situate this sudden and fantasmatic utterance of the word *Jew* in *Les Diaboliques,* for literally and symbolically the film has nothing to do with French representations of Jewish identity. Yet given the particular staging of this scene, the lines from Racine are very striking, if for no other reason than the fact that they appear so out of place. And that may well be the point—that the density of this moment in the film is a function not only of its formal characteristics but also of a complex historical allusion that appears and then evaporates, somewhat like the lesbian herself.[3]

This sudden change in the representation of cinematic space marks a transition to the resolution of the film. This transition is abrupt, and it has no precedent in the film. Nowhere does a body disappear so magically, not even Michel's body, which of course we soon discover has not disappeared at all. Nowhere does a disembodied voice appear out of nowhere. The remaining minutes of the film trace Christina's anguished trip down the corridor—she hears noises—and the final revelation that Michel and Nicole had planned the entire murder plot together. While the sight of Michel emerging from the bathtub is the primary shock of the film, I find the revelation of Nicole's heterosexuality equally shocking. And it isn't just the fact of her love for Michel that shocks, but the way it is represented, for suddenly Nicole is no longer a tough broad but, rather, a simpering, fussing woman in love. The citation from Racine and the disappearance of the female body announce the dissolution of the lesbian plot, its unraveling into heterosexual resolution. A certain cinematic violence is required in order to get rid of the lesbian plot, a departure from the consistent patterns that characterize the rest of the film: of surveillance and paranoia, of domesticity and mystery, all rooted in the ordinary, the daily routines of the everyday. But while the lesbian plot may be banished, it can also be read as enabling the heterosexual resolution of the film. For Nicole and Christina begin to change places in the scene just preceding Nicole's disappearance in the hallway, and without that exchange, that inversion of roles, Nicole's emergence as co-conspirator and dedicated lover of Michel would be even less believable than it is.[4]

There is yet another echo in this astonishing passage of the film, and yet another inversion. Françoise Mallet-Joris's 1951 novel *Les Remparts de béguine (The Illusionist)* was enormously popular and brought lesbian desire center stage in the realm of popular fiction in France. Mallet-Joris was one of a number of young female novelists whose works signaled the culture of modernity in France in the 1950s. Kristin Ross (1995) has noted the extent to which the novels of writers like Mallet-Joris, Françoise Sagan, and Christiane Rochefort embody anxieties about the heterosexual couple. These novels might also signal the fascination with lesbianism that made its way into both Boileau and Narcejac's novel and Clouzot's film.

In Mallet-Joris's novel, a teenage girl has an affair with her father's mistress. This triangle of overlapping heterosexual and lesbian desire is announced by the quotation of famous lines from Racine's play *Phèdre.* In the novel, the quotation signals both the known and the unknown—that is, the institutionalized knowledge associated with the classics of French literature and the discovery of a passion that is taboo:

> A phrase kept running through my head, confusedly, like a fugitive glimmer of light, like a dancing firefly. It was absurd of me, I was ashamed of it, but I couldn't help repeating it over and over without even understanding or realizing for a second what it meant: "Et Phèdre au labyrinthe avec toi descendue, se serait avec toi retrouvée ou perdue"—And

> Phèdre would have gone down into the labyrinth with thee, and with thee would have been either rescued or lost. (40)

The citation of famous lines from the play provides a screen onto which are projected virtually all of the teenager's anxieties about Tamara, her father's mistress, before their first sexual encounter. If Racine "accompanies" the initiation of the lesbian plot in Mallet-Joris's novel, the practice is inverted in Clouzot's film, here marking the end of the lesbian plot.

The simultaneous evocation and suppression of a lesbian plot in Clouzot's film thus suggest a connection between the film and France's recent past, and between film and popular fiction of the time in France, whether mystery novels or novels about young women and modernity. Another connection, between Clouzot's film and the film culture of 1950s France as shaped by the influential journal *Cahiers du cinéma,* suggests a very different way of reading the significance of lesbianism. I wonder if François Truffaut might have included a discussion of *Les Diaboliques* in his famous essay "Une certaine tendance du cinéma français" (A certain tendency in French cinema) had the film come out earlier than it did (Truffaut's essay was published in 1954; Clouzot's film came out in 1955). In that famous (and infamous) essay, Truffaut lambastes what he calls a scenarists' cinema (exemplified by the writing team of Aurenche and Bost), more commonly known as the tradition of quality, and opposes it to the true cinema of auteurs embodied by directors such as Jean Cocteau, Jacques Tati, and Jacques Becker. My purpose here is not to rehearse the implications of Truffaut's argument for the division between, say, commercial cinema and artistic cinema, or for the way in which this essay has stood, unproblematically, as a way of understanding a decade that is far more complex than his pronouncements would suggest. For the sake of the present discussion I want to draw attention to how Clouzot is situated in Truffaut's famous essay, and to suggest that beneath the division between the cinema of quality and the cinema of authors, there is another preoccupation that is never articulated so clearly but that suggests a vital perspective on films of the 1950s in general, and on Clouzot's films (and *Les Diaboliques*) in particular.

While Clouzot was not a favorite of the *Cahiers* writers in the 1950s, he emerges in Truffaut's essay in a very peculiar way. For most of the film directors mentioned in the essay, it is clear whether they qualify as hacks or auteurs. While screenwriters Jean Aurenche and Pierre Bost are the worst offenders insofar as the tradition of quality is concerned, they have their counterparts in directors like Yves Allegret and Jean Delannoy, who

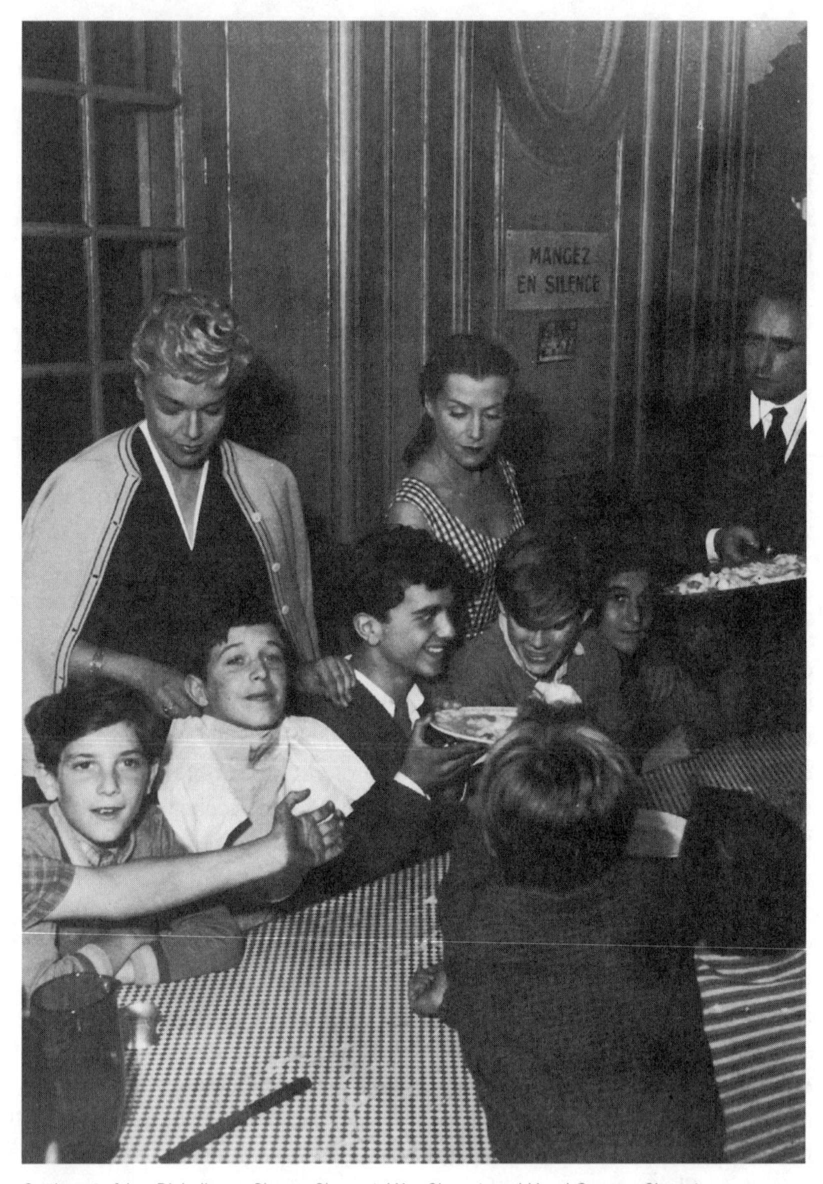

On the set of *Les Diaboliques*: Simone Signoret, Véra Clouzot, and Henri-Georges Clouzot.

in turn are opposed to the true auteurs of French cinema: Jean Renoir, Robert Bresson, Jean Cocteau, Jacques Becker, Abel Gance, Max Ophüls, Jacques Tati, and Roger Leenhardt (Truffaut 1954, 26). But when this particular list appears, near the conclusion of the essay, a curious slippage occurs. "Finally I can't believe in the peaceful co-existence of the *Tradition of Quality* and the *Cinema of authors,*" Truffaut writes. "Fundamentally, Yves Allegret and Delannoy are only *caricatures* of Clouzot and Bresson" (26). Oddly, Clouzot, unlike Bresson, did not make it into the list of true auteurs immediately preceding this statement, and given the comments that follow, it would appear that Truffaut was ultimately not quite sure where to situate Clouzot. For in his quick survey of the year 1953 in the cinema, Truffaut quickly writes off Clouzot's film *The Wages of Fear (Salaire de la peur)* in contrast to truly audacious films like *Madame de . . ., Monsieur Hulot's Holiday,* and *Carosse d'or.* Truffaut's condemnation of *The Wages of Fear* is curious indeed; it isn't the "scenaristic" quality of the film that is in question but, rather, "the pederastic relationships between characters" that are featured in the film (27)!

Two issues are at stake here, both concerning the symptomatic quality of Truffaut's essay. First, in a polemical essay so preoccupied with an absolute division between the cinema of scenarists and the cinema of authors, it is of course enormously interesting to examine how that division is upset, problematized, or otherwise put into question. Clouzot would appear to be a director, as the preceding discussion makes clear, who can be situated in either camp, or perhaps cannot be situated at all within this particular binary opposition. In other words, Clouzot might well be a figure through whom we can read the cinema in 1950s France otherwise—not in terms of a rigid division between the tradition of quality and the auteur cinema, but in terms, say, of a prodding of those very categories, and of more flexible approaches to the art of adaptation than Truffaut's essay would suggest are possible.

Second, why the sudden mention of "pederasty" in Clouzot's film? Why would Truffaut even bother to mention sexuality in a polemic about the politics of adaptation? It has been argued persuasively by John Hess (1974a, b) that Truffaut's essay is about many things other than adaptation and cinematic authorship. I would suggest that the politics of adaptation is also a sexual politics of adaptation, and that much of Truffaut's discomfort with certain works has more to do with "blasphemy" (a word he himself uses in the essay) understood in a sexual as well as a religious sense. Indeed, one of Truffaut's complaints about Aurenche and Bost is that in their adaptation of Colette's *Le Blé en herbe* the duo wanted to add a lesbian character not present in the original text (Truffaut 1954, 29)!

Clouzot's status as an auteur, as that concept was being theorized in the 1950s, and as exemplified in Truffaut's famous essay, is unclear. My point here is not to refute Truffaut but, rather, to take him at his word, and to situate Clouzot as preoccupied with a realm (sexual identity) and with a practice of adaptation (which in relationship to *Les Diaboliques* I've characterized as inversion) that were not readable in terms of the prevalent theoretical language of the time. Clouzot's work *was* enormously readable in terms of popularity, and one of Truffaut's gripes about the tradition of quality is that it pandered to popular taste, always remaking the same formula. While I do think that Clouzot has been unfairly marginalized as a result of the somewhat narrow ways in which the *politique des auteurs* was formulated by *Cahiers du cinéma,* my point is not just that Clouzot's work deserves more critical attention, but that a rethinking of the 1950s in French cinema is called for.

The lesbian plot in *Les Diaboliques* connects with two fundamental aspects of French cinema in the 1950s—adaptatation and authorship. Truffaut's famous denunciation of the "tradition of quality" in post–World War II French cinema, and his subsequent opposition between the tradition of quality and the true art cinema of directors like Bresson and Cocteau, has tended to obscure the extent to which the practice of cinematic adaptation in 1950s French cinema was often provocative and daring, a process of "reading" novels cinematically and not simply transposing them to the screen. (Somewhat paradoxically, one of Truffaut's major complaints about the tradition of quality is that it takes far too many liberties with literary sources.) Clouzot's adaptations are not only models of this process; they also demonstrate a consistent preoccupation with sexuality and gender as forces that shape and define what is visible, what is cinematic, what can be screened. Clouzot is not an isolated case in this regard. At least he was mentioned—usually ambivalently, but mentioned nonetheless—by Truffaut. Jacqueline Audry, virtually the only woman working in the studio system of the 1950s, was ignored by the *Cahiers* group, her work considered so unproblematically a part of the tradition of quality as to be unmentionable. Yet Audry's work is far more complex than any simple denunciation of the tradition of quality would suggest. It is more likely the case that the explorations into gender and sexuality so evident in her work simply had no frame of reference for the *Cahiers* folks (see Flock 1999).

At the opposite end of the spectrum, Jean Cocteau may well have been one of the directors cited approvingly by Truffaut and the critics of *Les Cahiers du cinéma,* but the price paid for this recognition was a consistent marginalization of how Cocteau's "art cinema" was informed by probing and testing the limits of the distinction between homosexual and heterosexual desire. Ultimately, the practice of cinematic authorship in the 1950s was not always so easily divided between the true auteurs and the industry hacks. Clouzot is a prime example of another path not really given credit by Truffaut: a director engaged with the traditions of popular film and popular literature, suggesting other ways of imaging a cinema that would be distinctly French and distinctly part of the culture of everyday life of the 1950s.

To raise the question of a lesbian plot is to suggest that lesbian desire is far more central than is usually acknowledged either vis-à-vis this particular film or films of its era, the ubiquitously repressive 1950s. Consider, by way of conclusion, the most recent remake of the film, starring Sharon Stone and Isabelle Adjani, which has been defined by its stars and its director as an attempt to restore some of the lesbianism that was presumably repressed in Clouzot's film.[5] Director Jeremiah Chechik says of the 1955 film that there was "so much of the relationship between the two women [that] was not and could not be dealt with culturally at the time. I just felt that [we had the opportunity] to stay emotionally truer to the book, the original material, and do a much more complex version" (quoted in Pizzello 1996, 37).

This "truer" and "more complex" version thus attempts to "update" the original film in several ways: by foregrounding the flirtation between the two women who plot to kill the man who makes their lives miserable; by changing the ending of the film and thereby supposedly weakening the motivating force of heterosexual passion; and by making the male detective a woman who affirms the death of the husband as a blow against patriarchy. Critical and popular opinion would suggest that these changes have been less than successful. Curiously, the supposedly new and improved *Diabolique* has drawn attention to the lesbian attraction that underscores Clouzot's film. As Janet Maslin noted in her review of the 1996 remake, "[in Clouzot's film] the very sight of the victim's dainty wife and his tough, steely mistress . . . is enough to suggest all manner of forbidden possibilities. Not least of which is that the women care more about each other than either ever cared about a man" (1996, 19).

It is perhaps not too surprising that in the process of revising Clouzot's original film, the recent *Diabolique* shares less with the 1955 film and more with recent popular films about women conspiring to get rid of the obnoxious men in their lives (e.g., *Mortal Thoughts,* 1991), as well as with those American remakes of European films that supply more upbeat endings (e.g., *The Vanishing,* 1993). In addition, Sharon Stone's performance, in the role created by Simone Signoret, plays off of her bisexual femme fatale in *Basic Instinct* (1992), the role that made her a star. Even though the remake compares unfavorably to Clouzot's classic, the supposed honesty of its portrayal of the relationship between the two female protagonists offers an opportunity to consider whether it is indeed so easy to define the 1950s generally, and French cinema of that period specifically, as a cultural wasteland insofar as sexual marginalities are concerned.

Yet the lesbian plot is banished in *Les Diaboliques,* and so I find myself caught in the very ambiguities of the spectral lesbian. Her banishment may well be homophobic. But her presence throughout the film is so powerful that the banishment requires an arsenal of obviously manipulative cinematic techniques. Nicole must literally disappear—or, rather, be disappeared—from the corridor before she can resurface as Michel's partner in crime. Thus the lesbian plot of *Les Diaboliques* effects a significant rupture in the overall style and logic of the film. In the original screenplay of the film, there is no description of Nicole's disappearance in the corridor, and the voice of the child reciting the passage from Racine's play is heard coming from Nicole's classroom at a point when Christina is overcome with anxiety about the disappearance of her husband's body (Clouzot 1954). Originally, then, the citation of Racine was meant to function in much the same way as the other voices of the boys do. Of course, one fully expects there to be changes, adaptations, and discrepancies between a script and a finished film, but such changes can also be enormously productive when read in light of the effects they produce, particularly when they result in a scene that stands out so startlingly as the vanishing of Nicole's body does. Something in *Les Diaboliques* required reworking and refashioning; the lesbian plot demanded another scene of representation. Signoret's Nicole may well vanish into thin air, but her decidedly complex presence casts a spell over the entire film.

Notes

1. The novel has become so identified with the success of the film that it is now sold under the title *Les Diaboliques,* with *Celle qui n'était plus* as a subtitle. Boileau and Narcejac were not entirely satisfied with Clouzot's adaptation of their novel (1954, 7–9).

2. I am grateful to Marie-Claire Vallois for pointing out the significance of *Athalie* in this context.

3. Thanks to Nelly Furman for discussing the scene with me, and for suggesting the relevance of Sartre.

4. Thanks to Kelly Hankin for suggesting the extent to which the de-lesbianizing of Nicole facilitates the heterosexual resolution of the film.

5. In addition to the 1996 remake, *Les Diaboliques* has been remade as two television movies: *Reflections of Murder* (1974) and *House of Secrets* (1993).

Works Cited

Barbey d'Aurevilly, Jules. 1973 (1874). *Les Diaboliques.* Paris: Editions Gallimard.

Bertin-Maghit, Jean-Pierre. 1996. "*Les Diaboliques* ou le Discours de la Terreur." In *Terreur et Représentation,* ed. Pierre Glaudes. Grenoble: ELLUG (Université Stendhal), 271–86.

Bocquet, José-Louis, and Marc Godin. 1993. *Henri-Georges Clouzot Cinéaste.* Sèvres: Editions La Sirène.

Boileau, Pierre, and Thomas Narcejac. 1954. *The Woman Who Was No More.* New York: Rinehart.

———. *Les Diaboliques (Celle qui n'était plus).* 1952. Paris: Folio. Reprinted in 1994.

Castle, Terry. 1993. *The Apparitional Lesbian: Female Homosexuality and Modern Culture.* New York: Columbia University Press.

Chauncey, George Jr. 1989. "From Sexual Inversion to Homosexuality: The Changing Medical Conceptualization of Female 'Deviance.'" In *Passion and Power: Sexuality in History,* ed. Kathy Peiss and Christina Simmons. Philadelphia: Temple University Press, 87–117.

Clouzot, Henri-Georges. 1954. "Les Veuves." In *Collection scénarios.* Paris: Bibliothèque du Film.

Doane, Mary Ann. 1987. *The Desire to Desire.* Bloomington: Indiana University Press.

Ehrlich, Evelyn. 1985. *Cinema of Paradox.* New York: Columbia University Press.

Faderman, Lillian. 1991. *Odd Girls and Twilight Lovers.* New York: Columbia University Press.

Flock, Jennifer. 1999. "Jacqueline Audry, Adaptrice de Colette: Le Désir Féminin au Premier Plan." *Iris* 26: 49–64.

Foster, Jeanette. 1985 (1956). *Sex Variant Women in Literature.* Tallahassee: Naiad Press.

Hadleigh, Boze. 1993. *The Lavender Screen.* New York: Citadel Press.

Hall, Radclyffe. 1990 (1928). *The Well of Loneliness.* New York: Anchor Books.

Hayward, Susan. 1995. "Simone Signoret 1921–1985: The Star as Sign—the Sign as Scar." In *Women and Representation,* ed. Diana Knight and Judith Still. Nottingham: WIF Publications, 57–74.

Hess, John. 1974a. "La Politique Des Auteurs, Part One: World View as Aesthetic." *Jump Cut* 1: 19–22.

———. 1974b. "La Politique Des Auteurs, Part Two: Truffaut's Manifesto." *Jump Cut* 2: 20–22.

Hottell, Ruth A. 1996. "The Diabolic Dialogic: *Les Diaboliques* by H. G. Clouzot." *Film Literature Quarterly* 24, no. 3: 255–60.

Mallet-Joris, Françoise. 1975 (1952). *The Illusionist.* Trans. Herma Briffault. New York: Arno Press.

Marks, Elaine. 1979. "Lesbian Intertexuality." In *Homosexualities and French Literature,* ed. George Stambolian and Elaine Marks. Ithaca, N.Y.: Cornell University Press, 353–77.

Maslin, Janet. 1996. "Oh, Forget the Cerebral. Just Kill Him." *New York Times,* 22 March, 19.

Newton, Esther. 1984. "The Mythic Mannish Lesbian: Radclyffe Hall and the New Woman." *Signs: Journal of Women in Culture and Society* 9, no. 4: 557–75.

Petit, Jacques, ed. 1974. *L'Histoire des Diaboliques.* Paris: Lettres Modernes.

Philbert, Bertrand. 1984. *L'Homosexualité à l'Écran.* Paris: Henri Veyrier.

Pizzello, Chris. 1996. "Bringing the Dark Side of Character to Light in *Diabolique.*" *American Cinematographer* April: 36–43.

Racine, Jean. 1960a. "Athaliah." In *Jean Racine: Five Plays,* ed. Kenneth Muir. New York: Hill and Wang, 227–88.

———. 1960b. "Athalie." In *Théâtre Complet de Jean Racine,* ed. Maurice Rat. Paris: Editions Garnier Frères, 647–715.

Roberts, Mary Louise. 1992. "'This Civilization No Longer Has Sexes': *La Garçonne* and Cultural Crisis in France after World War I." *Gender and History* 4 (Spring): 49–69.

Ropars-Wuillemier, Marie-Claire. 1972. *De la Littérature au Cinéma.* Paris: Armand Colin.

Ross, Kristin. 1995. *Fast Cars, Clean Bodies.* Cambridge: MIT Press.

Sartre, Jean-Paul. 1965 (1946). *Anti-Semite and Jew.* Trans. George J. Becker. New York: Schocken Books.

Siclier, Jacques. 1981. *La France de Pétain et Son Cinéma.* Paris: Henri Veyrier.

Truffaut, François. 1954. "Une Certaine Tendance du Cinéma Français." *Cahiers du cinéma* 31: 15–29.

White, Patricia. 1991. "Female Spectator, Lesbian Specter: *The Haunting.*" In *Inside/Out: Lesbian Theories, Gay Theories,* ed. Diana Fuss. New York and London: Routledge, 142–72.

II

In and Out: Feminism in Mass Culture

4. Walking the *Tightrope* of Feminism and Male Desire

This essay originated at the Modern Language Association meeting in 1984, where Paul Smith and Alice Jardine organized two panels on "Men in Feminism." The presentations from those panels, as well as several other additional essays, were eventually published in an eponymous volume (Jardine and Smith 1987). While the panels and the subsequent book were meant to be provocative, it was certainly not the case then (or now) that men have been absent from feminism. Over the years, earnest discussions have taken place in women's studies classrooms about the necessity to "educate" or to "include" men, for instance. "Men in feminism" is hardly a new formulation.

What distinguished this particular forum was, precisely, its *theoretical* dimension. The negotiation of men's relation to feminism evident in the panels and the book thus marks perhaps a new stage of theoretical sophistication within feminism. The relative merits of that theoretical sophistication might then be tested by examining the relationship to feminism of a certain kind of man, equally theoretically sophisticated. The task of any theoretical project is to examine the working field of oppositions that constitute the scope of inquiry, in this case, feminist inquiry. Feminist theory is thus assessed in the essays by Stephen Heath, Paul Smith, and Andrew Ross that were included in *Men in Feminism.* Heath describes man's "impossible relationship" to feminism as a sign, a symptom of feminist theory as a simultaneous investment in and distance from the persistent dualisms on which our most fundamental, and problematic, notions of identity are based. Smith situates the theoretical sophistication of feminism as a problem, the danger of a theory with a limited academic field of application: hence the familiar yet problematic fit between theory and practice defines his engagement with feminism. In Ross's discussion of the Yorkshire Ripper, the theoretical issue is most succinctly understood as a battle of opposing views. His demonstration of the "dangers of failing to distinguish between the natural and the sexual" (1987, 49) collapses the distinction between the law and a certain kind of feminism that wants to speak in the name of "all women." Thus there are two theoretical protagonists in Ross's discussion that correspond to the poles of "essentialism" and "antiessentialism" (and their attendant implications of French and American allegiances) in debates within feminism.

My purpose in this essay is to look at the theoretical agenda that frames these discussions of "men in feminism" from a perspective that is more appropriately described as a narrative vantage point than a theoretical one per se. The essays by Heath, Smith, and Ross to which the participants on the panel "Men in Feminism II" (the second panel at the 1984 MLA conference) were asked to respond are obviously theoretical texts; but they are as well narratives that possess a point of view (unified or otherwise) and unfold (problematically or not) across a field of binary oppositions. The narrative to which I turn is of a distinctly different (but not unrelated) kind, for it is a commercial film defined throughout by the persona of an actor who would appear to have an antagonistic relationship at best to the issue of men in feminism.

The film is *Tightrope* (1984), in which the image of Clint Eastwood as it has evolved over the years is pondered and interrogated. (Noting that the film was scripted and directed by Richard Tuggle, J. Hoberman speculates that "*Tightrope* is so personal that Eastwood couldn't sign it" [1984]). In *Tightrope* Clint Eastwood portrays a policeman, Wes Block, who is investigating a series of murders of women, all of them sex related. *Tightrope* is a film obsessed with division, with separation, with the tension of opposition, most graphically portrayed in the spatial opposition between the Tenderloin district of New Orleans, where many of the murders occur, and the suburban neighborhood where Block lives with his two daughters. (Block's ex-wife, glimpsed only briefly in the film, has left him and the family.)

The film is equally obsessed with sexual difference, and with the difference between two kinds of females—sexual partners and daughters. Wes Block walks a tightrope in that the separation of the two worlds of the film is fragile, and the narrative of *Tightrope* occupies the threshold space between the two realms. While the imagery of the film conveys the tightrope of the film's title, a brief discussion between Block and a

Clint Eastwood as Wes Block in *Tightrope*.

woman in a courthouse makes clear that the tightrope on which Block is poised is first and foremost a function of his own balancing act in relation to the worlds of law and sexual desire that he inhabits. The woman speculates about the killer's motivations and tells Block that "there's a darkness inside all of us . . . you, me, the man down the street. Some have it under control. The rest of us try to walk a tightrope between the two." The killer sought by Block is not out to get all women, or even all prostitutes (in any case, the film is unsure what the difference is). The killer is out to get Wes Block. He knows Block's fears and desires better than Block himself. Block's investigations lead him to sexual liaisons with several prostitutes, where his fancy for bondage in handcuffs becomes particularly evident. The murderer is an omnipresent voyeur, and each woman with whom Block makes contact becomes a victim of the killer. Block's double eventually transgresses the boundary line separating the two worlds of the film, penetrating the suburban house and assaulting Block's older daughter. Block's pursuit of the killer is an encounter with himself, with his own repressed—and some not-so-repressed—desires, until the final, inevitable showdown between the two men when the murderer is killed.

What makes *Tightrope* if not an exceptional film then at least an interesting one is that this is a Clint Eastwood film "with a difference."

Tightrope is a confessional film, and one to which a formula invoked in some discussions of pornography is particularly appropriate: *Tightrope* is the theory, Dirty Harry the practice. And even though *Tightrope* is not explicitly about pornography but, rather, about the network of relationships of which pornography is one expression, and even though Clint Eastwood may not be one of the "legions of feminist men," the film addresses more convincingly than many other texts the question raised by B. Ruby Rich: "If the legions of feminist men want to do something useful they could undertake the analysis that can tell us why men like porn" (1982, 30).

As a self-reflexive Eastwood film, *Tightrope* ponders questions and connections that might be unspeakable in another kind of film: between pleasure and danger, between heterosexual and homosexual desire, between paternal affection and incest, between sexuality and violence. More precisely, *Tightrope* problematizes the connections. The connections take on a particularly interesting narrative configuration. For the obligatory romance transpires with a woman, Beryl Thibodeaux (portrayed by Geneviève Bujold), who as director of a rape crisis center is concerned about the status of the investigations and is concerned in the name of "all women." It's worth pointing out here how unusual this designation of a female lead is in contemporary Hollywood cinema. If feminism has been mainstreamed into Hollywood, it is usually in terms of female heroism, or the conflict between love and career, and rarely in terms of a discourse or a perspective or a character that can be even remotely described as *feminist.* I mention this not in order to praise *Tightrope* as a progressive film but to ask what is served, within the narrative logic of this film, by such an allusion to feminism. This is an allusion that transcends the *Tootsie* school of feminist impersonation, for the representation of Geneviève Bujold as a feminist emphasizes her initial separation from the world occupied by Wes Block, a separation that is too profound to be bridged by a simple masquerade.

Tightrope is a love story of sorts, a heterosexual romance where desire leads, in however different ways, to connections between sexuality and violence. What Eastwood does in practice, Bujold ponders in theory. The connection between sexuality and violence is for Wes Block a symptom of the split between the two worlds of the film, and it is the function of Beryl Thibodeaux to heal that split. The feminist here is defined not only as the woman who defends female sexuality against male violence, but also as a figure who presumably comprehends the links between sexuality and violence.

If *Tightrope* is the theory and Dirty Harry the practice, then the links between sexuality and violence so central to *Tightrope* can be read in relation to the Dirty Harry films. In the first, *Dirty Harry* (1971), the narrative relies on an obsessive division of the world between good and evil. Harry Callahan pursues a killer who has raped a fourteen-year-old girl and buried her alive. The villain is unquestionably "other" in this film, an otherness emphasized by his hatred of yet simultaneous identification with gays. Early in the film, we see the killer attempt to shoot a gay man. Later, the killer arranges a meeting with Harry in a park known as a gay hangout. When he enters the park, Harry comes across a gay man whom he mistakes for the killer, and when Harry introduces himself, the man, called "Alice," assumes that Harry is flirting with him. The first encounter between Harry and the killer, then, is mediated and shaped by Harry's encounter with Alice. In the logic of this film, Dirty Harry and the villain are of two entirely different worlds. The only characteristic shared by the two worlds is the complete absence of women. In *Magnum Force* (1973), Dirty Harry is still a lone force of law and order, but the police department, which in the first Dirty Harry film was portrayed as hopelessly bound up in excessive liberal concern for the rights of criminals, here is seen as corrupt in its own right. For the villains that are the object of Dirty Harry's search turn out to be four young policemen and a police official who are members of a vigilante group. The gay sexuality hinted at in *Dirty Harry* is present in *Magnum Force* as well; as Harry's partner tells him, everyone in the department used to think the four young cops were "'queer." Women are by and large excluded from the configuration of this film as well.

In *The Enforcer* (1976), Dirty Harry confronts affirmative action and is forced to work with a female partner, portrayed by Tyne Daly. By some stretch of the imagination, she could be construed as a "positive image" in the sense that she turns out to be quite a good cop indeed—by saving Harry's life and losing her own. Here, too, Harry makes a foray into a massage parlor (posing as "Larry Dickman"), which, although strictly in the line of business, could be seen as a prelude to Wes Block's journeys into the sex commerce in *Tightrope.*

The Dirty Harry film that is perhaps closest thematically as well as chronologically to *Tightrope* is *Sudden Impact* (1983), in which a woman artist (portrayed by Sondra Locke) systematically kills off a number of men, and one woman, who had gang-raped her and her sister some years before. Harry's investigation proves to be somewhat more complex than in the earlier Dirty Harry films, for the woman's decision to take the law into her own hands (one of the rapists was the son of the local sheriff, who helped the criminals avoid punishment for their crime) makes her an appropriate double for Dirty Harry. In *Sudden Impact,* the sexual relationship between the woman and Dirty Harry leads to the somewhat predictable conclusion that she may be guilty of the murders but innocent of any crime. Her real crime—or disease—is man hating, for which Dirty Harry provides the cure. He thus protects her in the name of a higher law.

When seen from the vantage point of *Tightrope,* two themes that circulate in the Dirty Harry series of films are particularly striking. The first is the strong suggestion of homosexuality, which increases in direct proportion to the invisibility of women. It is almost as if the characters portrayed by Tyne Daly and Sondra Locke are significant in direct proportion to their ability to ward off the simultaneous attraction and repulsion of male homosexuality. In *Tightrope* the killer leads Block on a sexual chase that includes a stop in a gay male bar and a rendezvous with a male prostitute. Block refuses the man, but when asked, "How do you know you don't like it if you haven't tried it?" Block replies, "Maybe I have." Even in sarcasm, the suggestion of such a possibility loosens up the boundary lines between gay and straight that are so central to the Dirty Harry films.

Second is the simultaneous attraction and repulsion of women themselves. If women are virtually absent from the narrative configurations of *Dirty Harry* and *Magnum Force* as anything but cursory victims or imaginary reminders of the past (by way of brief reminders, for example, of Dirty Harry's deceased wife), the characters in *The Enforcer* and *Sudden Impact* are significant others. Daly, as Inspector Moore, is "plain" by Hollywood standards (and therefore "refreshing" by others); she wears sensible clothes and little makeup. What little sexual identity she has in the film is expressed in a telling scene with Harry when she refers to a building as "phallic" (Harry, somewhat confused, asks her if everything has a sexual connotation for her). As a somewhat detached observer of sexual symbolism, she anticipates Bujold's role in *Tightrope.* As the artist, Jennifer, Locke is like Harry in her single-minded pursuit of revenge, and the crossing of their paths keeps her hatred of a group of rapists from becoming a hatred of all men. (The designation of one woman, occasionally referred to as a "dyke," as a member of the gang sets up an opposition between gay and straight women that is not transgressed.)

Seen against the background of the Dirty Harry cycle, the narrative logic whereby feminism is "named" in *Tightrope* facilitates the opening up of the space between opposing terms—the blurring of the boundaries between the realms of gay and straight, between desire and violence, between men and women, between good and evil. Like the female leads in *The Enforcer* and *Sudden Impact,* Bujold's character represents a kind of otherness with which Dirty Harry contends. But as a feminist, the Bujold character has something that the other female leads do not. For in *Tightrope* feminism becomes a principle of law and order unavailable in the tightrope configuration of Wes Block's identity and identification with the killer. Daly's character becomes an acceptable partner by showing that she shares the same sense of law as Harry, and Locke's is motivated by personal rage. As a feminist, then, the Bujold character kills the proverbial two birds with one stone: she is distinctly "other" than Block, yet she represents a set of social values that, however strange or foreign they might be to him, are values to be contended with. Feminism as it is represented in the film thus allows a reshuffling of the polarities of desire and violence.

However novel the role ascribed to the woman in *Tightrope* might be in the context of the Dirty Harry films, the function of Beryl Thibodeaux, when defined in this way, rings stereotypically true: woman as a principle of morality, the icon that in a long history of Hollywood genres (the Western in particular comes to mind) allows the passage to resolution of one male identity crisis or another. But in the narrative of *Tightrope,* woman alone cannot function to this end: feminism is required. Put another way, the film needs to introduce a working opposition between *female* and *feminist.*

All females—and again, one can't really say *woman* here, since the detective's own prepubescent daughters figure so centrally—are potential objects of the conflation of desire and violence, whereas the feminist observes the conflation from a theorist's point of view. *Tightrope* appears to resolve quickly the distinction by having Block come to the rescue when the Bujold character is attacked by the killer. She defends herself—she teaches self-defense classes, after all—but it appears as though she is about to be killed when Block arrives on the scene. This is the first woman Block has been able to "save."

If it appears as though the film introduces the distinction between *female* and *feminist* only to collapse it quickly into heterosexual formula, it is important to note that the rescue is not quite as clear-cut as my description might suggest. In an earlier scene, Wes Block is attacked by the killer and is saved only because one of his dogs (the only one spared, or missed, by the killer) comes to his rescue. And Thibodeaux does use

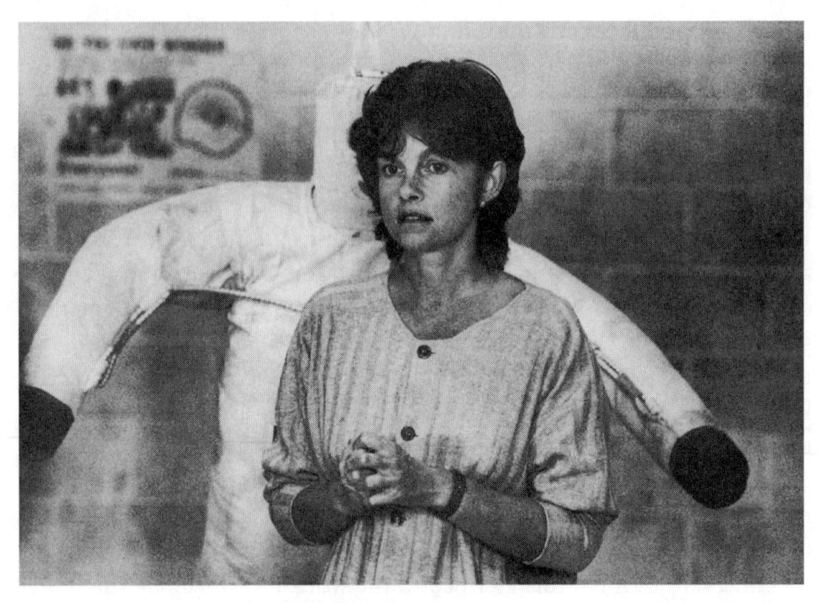

Geneviève Bujold as Beryl Thibodeaux in *Tightrope.*

every means imaginable to defend herself, from the techniques of self-defense to stabbing the villain with a pair of scissors (it worked for Grace Kelly in *Dial M for Murder*). Beryl Thibodeaux may well be rescued by a man, but the man himself was saved by a dog. Again, I point this out not in order to make claims for the "progressive" image of woman, or of male-female relations in this film, but rather to stress that the narrative resolutions are not as straightforward as they might initially seem or as one might expect. Indeed, for all the classic straightforwardness of the binary oppositions in *Tightrope,* the most distinctive overall tone of the film is confusion. To be sure, *Tightrope* has the proverbial happy ending, but virtually every step toward the resolution is marked by such uncertainty that it is not always clear what is being resolved. While Block tells the press that the murders are sex related, and while several of the women are clearly identified as prostitutes, the circumstances are unclear in several instances. Nor is it made clear the extent to which sexual abuse is a part of the murders. The most devastating violation in the film is the assault on Block's daughter, yet an easily dismissed aside by a police inspector assures the listener that no sexual assault occurred.

The very premise of *Tightrope* is a kind of confusion: Wes Block (once referred to as "Inspector Blocked" by Thibodeaux) doesn't know who he is, doesn't know how his desires are different from a killer's desires, doesn't know what a woman is. But in attempting to set right that confusion, *Tightrope* plunges deeper into another kind of confusion concerning male sexuality. Block's younger daughter, Penny—the only female in the film who escapes a sexual identity—asks a question, intended superficially as comic relief, which serves as a kind of pivot to the film: "What's a hard-on, Daddy?" Penny speaks from a position not unlike that of the feminist, a position of detachment (innocent in the daughter's case, critical and theoretical in the feminist's). The film has no answer for the question she asks. Wes Block sleeps with women, and the murderer kills them, but what indeed is a hard-on? Is it the desire to kill, or the desire for sex, and is it possible to resituate the polarities of violence and sexuality in any but either-or terms? If the director of a rape crisis center is a sexual being, how is she sexual? The only time we actually see Beryl Thibodeaux in the context of the crisis center is when she demonstrates attack points on a dummy to a female self-defense class. After showing kicks to various sensitive parts of the body, she tells her class that if the attacker continues to act "tacky," there is one final point of attack—a final, swift kick to the groin. *Tackiness* is, of course, a term that would be more applicable to the etiquette of dating than to sexual assault—again, a symptom of the film's confusion between the two. And when the kick is delivered to the groin of the dummy, its eyes light up. Block, who has been observing the class, winces in a gesture that can be read either as admiration or repulsion.

Tightrope is as unsure of what rape is as it is of what a hard-on is. Now the assertion that a Clint Eastwood film shares an affinity with feminism might seem somewhat delirious, but this confusion in *Tightrope* is analogous to the contradictory ways in which rape has been articulated as a theoretical and ideological issue within feminism. One feminist argument is founded on the incompatibility of sex and rape and thus defines rape as a crime of violence, not a crime of sex. Another argument claims that rape is the very paradigm of male sexuality, or of male heterosexuality. However different these positions, in both cases there is the desire to rescue sexuality—whether in the name of lesbianism as a moment outside of patriarchal relations, or in the name of a utopian heterosexuality between free and equal agents.

The feminist politics of rape crisis centers and feminist theories about rape do not leave much room for a discussion of men in feminism. In any case, the issue of rape evokes "radical feminism," and radical feminism seems to have become something of a specter haunting the discussion of men in feminism. Critics of radical feminism have focused on a variety of issues, such as the identification of men and women as belonging to inherently hostile and antagonistic camps, or the resurrection of the duality of oppression and emancipation, or the sometimes mocking attitude toward heterosexuality as a component of any kind of viable feminist identity. If, in the 1970s, the charges against radical feminism were reproaches against separatism, in the 1980s those charges tend to focus on the sin of essentialism as a naive belief in a female identity that escapes patriarchal contamination and erupts in certain privileged contexts.

Current debates about sexuality and pornography in particular have polarized feminists, and the terms of the polarity are often reduced to essentialist claims about the purity of female experience versus anti-essentialist positions, which while diverse in their points of emphasis, stress the difficult and contradictory nature of identity, whether male or female. While I don't question the necessity to be on the lookout for rampant essentialism, I do wonder about the usefulness of a so-called debate in which the same oppositions emerge again and again. And in particular I question the narrative logic and the theoretical agenda served by invocations, conscious or not, of "radical feminism" or "essentialism." A provocative *in,* like the one connecting *men* and *feminism,* has an implicit "other"—the other of radical feminism, of separatism (whatever that may be construed to mean). The radical feminist thus caricatured is part of a community (lesbian, or feminist, or both) in which men are not only not addressed but irrelevant. She is thus unwilling to engage with real men or masculinity. That there may be or have been historical reasons for separatist activity, or that the term *radical feminism* may include more diversity than the often-repeated slogan "porn is the theory, rape the practice" would suggest; that radical feminism might be about something more than, *other* than, the exclusion of men—in short, that radical feminism may itself be part of a complex *narrative* rather than the bad object of essentialist theory—is thus obscured.

Male desire in *Tightrope* also demonstrates a fear of irrelevance and a subsequent repression that makes the portrait of a feminist slightly askew. The portrayal of the Bujold character is surprisingly "accurate," remarkably free of the "libber" stereotype one might expect in an Eastwood film. But there is a mistake, a gap, in this portrayal of the discourse of feminism. Except for her relationship with the detective's daughters, Beryl Thibodeaux has virtually no relationship with women, no connection to anything remotely resembling a community of women. Feminism in terms so irreducible or inapplicable to the problematic nature of male sexuality is unrepresentable. Feminism in *Tightrope* is the object of a certain kind of male desire—the desire for resolution, to be sure, but also the desire for a heterosexual relationship where the transgression of boundaries can be pondered without losing one's self.

That the creation of a feminist in *Tightrope* is an ideological as well as a narrative gesture hardly needs to be emphasized. *Tightrope* is located within that ubiquitous and nebulous entity, "classical Hollywood cinema," many analyses of which have demonstrated that narrative resolution often not only incorporates but turns on such blind spots. However much the projects of theory and narrative might overlap, it is the task of theory to interrogate the patterns of opposition and resolution, not to replicate them. The desire, in *Tightrope,* for a feminism that comforts and affirms is not unlike the desire of a male theorist to be "in" feminism or to dismantle feminism from the comfortable vantage point of a certain kind of theoretical discourse. This is not to say that there is something "wrong" with that desire. But there is a fit between theory and narrative, and the intersection of feminism and male desire needs to be thought—and rethought—out by submitting theory to the test of narrative.

Works Cited

Heath, Stephen. 1987a. "Male Feminism." In Jardine and Smith, 1–32.

———. 1987b. "Men in Feminism: Men and Feminist Theory." In Jardine and Smith, 41–46.

Hoberman, J. 1984. "Double Indemnity." *The Village Voice,* 28 August, 46.

Jardine, Alice, and Paul Smith. 1987. *Men in Feminism.* New York and London: Methuen.

Rich, B. Ruby. 1982. "Anti-Porn: Soft Issue, Hard World." *The Village Voice,* 20 July, 1, 16–18, 30.

Ross, Andrew. 1987. "Demonstrating Sexual Difference." In Jardine and Smith, 47–53.

Smith, Paul. 1987. "Men in Feminism: Men and Feminist Theory." In Jardine and Smith, 33–40.

5. *L.A. Law* and Prime-Time Feminism

The reference to "prime-time feminism" in my title might seem initially to be a contradiction in terms, or at the very least a tongue-in-cheek starting point from which, if I were speaking from the vantage point of "authentic" feminism, I would be expected to demonstrate that prime-time feminism is not feminism at all. I am not concerned here, however, with the authenticity of representations of feminism but, rather, with the significance of the fact that increasingly feminism is being appropriated by various mass cultural forms. At a time when the crazed demands of the most famous American female villain of 1987, Glenn Close's Alex in *Fatal Attraction,* evoke striking parallels with the feminist critique of male privilege, it is important for feminist critics to continue to examine and rethink the links between feminism and mass culture (Modleski 1984). If the limitations of the progress model—according to which feminist pressure on the media has resulted in supposedly better images of women—are fairly self-evident, there remains nonetheless a cynicism on the part of many feminists about the ways in which feminism has been appropriated and assumed by, or otherwise grafted onto, mass cultural forms.

My concern in this essay is with the relationship between feminism and television narrative in a series that has been praised widely for its engagement with issues of gender and sexual politics. The product of a collaboration between Terry Louise Fisher (formerly of *Cagney & Lacey*) and Steven Bochco (the co-creator of *Hill Street Blues*), *L.A. Law* began its regular run in 1986. There are, of course, other television programs in which feminist questions have been raised, and still others that feminists have found more progressive and satisfying than *L.A. Law*—from *Golden*

Girls with its focus on female bonding and aging to *Cagney & Lacey*'s female, and occasionally feminist, heroics. Yet *L.A. Law* is distinctly interesting for the feminist questions it raises, due in large part to how those questions are given narrative shape and definition within the particular format of the multipart and overlapping narrative and ensemble cast structure. Put another way, *L.A. Law* represents feminism not only as a thematic issue but also as a narrative one.

That *L.A. Law* is the successor to *Hill Street Blues* is fairly obvious, not only through the Bochco connection but also through *L.A. Law*'s position in the NBC Thursday night lineup in the spot previously held by *Hill Street Blues.* Like *Hill Street Blues,* as well as other MTM productions, including *The Mary Tyler Moore Show, L.A. Law* focuses on the surrogate family of the workplace, where a benevolent patriarch (Leland McKenzie, corresponding to Lou Grant in *The Mary Tyler Moore Show* and Frank Furillo in *Hill Street Blues*) presides over a family of coworkers (Feuer et al. 1984). Now it is tempting to view *L.A. Law* as the upscale, yuppie revision of *Hill Street Blues,* with some significant changes: more women in *L.A. Law,* a more distinctly heterosocial environment (as opposed to the homosocial world of *Hill Street Blues*), and less "messiness," that is, *L.A. Law* is much cleaner, much more straightforward, and despite its overlapping story lines, much easier to follow than *Hill Street Blues.*

While I do not disagree that *Hill Street Blues* was a more innovative program, the very term *innovation* can be misleading in television criticism since, as many critics have argued, television innovation has more to do with recombining other components of television programming than with inventing startling new forms (Gitlin 1983, esp. chap. 5). Hence, *Hill Street Blues* was innovative to the extent that it combined elements of live television, soap opera, and episodic comedy and drama (Gitlin 1983, esp. chap. 14). *L.A. Law* may thus be innovative in a different way, for it takes the "feminism" that previously had been associated with relatively one-dimensional formats (the cop show in *Cagney & Lacey,* the sitcom in *Golden Girls*) and combines it with the multinarrative, large-cast format associated with MTM productions like *Hill Street Blues* and *St. Elsewhere.* But I would argue as well that the overlapping narrative structure of *L.A. Law* is qualitatively different from its predecessors, for in it the very possibility of multiple narration is predicated on the terms of gender.

In the pilot for *L.A. Law,* one of the central story lines focuses on the relationship between Michael Kuzak, a partner in the firm of McKenzie, Brackman, Chaney, and Kuzak, and Adrienne Moore (portrayed by

The original cast of *L.A. Law*: Last row, left to right: Alan Rachins as Douglas Brackman Jr.; Jimmy Smits as Victor Sifuentes; Richard A. Dysart as Leland McKenzie. Middle row: Jill Eikenberry as Ann Kelsey; Michael Tucker as Stuart Markowitz; Michele Greene as Abby Perkins; Susan Ruttan as Roxanne Melman. Bottom row: Harry Hamlin as Michael Kuzak; Corbin Bernsen as Arnie Becker.

Alfre Woodard), who appears in court to testify against a group of young men accused of gang-raping her and throwing her in a dumpster. Kuzak is the reluctant lawyer for one of the young men, the son of a wealthy client of the firm. Moore suffers from leukemia, a fact that gives the defense an opportunity to pursue a peculiarly twisted logic: since she has so little time left to live, she had been undoubtedly on the prowl for some wild group sex with the young men. "Gather ye rosebuds while you may, Miss Moore," says the lawyer who questions her. Moore's response is not only outrage but failure to comprehend the lawyer's turn of phrase and genuine perplexity as to why she cannot explain *her* side of the story. Moore becomes enraged and stands up and shouts, "I want to know who is on trial here." The judge warns her that if she continues, she'll be held in contempt, to which Moore responds tearfully and angrily that the feeling is mutual. The lawyer questioning her proposes a continuance, and Moore accuses him, and the court, of delaying the trial until she dies. The judge interrupts Moore's impassioned response by saying, "I warn you." Moore responds furiously, "I warn *you*—this door swings both ways," and threatens to get a gun in order to take justice into her own hands. She is then cited for contempt and temporarily removed from the courtroom until she agrees to apologize.

The image of a door swinging both ways, here a function of helpless outrage, is particularly emblematic, not only of this particular story line but of the overall movement and development of *L.A. Law.* For in the pilot Kuzak's manipulation of a situation he finds repugnant is also very appropriately described as swinging a door both ways, but now in a way that allows for a more decisive articulation of justice. Kuzak is identified here as he will be throughout the series as the moral center of *L.A. Law,* the lawyer who agonizes most over what is right and wrong, and whether the law can take the human factor sufficiently into account. Adrienne Moore recognizes that there is not only no hope for justice but no hope for her to tell *her* story in a court of law. She makes the required apologies to the court, retakes the stand, and gives the defense an obvious opportunity to dismiss her testimony when she acknowledges deliberately that the drugs she takes for her disease often produce memory loss and clouded perception. As a result, Kuzak's client, a true stereotype of the obnoxious rich boy, goes free. Kuzak, however, gives a prosecution team member a tip that leads to his client's arrest on other charges, and eventually to his conviction on the rape charge. If the law is a narrative system—and *L.A. Law* emphasizes again and again that the law is first and foremost about storytelling and image making—then the stories of the Adrienne Moores of this world are hopelessly fragmented and ineffective until they are retold by master narrators like Michael Kuzak, for whom doors that swing both ways are fundamental tools of the trade.

That Michael Kuzak is a white male and Adrienne Moore a black female suggests yet another way in which the image of a door swinging both ways is particularly appropriate to describe the TV series. After Kuzak's client has been sentenced to prison (where, as the senior partner of the firm later puts it to Kuzak, he will "learn more about rape than you bargained for"), Kuzak extends an offer of friendship to Moore. In the concluding scene of the pilot, the woman comes to his office and confesses tearfully how afraid she is. The two embrace. Now this conclusion practically begs for a critical reading, for taken at face value it presumes that offers of friendship, not to mention the narrative of the law, can transcend the boundaries of race, class, and gender. Such strains on ideological credulity are common in *L.A. Law,* but they are more significant for the multiple readings that they inspire than for their more obvious melodramatic or humanistic flourish. For depending on your point of view, *L.A. Law* may be read as a "realistic" portrayal and critique of lawyers and the practice of the law, or as a smug portrayal of an us-against-them dichotomy with a liberal veneer. Accordingly, critical response to the series has varied widely, from praise for its satirical and critical presentation of lawyers, to dismissal of its idealized image of the law profession (Kort 1987; Waters and Huck 1987; McWilliams 1986).

L.A. Law is by no means the first prime-time series to capitalize on the door that swings both ways. From sit-coms like *All in the Family* to prime-time soaps like *Dallas,* television narrative has relied centrally on principles of multiple identification and of narrative structure in which there is a fine line, if any line at all, between irony and rhetoric, between critique and celebration (Newcomb 1974, 221–25; Ang 1985, chaps. 3, 4). Indeed, one of the most distinctive characteristics of contemporary television narrative might well be the breaking-down of familiar boundaries—between fiction and nonfiction, transparency and self-reflexivity, progressive and reactionary vantage points (Ellis 1982; Feuer 1984). What is particular to the narrative ambiguity of *L.A. Law* is its constant return not only to issues of gender, which is not so uncommon in television narrative, but also to the ways these issues have been raised in feminist discourse.

For the door that swings both ways in the *L.A. Law* pilot is shaped by the opposition between a woman prevented from telling her story in a court of law and a man who despite his own vested interest in the practice of law is capable of hearing what she has to say *and* of turning the law around in her favor. Michael Kuzak is one of several sensitive male lawyers in the series who are located, in different ways, in an ambiguous space between objectivity and subjectivity, between the law as institutionalized objectivity and the more subjective considerations irreducible to the law. To be sure, Kuzak's narrative and legal desires have to do with his own position as subject. But even if his story is no adequate substitute or replacement for her story, it nonetheless assigns her a vantage point from which some satisfaction, some resolution, is possible. If this particular story line is any indication, *L.A. Law* can only tell its stories by acknowledging, however subtly or indirectly, that men and women occupy radically different positions vis-à-vis the law.

The figure of the swinging door reappears in the first episode of *L.A. Law*'s 1987–88 season. Arnold (Arnie) Becker, the resident womanizer and divorce lawyer of the firm, meets with a male client who is being sued for divorce by his successful and wealthy wife, a television star. Becker describes his client as a man who gave up his own career as an athletic trainer in order to be a full-time homemaker. Thus Becker attempts to convince his client to demand alimony, arguing that "the feminist door swings both ways." The obvious point is that what gains women have made in the name of feminism should be available for men to enjoy as well. In other words, unlike the story line in the pilot, this door evokes the sameness of men and women before the law. According to this logic, feminism guarantees equality, thereby dispelling the fear that women might (again in the name of feminism) usurp male privileges. And while the door that swings both ways in the pilot engages with issues of difference—gender and sexual politics as well as race and class—the swinging door at the beginning of *L.A. Law*'s second season is identified explicitly and exclusively as a *feminist* door. In identifying feminism as an explicit or implicit protagonist, as it has been throughout the first two seasons, the narrative of *L.A. Law* shifts constantly between the two different swinging doors—one suggestive of the radical difference between men and women vis-à-vis the law, and the other of the applicability of the law to men and women alike.

The precredits sequence about the feminist door concludes when Becker, having asked his client for advice about weight training, removes his shirt so that the man can examine his pectorals. Roxanne Melman, Becker's secretary, enters the office unannounced and is suitably shocked at what she sees. The mention of feminism thus serves to inflect the strategies of narration with yet another theme, namely, gayness or bisexuality. And making this inflection even more shocking, few characters on *L.A. Law* have given less indication than Arnold Becker of swinging both ways. While *L.A. Law* often romanticizes excessively about heterosexuality and male-female couples, a tentative but recurrent theme in the series is indeed gay sexuality. Sometimes the topic is explicit, as in a story line on AIDS, or with a lesbian character who rejects Becker's advances. Sometimes it is implicit: the only character whose heterosexuality is not emphasized from the outset is Victor Sifuentes, provoking some viewers to ponder whether his earring was a wandering signifier of difference or, rather, a more precise sign of sexual allegiance. (Eventually, Victor's heterosexuality is established.)

The evocation of gay sexuality in *L.A. Law* seems to me a fairly clear example of "wanting to have it both ways," to quote the gay lawyer who confronts Grace Van Owen in the AIDS case. In other words, allusions to gay sexuality are flirtations with sexual difference that assure rather than challenge heterosexuality as norm. Yet such allusions also suggest a destabilization of that very norm. That feminism permits a gay joke in Arnie's encounter with his client is thus symptomatic of a fundamental narrative link between the two, as simultaneous lure and threat. The lesbian character and story line, for example, appear in a episode that was designed and widely publicized as a response to women viewers who complained that Roxanne Melman's excessive devotion to Arnold Becker was offensive (Kort 1987, 43). In the episode, Roxanne stands firm in her demands for a raise. Her refusal to be seduced by Arnie's attempts to dissuade her is not unlike the lesbian's rejection of his sexual advances. When the two story lines cross and Roxanne responds with shock and disgust to the lesbian's open display of affection with her lover, Roxanne (and the series) gets to "have it both ways": assertiveness is affirmed without the dreaded taint of sexual rejection of men. Yet at the same time, the lesbian represents a detachment from Arnold Becker's sexual bravado, a detachment that is seductive in its own way.

In both the pilot and the second season opener, the doors that swing both ways are defined within terms central to feminist discourse: rape as the ultimate test of whether the law is patriarchal or not; female narration as difficult and marginal; the appropriation of feminism by men to recapture those privileges challenged by feminism in the first place; the definition of feminism as a threat to the heterosexual status quo. But perhaps where *L.A. Law* is most obviously and strikingly feminist is in its cast of characters, all of whom are engaged in various stages of door swinging. The female characters may not necessarily be identified as feminists, but all four major female leads—partner Ann Kelsey, District Attorney Grace Van Owen, associate Abby Perkins, and secretary Roxanne Melman—exhibit variations of two features commonly associated with a popularized view of feminism: power dressing and assertiveness training. The four characters fall into two distinct groups and offer two kinds of pleasure particularly pertinent and interesting to female spectators: on the one hand, there are the two lawyers who have made it and whose power and skill are measured frequently by their abilities to undermine, challenge, or otherwise mock the discourse of patriarchy; and on the other, there are the devoted, underpaid secretary and the insecure, beginning lawyer, who have a more tentative relationship to success and who struggle to affirm an identity within the realm of the law. During the second season, Abby Perkins begins to make the transition from one group to the other. She is the lawyer who is most attentive to people's feelings. The case that marks her initiation into the realm of success concerns a feud between former business partners; her recommendation, which is scoffed at by virtually all the other lawyers in the firm, is that they attempt to reconcile their differences. They do and hire Abby as their lawyer. Abby's success thus implies that the stereotypically female preoccupation with feelings and relationships is compatible with the law.

L.A. Law is not of course the only series on television to equate *feminism* with the styles of power dressing and assertiveness. Prime-time programs such as *Who's the Boss?* come to mind, and the stock figure of the female villain on both prime-time and daytime soaps has not infrequently been given such a "feminist" inflection. Witness, for example, the ruthless businesswoman Lee Halprin on the ABC daytime soap *One Life to Live,* who runs an all-woman consulting firm called Dynawoman and who frequently calls men on their sexism in between planting dead mice in punchbowls and making unscrupulous business deals.

However, the appropriation of feminism in *L.A. Law* is better described in terms of narrative structure than in terms of character per se. Put another way, the cast of characters in the series is more interesting for the ways in which different functions of narration are assigned across gender lines. Individual episodes of *L.A. Law* tend to include anywhere from two to four major story lines, at least one of them a courtroom trial. The story lines are complicated not only by the relations between them but also by the overlapping personal and professional lives of the lawyers. Recurrent scenes and motifs include the staff or partners' meetings, characterized by multiple reaction shots and summary of what has preceded or exposition of what is to come; standard punctuation marks, such as the sweeping pans of the city with which each program begins; and a poignant conclusion, always of two people, usually embracing, frequently Kuzak and Van Owen (again, shades of the bedroom scenes between Joyce Davenport and Frank Furillo that form the coda to *Hill Street Blues* episodes).

Depending on the kinds of cases they are involved in, individual lawyers vary in the amount of narrative authority they possess. Three male characters exercise what might be called a capacity for omniscient narration: Leland McKenzie, the patriarch of the firm and its sole remaining founding partner; Douglas Brackman, son of one of the founders, who oversees the staff meetings and insists constantly on productivity and generating large fees; and Arnold Becker, the most overtly manipulative lawyer of the firm, largely because he recognizes each and every case he takes on as a familiar scenario to which he can, most often, predict the outcome. These three overarching perspectives are consistently mocked in the series: gently, in the case of McKenzie (the partners rise up in virtual revolt when it is revealed he used an old-boy tactic to remove a lawyer from a case); broadly, in the case of Brackman (whose style of "office management" is an ongoing joke); and a little of both in the case of Becker (a perpetual pleasure in the series is watching his narrative predictions backfire). The narrative center of *L.A. Law* is occupied, however, by those lawyers with no pretense to omniscience, and with a more limited narrative range: Ann Kelsey, Grace Van Owen, Michael Kuzak, and Victor Sifuentes in particular. In other words, the overarching narrative perspective of *L.A. Law* comes from juxtaposition and combination, rather than from the identification of a single narrator or a single perspective as the voice of narrative authority and cohesion. Sometimes the interconnectedness of the segments—the thematic overlap between story lines, or an "'echo" effect where story lines reflect off of each other—is made quite evidently, and sometimes it is made more subtly. But almost without exception, the relationships between the different segments in an individual episode are not acknowledged or articulated by the individual lawyers themselves, giving the series its much-acclaimed quality of open-endedness.

L.A. Law has shown a particular preference for story lines on rape. The centrality of multiple and overlapping narration in the series suggests the possibility of a more complex engagement with rape, defined as a problem of representation as well as one of sexual violence, than is usually the case on prime-time television. Now given that one of the most distinctive features of *L.A. Law* is this overlapping and interweaving of story lines, any consideration of narrative must take into account the juxtaposition of segments as a narrative device in its own right. One of the appeals of the law as a framework for narrative, and for television narrative in particular, is that it engages with a multiplicity of narrative perspectives and yet also allows sharp and clear definitions of what is right and what is wrong. In Patrice Petro's terms, television law allows a folding of the hysterical text into the criminal text (Petro 1988). If feminism for *L.A. Law* is a prime example of the door that swings both ways, then where the series is most provocative in feminist terms is in the ways that feminism is narrativized, situated in the context of multiple story lines, and defined as a narrative perspective in relationship to others.

I've suggested that in the pilot a basic structure is articulated whereby the white male lawyer intervenes and manipulates the law so that a black woman's story might be told. That Kuzak's position as narrator can be read as both a form of manipulation in its own right and as an enlightened reach across the boundaries of race, gender, and class is typical of *L.A. Law*'s own status as a door swinging both ways. The definition of the lawyer as narrator when the lawyer in question is female raises some of the most interesting questions concerning *L.A. Law* and feminism. In the pilot another story line involves a black woman who is never seen on camera, a woman who has been brutally exploited by her insurance company. In this story the black woman functions as nothing more than a pretense for Ann Kelsey to fight the insurance company; indeed, Kelsey says as much herself in the conclusion of the story in the following episode. After she has won a large settlement for her client, Kelsey acknowledges to Leland McKenzie that she had virtually no relationship with her client and fought the case for her own sake, not the client's. Two black women function, then, as central narrative figures: the one, Adrienne Moore, very much the visible center of the pilot, and the other a most conspicuously absent and marginal figure. More central to Kelsey's case are her showdowns with the insurance agent, an obnoxious and somewhat pathetic sexist who bears a strong physical resemblance to Stuart Markowitz, the lawyer who will soon become Kelsey's significant other. Kelsey's role as narrator is staked out in the pilot as calling the bluff of macho behavior and puncturing masculine pretense, whether by icy detachment, witty repartee, or deflation of male superiority.

If Kelsey acknowledges that this particular legal battle has more to do with her male opponent than with her client, then her relationship to the law can be seen as either the opposite of Kuzak's (he, the enlightened liberal; she, the ruthless one) or its repressed side (she thus making explicit the self-serving and performance-like aspects of the law displaced in Kuzak's story line), or, more in keeping with the swinging doors of the series, as both simultaneously. While it is tempting to regard *L.A.*

Law as one of the few truly equal-opportunity programs on prime time, Ann Kelsey's function in this respect is remarkably evocative of a more familiar definition of woman: the feminine as a return of the repressed, the eruption of a connection not otherwise speakable.

Consider, for example, a juxtaposition of scenes in the pilot from two separate story lines. In one scene, the insurance agent makes a settlement offer that Kelsey refuses. In response to his remark that "juries don't like bulldozing, chop-busting, butch lady lawyers any better than I do," Kelsey remains cool: "Thank you for sharing that insight with me, Mr. Messman," she says and rejects the offer again. That scene is followed by an equally tense encounter pitting Arnold Becker and his female client against her husband and his lawyer. The husband occupies much the same position as the insurance man in the previous scene, for he speaks the same language of sexual putdown. But here the woman responds in kind, screaming at her husband and calling him, in what is one of the more memorable epithets in the show, an "impotent piece of snot." While the argument could be made that the two scenes draw parallels between what happens to women in the workplace and what happens to them in marriages, the far more immediate connection drawn is that Becker's client vents the rage suppressed in Kelsey's lawyerly façade.

At stake in the strategies of undercutting, of double entendre, of narrative ambiguity in *L.A. Law* are the claims of feminism itself. Teresa de Lauretis defines the goal of feminist criticism as accentuating and insisting on the gap between "woman": "the other-from-man (nature and Mother, site of sexuality and masculine desire, sign and object of men's social exchange)" and "women," "the real historical beings who cannot as yet be defined outside of those discursive formations" (1984, 5). Indeed, *L.A. Law* draws on feminist discourse in order both to open up and to close down the analogous gap between *feminine* and *feminist.* Consider, for example, another episode in which overlapping story lines, again involving Kuzak and Kelsey, accentuate the radical difference in narrative mode between male and female practice of the law. The principal story in the episode is a case of date rape, in which Kuzak defends a woman who was raped by a man after she had gone back to his room following a party. The jury makes a decision that is most ambiguous: it rules in the woman's favor but gives her a cash award of $1, thus suggesting that there are some rapes that are not quite so criminal as others. Although Kuzak makes a convincing case for the seriousness of date rape, it is later revealed that he is not completely convinced of his client's innocence either. Only when another woman comes to his office to tell him that she, too, was raped by the same man does the episode seem to affirm, unequivocally, the woman's point of view that she was indeed raped. (Note the striking narrative logic here: the man is not a real rapist until he does it twice.) Yet the discourse of the date rape case slides into another story line, almost as if there is a narrative price to be paid for the woman's vindication, a vindication virtually indistinguishable from the feminist insistence that acquaintanceship in no way mitigates the criminality of rape. The attorney for the defendant, a woman, argues in her summation that

> every woman in this courtroom knows it is more respectable, more feminine, and sometimes more alluring to manifest the sign of resistance—at least initially. You know something else? The men know it, too. The simple fact is sometimes we say no when we really mean yes, and sometimes we say no when we really mean no, and sometimes men can't tell which is which.

This narration describes with remarkable accuracy the accompanying story line in which Kelsey decides to sell her condominium and agrees to a rather elaborate deal arranged by her lover, Stuart Markowitz. Suddenly, in an inexplicable burst of fickleness, she changes her mind and tells him and the potential buyer that the deals are off. At the conclusion of the program, she apologizes to Stuart and asks if it is too late to change her mind about the sale. Stuart, another of the legions of men who "can't tell which is which," throws up his hands in the air in exasperation. The two kiss and make up, as if to prove the lawyer's point that sometimes it is "more alluring" to say no. The episode thus trivializes the very issue that it attempts to present, through Kuzak's crisis of conscience, as worthy of serious legal attention. In addition, it is once again the woman on whom the narrative contradictions are projected.

This projection of contradictions onto the body of the woman occurs in a particularly complex and interesting way in another story line, this one devoted to Stacy Gill (portrayed by Steven Bochco's real-life wife, Barbara Bosson), a woman television news anchor who has brought charges of sex discrimination after being fired, according to the television station, purely because of poor ratings, and according to her, because of a story she agreed to do at the station's request on breast cancer, during which she demonstrated the various components of cancer detection and quite literally bared her breasts for the camera.

A secondary story during the two episodes in which the Stacy Gill trial was aired concerns Douglas Brackman's transformation from a slumlord into a concerned, responsible landlord. During his slumlord phase, Brackman meets his wife in a restaurant for her birthday and asks her to sign papers so that their property can be turned over temporarily to his mother. Sheila, his wife, mistakenly assumes that he wants a divorce and begins bemoaning her fate, making quite a spectacle of herself in the process. After telling Douglas that she "doesn't snap back like some twenty-five-year-old with elastic breasts," she proceeds to sing "Happy Birthday" quite loudly, while everyone in the restaurant gapes and stares. In an earlier scene in the episode, Stacy Gill and Kuzak chat in a bar about her case, and Gill cries as she describes her discomfort at being seen as a "breast with a woman attached." Sheila Brackman, in making a spectacle of herself, thus becomes the hysterical version of Stacy Gill.

Rarely do the characters in *L.A. Law* draw connections between individual story lines; those connections emerge, rather, through other narrative devices, such as the principles of overlap I've described. An exception to this rule occurs during the Stacy Gill episodes. Kuzak defends Gill passionately and, as is usually the case in his arguments, emphasizes the human factor over the narrowly legal one. The station makes a generous settlement offer, which Gill refuses, against Kuzak's recommendation, primarily because it would require her to drop the sex discrimination charge. Only after the jury rules in her favor, with a huge award, does Kuzak discover that Gill has an advance book contract contingent on going through to a jury verdict. As a result, he feels exploited. Gill tells him that had she informed him of the contract, he would have been less fired up, less passionate in her defense. In a secondary story line, Kuzak does exactly what he is miffed at Stacy Gill for doing: he gives a case to Sifuentes, tells him to ask for a continuance, and neglects to inform him that there are no more continuances to be had, so that Sifuentes has to prepare the case cold. Kuzak defends his actions with a logic that echoes Gill's. The more typical pattern in *L.A. Law* would be for the ironic echo to remain implicit—obvious, perhaps, but nonetheless not narrated or called attention to by an individual lawyer. However, in this case, Grace Van Owen confronts Kuzak with the recognition that what Gill did to him was no different from what he did to Sifuentes.

This atypical narrative development is enormously instructive, particularly given its position at the conclusion of a story that was introduced with the parallel between a distraught Stacy Gill and a hysterical Sheila Brackman. Grace Van Owen is given a position of narrative authority that seems initially to oppose that previous equation of a woman fighting a sex discrimination suit with a woman making a spectacle of herself. Like the juxtapositions that contrast Ann Kelsey's professional behavior with its repressed opposite, the Stacy Gill/Sheila Brackman parallel closes down the gap between "feminist" (the woman who agreed to expose her experience with breast cancer to the public in order to help other women, and who accuses her employer of sex discrimination) and "feminine" (the woman who is distraught about the elasticity of her breasts, and who fears her husband is having an affair). Yet in both instances, the eruptions of the feminine offer possibilities for opening up the gap as well, if for no other reason than the fact that the need to eliminate the distinction speaks to a narrative anxiety, a problem of representation.

I am not arguing here for reading these strategies against the grain, which implies an initial coherence that might then be turned around, but rather for identifying the ambivalence central to the strategies themselves. Ambivalent or not, however, Grace Van Owen's function as a narrator could be read as an alternative strategy, an instance of female authority that is distinctly unambivalent. Van Owen affirms a principle of equality that may be somewhat cynical but is nonetheless of feminist inspiration: that women and men have the same rights to exploit the law, and lawyers, to their benefit. While the position Van Owen is assigned in this episode is, as I've said, unusual for *L.A. Law,* the perspective she articulates here is one she represents fairly consistently in the series. Van Owen represents the notion that the polarities of "male" and "female" are simply roles that men and women can adopt at their discretion and will. But her "feminism" is, to use again one of *L.A. Law*'s pet phrases, a door that swings both ways. When an attempt is made on Van Owen's life after she has argued successfully for a death sentence, she neglects to recognize a gender component to her vulnerability, a component underscored ironically when she decides, nervously, to buy a handgun and then changes her mind after agreeing with the salesman who says to her, somewhat sleazily, "Sexy, isn't it?" In another episode, she even appropriates the language of rape to describe her own desires. In the episode, Van Owen comes on to a man in a gorilla suit, thinking it is Michael Kuzak. When she later describes the incident, she tells Kuzak that she "practically raped the guy."

These two strategies (the echo effect, through which the stereotypically feminine seems if not necessarily to undermine then at least to complicate female challenges to male power; and female narration, which theorizes the symmetry of male and female behavior) correspond to the two types of swinging doors that I've described as symptomatic of *L.A. Law*'s engagement with feminism. The echo effect represents an essential difference of men and women vis-à-vis the law, while the unusual identification of a female narrator suggests a more equal-opportunity approach, whereby men and women are the same before the law. These options are remarkably evocative of what Catharine A. MacKinnon has described as the "two routes to sex equality" (1987, 71):

> The primary avenue views women as if we were men. It measures our similarity with men to see if we are or can be men's equals. This standard is called the equality rule. . . . The second approach . . . views women as men view women: in need of special protection, help, or indulgence. To make out a case, complainants have to meet the male standard for women: femininity. . . . In other words, for purposes of sex discrimination law, to be a woman means either to be like a man or to be a lady. We have to meet either the male standard for males or the male standard for females. (74)

MacKinnon goes on to say that for a woman lawyer, both standards are applicable simultaneously: "Available to women in the practice of law are the same two roles as those in standards of sex discrimination law, except that women lawyers are held to both at once." In the terms of television narrative, then, the woman lawyer is an emblem of ambiguity and contradiction; as MacKinnon puts it, "Now, given that you are a woman lawyer, are you feeling a little schizoid?" (75).

I don't think it is inappropriate to describe *L.A. Law* as a series of endless ambiguities about the law and sexual politics, and about feminism itself. But there is something suspicious about this delight in ambiguity, both within narrative, where it can function so often as a ruse or a decoy, and within criticism, where it can harden into an idealized abstraction. However complex the desire in the series to both open up and close down the difference between femininity and feminism, its narrative strategies all lead to a virtually identical point of closure: the poignant two-shot that concludes each episode. Indeed, the very regularity and consistency of closure suggest its importance within the narrative economy of the series. The most common closing shot of *L.A. Law* is an image of one of the couples: Ann Kelsey and Stuart Markowitz or, more frequently, Grace Van Owen and Michael Kuzak. Sometimes the closing shot predicts a couple-to-be, like Abby Perkins and George Handelman, a lawyer in the district attorney's office. While the closing shot does evoke, as I've suggested, the concluding images of *Hill Street*'s Joyce Davenport and Frank Furillo, the narrative functions are quite different. For the steamy love scenes between Davenport and Furillo often seem like reminders that the series does exist in a heterosexual world, after all. As Steve Jenkins puts it, *Hill Street Blues,* through the Furillo-Davenport relationship, "asserts a sense of heterosexual, male-female, private/professional balance in the face of its own imbalance; it returns the spectator, after the supposed chaos, to a space where things are in their correct place, as they should be" (1984, 192). Jenkins also suggests that the Furillo-Davenport finale can be read just as persuasively as a "logical extension of the narrative, rather than as a kind of calming coda to it" (196). The point is that, like the door that swings both ways in *L.A. Law,* both readings are encouraged simultaneously.

The comparison with *Hill Street Blues* is instructive. While *L.A. Law* may have plenty of chaos of its own, it does not lack in female characters or in heterosexual interaction. Hence the final shots do not really function as tacked-on conclusions, second thoughts that represent what has been by and large repressed. Rather, the final shot of each episode reiterates what is one of the show's most obvious and insistent fantasies: a utopian heterosexuality, a complementarity of men and women in the face of the massive disorder instigated, in the previous fifty-five minutes, by the intersection of law and gender. Frequently, the concluding shot assures that however tough the women of *L.A. Law* may be in their legal battles with men, their challenge to patriarchy does not extend into the realm of sexual orientation or desire. The point was made strikingly in a second-season episode in which Grace Van Owen was accused of being a "humorless radical feminist" in defending a teenage stripper sexually molested by a group of lawyers. In the concluding shot of the episode, Van Owen and Kuzak inhale helium from a balloon and talk in funny voices as they embrace, so that at least the "humorless" and the "radical" parts are temporarily dispelled.

During the first season a few concluding images of episodes do not feature the male-female couples of the show. One is the pilot, which I've described as setting out the overlapping boundaries of law and gender through the final embrace of Kuzak and Adrienne Moore. Two other episodes conclude with images suggestive of a disruption in the law: one features the story line of a judge accused of taking a bribe and ends with the judge and Leland McKenzie in a face-to-face, and another, in which Kuzak overidentifies with Sid Herschberg, a lawyer who cracks under pressure and is institutionalized, concludes with Kuzak's visiting Herschberg in a mental institution and embracing him. These occasional departures from final shots of men and women in love focus on the law as a fraternity, a brotherhood. One is, of course, reminded of Luce Irigaray's observation that heterosexuality is a ruse, "just an alibi for the smooth workings of man's relations with himself, of relations among men" (1985, 172). In the former episode, the judge calls Leland McKenzie a "wizard of ambiguity" and takes great glee in forcing his longtime associate to answer a question "yes" or "no." The brotherhood of the law may not erupt in quite the same way that stereotypical femininity does within individual episodes, but I would argue that this male fellowship of the law disrupts the utopian heterosexuality that provides *L.A. Law* with one of its most distinct continuous threads, and certainly with its strongest sense of closure.

While there is much to be said about the conspicuously ideological dimensions of this utopian heterosexuality, I am more interested in its narrative dimensions. For the feminism that is appropriated in *L.A. Law* is, at the very least, capable of making a good story. *L.A. Law* makes for an interesting comparison, in this respect, with another recent articulation of feminism and the law. In a November 8, 1987, piece on the *New York Times* editorial page, Stephen Gillers, a professor of law and a member of the board of the New York Civil Liberties Union, criticized feminism for not letting some stories be told. Gillers's piece was occasioned by the acquittal of Karen Straw for the murder of her husband on the basis of evidence that she was a battered wife. Gillers draws a rather remarkable connection between the feminist defense of Karen Straw and the feminist criticism of a completely unrelated case, the trial of Robert Chambers for the murder of Jennifer Levin. In the Chambers case, feminists have criticized the attempt by the defense to introduce as relevant material Jennifer Levin's supposed history of sexual "aggression" with other men. As Gillers so strikingly puts it in an amazing turn of convoluted narrative logic, feminists "would permit Karen Straw but not Robert Chambers to pin blame on someone else." Feminists are thus guilty, in Gillers's view, of "denying Mr. Chambers the right to tell his story."

If, in Gillers's view of feminism and the law, feminism threatens to block the flow of narrative and to stifle a man's right to tell his story, feminism in *L.A. Law* has the opposite effect, for it encourages and stimulates the production of narrative. To be sure, the representation of feminism in *L.A. Law* is a function of feminism's capacity to disrupt and upset the categories of legal and narrative discourse. But if feminism, as a source of narrative tension, seems to be suspended momentarily with each concluding scene of *L.A. Law,* then the few concluding scenes that are not of one romantic couple or another are useful reminders that fantasies of integration and resolution, whether in male-female relations or in courts of law, are temporary and fleeting indeed.

Epilogue: *L.A. Law* and Prime-Time Lesbianism

On February 7, 1991, CJ, a newer character introduced in the fifth season of *L.A. Law,* kissed Abby. The kiss and its subsequent development—both within the series and in the reponses to it—highlight crucial issues concerning the representation in the media of lesbians and gay men. These issues include, first, continuing disagreements about what constitutes appropriate and viable political pressure on television networks, particularly in the face of well-organized campaigns by the Religious Right; second, the connections between media visibility (that is, any news is good news) and media analysis (most news is bad news when subjected to analytic and theoretical scrutiny); and third, attempts to uncover some kind of pattern that would explain why some programs suffer for the inclusion of gay/lesbian characters and story lines, while others do not. From the perspective of *Ellen* and its status as the most significant triumph—and ultimate failure—of not only the representation of lesbianism on television but the staging of coming out and its attendant televisual possibilities, the kiss on *L.A. Law* may seem minor indeed. But CJ and Abby's kiss was one of many events that paved the way for *Ellen.*

One of the most basic tenets of gay and lesbian studies is that sexuality and gender are not the same, that they are of course connected but not reducible one to the other. Further implicit in this distinction is that only through an initial separation of the dichotomies of gender (male and female, masculine and feminine) and sexuality (homosexual and heterosexual) is any understanding of the complex intersections between them possible. As Eve Sedgwick puts it, "Ultimately, I do feel, a great deal depends—for all women, for lesbians, for gay men, possibly for all men—on the fostering of our ability to arrive at understandings of sexuality that will respect a certain irreducibility in it to the terms and relations of gender" (1990, 16). While some feminist theorists have taken the separation of gender and sexuality as a point of departure, I fear that the terms of the separation may fail to account for the specificity of lesbian identities and representations, however complex and fragile they may be. My point here is not to criticize the absence of lesbianism in much of what is called queer theory and gay/lesbian studies, although the separation of gender and sexuality may well be no coincidence insofar as lesbian marginality is concerned. Rather, I want to examine how feminism is situated in relationship to gender and sexuality, for one implication of the distinction between gender and sexuality is that feminism, as a theory of gender, can only go so far in analyzing sexuality. More specifically, I want to read CJ and Abby's kiss on *L.A. Law* as it highlights issues that emerge when feminism and lesbianism encounter each other in mass culture.

I argue above that *L.A. Law* represents feminism in a very ambiguous way, and that the program offers both critiques of male supremacy and defenses against those critiques. The show consistently took on issues of enormous interest to feminism, such as rape and sex discrimination, and its cast of characters always included proverbially assertively trained, independent women. The structure of the program, with overlapping story lines, offers numerous possibilities for shifting perspectives and multiple points of view. One of the most characteristic features of these overlapping stories is the displacement, or echo effect, from one story line to another (for example, the date rape episode discussed above). Typically, the displacement effect occurs across figures of women.

When I wrote the above essay on *L.A. Law,* the series was new, popular, and (generally) praised. While the format of the show altered little over the years, its perceived quality did change. In the early years of *L.A. Law,* its success was analyzed, and then its failures were analyzed. CJ was one of a group of new cast members designed to revitalize the show, yet she never inspired the same acclaim as Michael Kuzak (played by Harry Hamlin) or Victor Sifuentes (Jimmy Smits). Whereas the show initially seemed innovative, later on it became passé. It is tempting, then, to see the lesbian kiss—like an interracial romance that occurred during the same season—less as an innovation and more as desperate maneuvering to acquire attention and viewership.

The popularization of feminism remains one of the most interesting features of *L.A. Law.* It is a well-known cliché that in popular conceptions of both feminism and lesbianism, there is a decisive connection between the two. It doesn't require too much imagination to see in the much-publicized, supposed disavowal on the part of many women of the label *feminist,* with its attendant qualifiers of *male-bashing* and *man-hating,* a fear and loathing of lesbian implications. The attraction between CJ and Abby plays on this popular association of feminism and lesbianism. Prior to this episode, CJ learns that Abby will not be offered partnership in the law firm. Despite rules of confidentiality, CJ tells Abby the news, while Ann Kelsey follows the rules and does not inform Abby of the decision. Hence, Ann Kelsey becomes defined as one of the boys, a dutiful daughter, while CJ's rejection of the old-boy network is established. In a spirit of feminist subversion, CJ encourages Abby to manipulate the firm's rejection of her to her own advantage, and an alliance is formed between the two women.

Three other stories are intertwined in the episode in which CJ kisses Abby: (1) Arnie Becker's marriage to Corinne disintegrates after her suspicions of his infidelity are confirmed by Roxanne, Arnie's secretary; (2) one of Leland MacKenzie's clients is threatened with a takeover, and he and Rosalind Shays—one of the most striking embodiments of the fear and loathing of female assertiveness run amok ever to have appeared on prime-time television—conspire to protect him; and (3) a man with multiple personalities is on trial for a murder committed by one of those personalities. The single, obvious theme uniting these stories is deception: Corinne is deceived by Arnie and Arnie by Roxanne; Rosalind deceives a man into thinking she is deceiving Leland in order to save the client's company; part of the prosecution's argument in the case of the murder trial is that the defense is using multiple personality disorder as a ruse. In the midst of these twists and turns of deception, Abby and CJ become allies because of the firm's deception of Abby (in the "previously on *L.A. Law*" recap at the beginning of the show, CJ informs Abby of the firm's decision not to make her a partner, to which Abby replies, "Lying sons of bitches"). After the kiss, CJ assures Abby that there was no deception on her part, that she did not scheme in order to act on her attraction to Abby.

Typically for *L.A. Law,* the thematic link is complicated by effects of displacement. Surely, it is no coincidence that a story line concerning multiple personality disorder appears on the same episode as CJ and Abby's kiss, particularly given the immediate framing of the kiss as bisexual, not lesbian, at least for CJ. Indeed, swinging both ways has always characterized the show, and with the kiss, swinging both ways is embodied in a single character. Interestingly, the swinging-door metaphor, prior to the 1990–91 season, was largely limited to questions of gender and sexual politics, and the occasional flirtation with gay sexuality (and more rarely, with lesbianism) served largely to assert heterosexual identity.

If *L.A. Law* offered viewers the possibility to have it both ways as far as feminism is concerned, the same applies to its representation of lesbianism. Lesbianism is negotiated in this episode in the following ways: first, the kiss confirms a connection between feminism and lesbianism to the extent that CJ and Abby are brought together by their annoyance with the patriarchal status quo of the firm. While several scenes from the accompanying story lines occur between Abby and CJ's departure from Douglas Brackman's office (where they are scolded) and the scene of the kiss, the mise-en-scène suggests a continuous movement from Brackman's office to the encounter. Additionally, Brackman's last words to the two women—"That's all, then. Dismissed."—suggest a school principal scolding mischievous students, thus framing the kiss as a childish or righteous revolt, depending upon your point of view.

Second, CJ and Abby's kiss is preceded by a dinner discussion between Rosalind Shays and the man with whom she is attempting to make a dirty deal (a bogus dirty deal, we learn later; at this point it appears as though Shays is indeed duplicitous). Shays agrees to help him with the takeover if he agrees to keep his firm's business with MacKenzie, Brackman—or with her. The man is suspicious of her motives and describes Leland MacKenzie's probable reaction to keeping him as a client: "He'd sooner die than get into bed with me." The purely metaphoric quality of sharing a bed with Leland is literalized, in its homosexual implications, in the scene that immediately follows, when CJ and Abby kiss. Yet the homosexual implications retain their male-business-bonding reference as well. For CJ's manipulations of the law firm to her (and Abby's) ends are a match for those of any of the male lawyers on the show, including master manipulator Arnie Becker, whose personal life, as coincidence would have it, is in shambles in this particular episode because of the women in his life.

Finally, the aftermath of the kiss occasions yet another displacement. The morning after, in the law office, Abby awkwardly raises the issue with CJ, and CJ assures her that she hadn't attempted to set her up, that she is "flexible," and that she doesn't want their friendship to suffer. After these expressions of good will, we cut to the multiple personality disorder murder case, where the defendant's psychiatrist is attempting to make the evil, murderous personality emerge. "Let Sean come out," he says. "Come out. . . ." This process of "coming out" is more complex than even the psychiatrist imagined, since yet another personality eventually emerges to complicate the three male personalities of the man on trial. It turns out that the murder was committed by a female personality who claims herself to be the protector of her two boys, and she reveals that their/his father sexually abused them/him.

What a curious itinerary a moment of lesbian attraction engenders, across a number of positions analogous to CJ in particular, from would-be disrupter of male bonding in the corporate workplace to psychiatrist encouraging a woman who has been seduced and abandoned by that workplace to "come out," however literally or figuratively. To be sure, the allusion to lesbian desire is as marked by simultaneous attraction and repulsion as *L.A. Law*'s ambiguous engagement with feminism. Yet the lesbian moment is specific, for it foregrounds the very separation between gender and sexuality that has been so crucial to gay/lesbian theory. The two male homosexual frames of reference, one metaphoric (Leland wouldn't want to "get in bed" with the client) and one literal (the father who sexually molested his son), correspond to bald forms of male power, men controlling corporations and fathers controlling and abusing sons. In some sense this episode acts out a certain anxiety about lesbianism vis-à-vis these uses of homosexuality. It is as if the narrative structure of overlap and displacement makes the episode a testing ground, an attempt to make lesbian desire fit into male heterosexual fantasies.

CJ and Abby's kiss also reads as a warning of the risk inherent in separating sexuality and gender, since lesbianism in the episode is embedded in the homophobic fantasies about male homosexuality that are indissociable from those of gender power. A lesbian moment may be visible briefly, but that moment is tenuous. And so I find myself critical of *L.A. Law* for its own desire to have it both ways, to "represent" lesbianism but to undermine the representation at the same time. But I also find it hard to disagree with GLAAD (the Gay and Lesbian Alliance Against Defamation) when the organization encouraged positive responses to NBC for making visible—however briefly—lesbian desire, particularly in the face of groups like the American Family Association, which included the show on their list of targeted series. In other words, I too want to have it both ways, and theorizing the lesbian moment on *L.A. Law* requires some . . . flexibility.

Works Cited

Ang, Ien. 1985. *Watching Dallas.* New York: Methuen.

De Lauretis, Teresa. 1984. *Alice Doesn't: Feminism, Semiotics, Cinema.* Bloomington: Indiana University Press.

Ellis, John. 1982. *Visible Fictions: Cinema: Television: Video.* London: Routledge and Kegan Paul.

Feuer, Jane. 1984. "Melodrama, Serial Form, and Television Today." *Screen* 25: 4–16.

Feuer, Jane, Paul Kerr, and Tise Vahimagi, eds. 1984. *MTM: "Quality Television."* London: British Film Institute.

Gillers, Stephen. 1987. "Feminists vs. Civil Libertarians." *New York Times,* 8 November, 20.

Gitlin, Todd. 1983. *Inside Prime Time.* New York: Pantheon.

Irigaray, Luce. 1985. *This Sex Which Is Not One.* Trans. Catherine Porter. Ithaca, N.Y.: Cornell University Press.

Jenkins, Steve. 1984. *"Hill Street Blues."* In Feuer, Kerr, Vahimagi, 183–99.

Kort, Michele. 1984. "Terry Louise Fisher: How She Dreamed Up the Women of *L.A. Law.*" *Ms.* June: 38, 42, 44.

MacKinnon, Catharine A. 1984. *Feminism Unmodified: Discourses on Life and Law.* Cambridge: Harvard University Press.

McWilliams, Michael. 1986. "The Biggest Snow Job in Prime Time." *Village Voice,* 7 October.

Modleski, Tania. 1984. *Loving with a Vengeance: Mass-Produced Fantasies for Women.* New York: Methuen.

Newcomb, Horace. 1974. *TV: The Most Popular Art.* New York: Anchor Books.

Petro, Patrice. 1988. "Criminality or Hysteria: Television and the Law." *Discourse* 10, no. 2: 48–61.

Sedgwick, Eve Kosofsky. 1990. *Epistemology of the Closet.* Berkeley and Los Angeles: University of California Press.

Waters, Harry F., and Janet Huck. 1987. "Lust for Law." *Newsweek,* 16 November, 84–91.

6. Fear of Falling

I have been following figure skating in a relatively informal but passionate way for years. By *informal* I mean that I have acquired a fair amount of knowledge about skaters, about the presentation of skating on television, and about controversies (concerning, say, judging); at the same time, I am a real neophyte in that I still really can't tell the difference between a triple flip and a triple Salchow. My limited knowledge hasn't prevented me from articulating firm opinions, and I have often found myself swept up by the frenzy of competition. For instance, during the famous 1988 Olympic showdown between Katarina Witt and Debi Thomas, popularly billed as the "dueling Carmens," I enthusiastically adopted the popular conception of Witt as female villain, as ice princess, and of Thomas as the earnest and forthright challenger. (At the 1994 Olympics I was equally taken in by the image of Witt as a wise old-timer.) I've cheered for Brian Boitano. I was appalled that Isabelle and Paul Duchesnay, the brother-and-sister ice dancing pair who challenged many of the gender stereotypes of the sport, didn't get the gold. And so on.

When Nancy Kerrigan was attacked and the subsequent involvement of Tonya Harding was revealed, I consumed news of the event as enthusiastically as anyone I know. What interested me in particular about the Harding/Kerrigan event was how it foregrounded and exaggerated issues that have been present in the presentation of figure skating as a spectator sport for years. Abigail Feder's study (1994) of the presentation of women's figure skating is a sobering reminder that in the one sport where women tend to be more visible than men, the price paid for such visibility is the excess of stereotypes of femininity. The fact that figure skating is virtually absent from such recent studies as Susan Cahn's *Coming On Strong: Gender and Sexuality in Twentieth-Century Women's Sport* (1994) and Mariah Burton Nelson's *The Stronger Women Get, the More Men Love Football* (1994) suggests that the battle between "femininity" and "female strength" is not really being waged in any particularly groundbreaking ways on the ice.

Yet however much figure skating seems to be ruled by extremely conventional representations of femininity, I find that analysis of spectatorship vis-à-vis figure skating raises more complicated issues. Just as the supposedly universal and ubiquitous male gaze of the classical Hollywood cinema functions quite differently when examined through the lens of female spectators and female pleasures in the cinema, so the spectacle of figure skating takes on a different look and set of expectations when viewed through the lens of female spectatorship.

Consider in this context one of the many peculiar devices employed in the NBC made-for-television movie *Tonya and Nancy: The Inside Story* (broadcast April 30, 1994). A series of fictionalized interviews with a range of commentators on the Harding/Kerrigan affair are featured in the telefilm. Taped rather than filmed (thus creating the illusion of authentic interviews), and featuring direct address to the camera in the style of talking-heads documentaries, these interviews included television producers, a former skater, a 1960s activist, and a skating judge. Two of the interviews included in the television movie serve as appropriate images of the issues at stake in this essay, a very speculative exploration of female spectatorship in relationship to figure skating.

Two individuals, one female and one male, are identified as "supporters" of Harding and Kerrigan, respectively. Both of these interviews occur in the last half-hour of the teleplay. The Harding supporter is middle-aged, and she wears an "I Love Tonya" button. "It's just so unfair," she says angrily and passionately to the camera. She continues: "The way the judges have always treated her. . . . And the media! That's why we started the fan club. Because the Nancy Kerrigans of the world get all the attention. And somebody like Tonya who's had to struggle all her life. . . . The Tonyas of this world just get pushed aside. It makes me sick."

The Kerrigan supporter appears a bit later, following images of Tonya and her husband Jeff Gillooly planning what they will say to the police. The Kerrigan supporter appears to be a bit younger than the Harding fan club organizer, but he is also middle-aged (and balding), wearing horn-rimmed glasses, a button-down shirt, and a cardigan around his shoulders. His tone is also angry, though not quite as personally involved as the woman's:

> Don't give me that bleeding-heart crap about unhappy childhoods. I mean, what are we saying here? That because she comes from a dysfunctional family that she's supposed to grow up and marry a jerk and commit a crime? What ever happened to free will? I mean, look at Nancy. Now she sacrificed, too. But she played by the rules. You get what you deserve.

While it might be appropriate to describe both of these fictional supporters as passionate in their defenses of their heroines, there is no question that the Harding fan is more emotional and seems to have more at stake personally in her identification with the skater. The Harding fan even seems somewhat deranged, whereas the Kerrigan fan utters what was quickly becoming popular common wisdom concerning the paths of the two skaters. In addition, the contextualization of the interviews creates an odd juxtaposition between the female fan who reacts and the male fan who comments. It is, of course, no coincidence that the more deranged and excessive fan is female, while the male fan embodies cool reason and sarcastic restraint.

While the gender dichotomy of these two presentations of spectatorship does not surprise me, I find it a matter of some curiosity that both supporters are distinctly middle-aged. One suspects perhaps that the Harding/Kerrigan affair, as retold in this made-for-television movie, offers the possibility to middle-aged spectators to take sides and to act out fantasies and projections of the meanings of success and failure for the female skaters. Both fans are identified as "supporters," which suggests an investment stronger than everyday, run-of-the-mill spectatorship. Yet the intensity of each supporter's defense of her/his favorite speaks to a particular quality of figure skating and its relationship to its viewers. For figure skating is notorious for its provocation of histrionics, from the outlandish and fluid standards of judging to the dramatic question that is raised every time a skater glides onto the ice: will shc fall?

Falls are the unconscious of figure skating, the dangerous id that can emerge at any time and upset years of preparation and devotion. There is a hierarchy of falling in skating: there are near falls and real falls. When a skater's hand touches down after a jump or a landing is two-footed, then we are witnessing a near fall, the possible prelude to a real fall. Among the real falls, there are variations of degree, from awkward but recoverable stumbles onto the ice to splats in which the graceful, athletic body is out of control. A real fall is always potentially catastrophic, but it offers the opportunity to witness the gumption of the athlete in his or her recovery time. More than one fall signifies a crumbling of confidence.

The fear of falling is a factor in all figure skating, whether the competitors are male or female. Brian Boitano's performance at the 1994 Olympics was ultimately reducible to a single moment, repeated on television replays over and over again (as such moments always are), in which he fell during his short program. But I want to argue that the fear of falling has special significance for women skaters, and in particular for the relationship that exists between female spectators and female skaters. Perhaps more than any other spectator sport, women's figure skating relies on the precarious balance between athleticism and the display of grace—that is, femininity. The fall shatters the balance and in particular disrupts the performance of femininity.

In addition to the anticipation of falling, figure skating offers a unique set of circumstances as a spectator sport. First, there is the visibility of women in the sport. Televised women's competition not only draws huge numbers of women viewers, but supposedly even more viewers than televised football games! Second, the visibility of femininity in figure skating is a proverbial knife that cuts both ways. For while femininity is an expectation for female skaters, it is also a specter haunting men's figure skating. Throughout the history of the sport, male athletes have had to contend with the associations of figure skating with a gay sensibility, and televised coverage of the men's competition often wavers uncomfortably between a submerged acknowledgment of that sensibility and an affirmation of heterosexual and/or firmly "masculine" identities. Indeed, both of these were on display during the 1994 Olympic games in the men's competition. Elvis Stojko's much-heralded innovative choreography based on the moves of martial arts (he has a black belt in karate) provided a stunning, if implicit, contrast to the gold medalist Alexander Urmanov, whose style is much more classical (that is, "feminine"). Stojko was referred to constantly as a new breed of figure skater, with the implication that he was bringing a more explicitly masculine presence to the sport.

The Harding/Kerrigan story foregrounded virtually all of these elements particular to figure skating. As a sport in which women are so central, it comes as no surprise that the coverage of women's figure skating competition often relies on excessively stereotypical views of women, from the good girl/bad girl dichotomy to variations on fairy tales. During the Harding/Kerrigan story, the two skaters became opposites even more rigidly defined than Katarina Witt and Debi Thomas in the 1988 Olympics. The tension between athleticism and artistry was polarized in the contrast between Harding (whose sturdy thighs were often commented on in this context) and Kerrigan. Obviously, Kerrigan was designated the more "feminine" of the two skaters, with Harding's fondness for hunting, pool, and cigarettes interpreted as signs of, if not "masculine," then at the very least "unfeminine" behavior. (Interestingly, one of the peculiarities of this distinction between the more and the less feminine is that Harding was also deemed the more obviously heterosexual of the two; in men's figure skating this would surely operate in the tension between gay and straight, but the operative distinction here is sexual/virginal.)

If the anticipation of the fall is a particular feature of figure skating, then the Harding/Kerrigan affair foregrounded that feature in a very dramatic way. Prior to the national championships in Detroit where Nancy Kerrigan was attacked, both skaters had particular histories of their relationship to the fall. Harding is best known for landing a triple-Axel jump in competition, but she is also known for failing to land that trademark. Kerrigan's relationship to falling was not focused on a particular jump but served, rather, to emphasize the troubles she had had with the strain of competition. At the 1993 world championships, Kerrigan was in first place entering the final stage of the competition, and she proceeded to stumble through her program, finishing in fifth place. The televised coverage of the event showed Kerrigan waiting for her scores, and the camera slowly zoomed in to capture the look of anguish on her face; at that moment Kerrigan uttered the words, "I'd like to die."

Even the attack on Kerrigan, and in particular the images of her screaming in pain that circulated widely, acquired some of the features associated with the fall. To be sure, Kerrigan was "felled" by a baton wielded by an attacker, not by her own inability to complete a jump, and she fell off, not on, the ice. But the image of a skater screaming immediately evokes the specter of the fear that haunts skating. Kerrigan's screams of pain and rage may have been in response to an attack, but they are precisely the response to the fall one imagines.

It doesn't require too much imagination to see that the fear of falling in figure skating represents more than a failed jump. It represents confidence in the spotlight, or the lack thereof, and during the Harding/Kerrigan story it represented a kind of moral gauge, particularly when Kerrigan completed her short and long programs "flawlessly," to use her own overused word (perhaps because she did not win the gold medal, Kerrigan defended her performance as "flawless"). Falling becomes an indication of a variety of syndromes that are presumed to be particular obstacles to female athletes—poor self-esteem, fear of success, terror of the spotlight. And in the most general and far-reaching sense, the fear of falling on the ice represents a discomfort with spectacle and public exposure in general. The significance of falling in this metaphorical sense during the entire Harding/Kerrigan affair did not just occur on the ice; both women are somewhat inarticulate off the ice. This is especially true of Harding, who had difficulty reading her prepared statement during the infamous news conference where she acknowledged that she knew that "people close to her" had participated in the attack and who, when interviewed during the Olympics after it became obvious that she would not win a medal, attempted in vain to make Kerrigan's patriotism an issue.

Given how central female spectatorship has been in film, television, and mass culture studies of the past decade, it is useful to consider how and to what extent the female spectators identified in other forms of mass culture might relate to female spectators of figure skating. Studies such as Tania Modleski's analysis of soap operas and popular fiction (1984) and Janice Radway's examination of romance novels (1991) have put into question the supposedly simple, transparent ways in which women respond to these examples of mass culture. For while neither Modleski nor Radway questions the strength of women's identifications, they do not assume that identification to be a simple matter of identifying with cultural ideals of femininity.

Figure skating offers a display of grace and femininity to which women in this culture are presumed to aspire; in this sense, figure skating offers a spectacle of identification. Indeed, one could go so far as to say that the presentation of figure skating keeps female athleticism within safe boundaries by constantly emphasizing the grace and prettiness of skaters. But then there is the nagging question of the fall—and of the fact that what spectators actually see in watching figure skating is less an idealized spectacle of femininity than the potential acting out of the *failures* of femininity.

Very schematically, and following work on female spectatorship in film, we could define the significance of falling in figure skating in two very different ways. Imagine yourself watching a favorite performer as she takes the ice. One of the minibios that often accompany televised coverage of ice skating has emphasized how much she has struggled to achieve perfection. As she takes the ice, you are excited and nervous for her. She glides, she spins, she turns, and then she is ready to jump. She falls. You gasp. You blink. You hurt for her. You share her pain. You have identified with her so closely. Now imagine yourself watching another skater, one about whom you have some suspicions. As she glides confidently across the ice, you find yourself a bit contemptuous of her. Who does she think she is? She completes her first triple combination, and you begrudgingly join in the praise of the television commentators. But then she two-foots a landing of a jump, and you find yourself becoming edgy and, if truth be told, hopeful. On her next jump she falters and spills, legs akimbo, across the ice. You laugh.

Those familiar with recent film theory concerning spectatorship and female spectatorship in particular will recognize these two scenarios: in the first case there is an excess of identification, leaning toward a masochistic desire; in the second, there is distance from the image produced by identifying with the imagined male spectator, and attendant sadistic pleasure in the falling apart of the image of femininity (Doane 1991, esp. chaps. 1, 2). In the first case there is imagined closeness to the skater; in the second, distance from her. For the purposes of this essay, the particular dynamics of cinematic identification as rendered through psychoanalysis are less significant than the simultaneity of closeness and distance. The relationship of female spectatorship to figure skating is to be found in the particular way in which identification and distance intersect. The most common popular conception of Nancy Kerrigan and Tonya Harding was that spectators "identified" with Kerrigan and "distanced themselves" from Harding, that there was hope that Kerrigan would succeed and that Harding would fall. The news reporter who functioned as the narrator of *Tonya and Nancy: The Untold Story* puts it quite bluntly near the conclusion of the televised movie. Over an image of Tonya Harding, he says: "Imagine how it would feel to know that 100 million people want you to fall." And over a contrasting image of Nancy Kerrigan, he says: "Imagine how it would feel to know that if you fall you would fail 100 million people."

But if Harding and Kerrigan embodied an opposition between distance and closeness, between hoping she falls and fearing she'll fall, it is far more typical for those responses to exist simultaneously. There is nothing particularly new about this hypothesis concerning the simultaneity of closeness and distance; this is precisely what many feminist theorists have argued about the nature of women's responses to many different forms of mass culture, from Modleski's argument that the female villain in soap operas provides both an object of scorn and a projection of power, to Radway's claim that women identify with romance novels because the male characters that inhabit them exhibit a utopian synthesis of male and female qualities. What is particular about spectatorship and figure skating is the significance of falling. Films, television programs, and novels may have symbolic ruptures; ice skating performances have real ones, when the fragility of performance is amply on display. Few televised spectacles offer such consistent possibilities for disruption. And when a skater falls, the performance is shattered, perhaps momentarily, but often irreparably. Put another way, the significance of the fear of falling lies in a particular contract established between spectator and skater; the rupture of performance is immediate.

In addition, there is another quality particular to figure skating, and that is its association with the desires and dreams of adolescent and preadolescent girls. It is well known that figure skating has a particular following among these two age groups of girls. Of course, adult women watch the sport as well, but I believe that one of the major appeals of figure skating for adult women is the recapturing, recollecting, and revisioning of the experience of adolescence. It is easy to trivialize that recapturing as a kind of simple-minded idealization of adolescent ideals, whereby the girl and the adult woman both fall into rhapsodized identification with the image of perfection, the object of all adoring gazes. It is also easy to pathologize the recollection of adolescence, which is implicit in the interview with the female supporter of Tonya Harding in the television movie; indeed, it doesn't require too much imagination to see in her anger over the unfairness of Harding's treatment a projection of her own anger about herself. But given how central the fear of falling is in figure skating, I think it is too simple to attribute female spectatorship to the mere mimicry of patriarchal ideals of womanhood, whether on the part of an adolescent girl who identifies passionately with a figure skater or an adult woman who relives adolescence. Indeed, so much of the experience of watching figure skating involves the anticipation of or reaction to the fall that one begins to suspect that part of the appeal of the sport for women viewers is less the simple exhibition of femininity than the exhibition of femininity as a performance fraught with danger and the possibilities of failure.

It is useful in this context to look at a series of fictional books about figure skating that are directed at an audience of adolescent and preadolescent girls. As narratives that extend the experience of watching figure skating, such books often function to mediate the fear of falling. In

December 1993, the *Silver Blades* series, by Melissa Lowell, began publication. At the time of this writing, six books have appeared in the series. Silver Blades is the name of a skating club in Pennsylvania to which the four heroines of the series belong. Each volume focuses on a different skater and a particular issue she must confront, usually having to do with the pressures of competition. Throughout the books, falling is a major motif. The first book in the series, *Breaking the Ice* (Lowell 1993a) introduces Nikki Simon, whose family has just moved to Pennsylvania so that she can be a part of the Silver Blades club. She tries out and is accepted into the club and is introduced to the three girls who will become her coheroines in the series: Jill Wong, Tori Carsen, and Danielle Panati. Each of the girls experiences the kinds of problems one might expect—fear of competition, conflicts between skating and a social life, and snottiness from other skaters.

The character of Tori Carsen is particularly interesting in this respect. In the first book she seems to embody the ice princess, in that she attends a private school and plots to denigrate any skater who she feels threatens her. Tori suffers from an overbearing mother (shades of Tonya Harding) who insists on attending all of her practice sessions. By the conclusion of the first book, Tori has apologized for her evil ways, and in the third book in the series, stage fright is shown from her point of view (she suffers a humiliating fall before her performance even begins). In other words, the series offers to its young readers not only the possibility of understanding why an ice princess might act the way she does, but also the opportunity to see her change for the better.

In order to become successful performers, the girls must also learn to be successful spectators. This simultaneous process of spectatorship and performance is developed quite succinctly in the second book in the series, *In the Spotlight* (Lowell 1993b), in which Danielle is chosen to be the soloist at the club's show. (Tori fully expected to be chosen.) Danielle has confidence problems that are multiplied by her fear of being overweight. In addition, she meets a boy she likes and suffers the conflict between romance and dedication to skating. While all of Danielle's conflicts are resolved in a fairly predictable way, her success on opening night is prefigured by her ability to appreciate the feats of her fellow skaters. Potential ice princess Tori saves a panicking skater who falls out of formation, and pairs Nikki and Alex perform so well that Danielle is "awed by how well they skated together in such a short amount of time" (1993b, 128). When it is Danielle's turn to perform solo, she has so identified with the entire spectacle of the show, and with the other skaters, that she does (as one might suspect) a superb job: "The audience began to clap, and Danielle actually found herself smiling. This wasn't so bad, she told herself. In fact it was fun!" (129).

Of course, skaters fall in the *Silver Blades* books, but when they do, it is always a learning experience through which the girls focus, practice harder, and succeed. At the same time, their own progress and maturity are equated with their learning not to revel in the misfortunes—that is, the falls—of other skaters. Everyone falls, the books suggest, but the results are never as catastrophic as they might seem. Falling and how one responds to it are measures of success and maturity in both performance and in spectatorship.

I imagine the young girls who read the *Silver Blades* book as acting out their own fantasies of being stars on the ice, certainly, but the books also function as primers on the art of watching skating. Girls are encouraged to be supportive of each other, to focus on their own performances, and not to gloat over the mistakes of others. In the first book of the series, when Tori claims that Nikki ran into her on the ice on purpose, the girls tell Tori that she has watched too many old movies. In that common retort is an interesting twist, for the *Silver Blades* books seek to rewrite Hollywood conventions of competition between women, arguing instead for an idealized community within which there is support and possibility beyond every fall. The imagined love and attention that come with a successful performance are always available, as long as one combines performance and spectatorship in the right proportions. As fiction for young girls, the *Silver Blades* series is supposed to present role models and life lessons. I think the books also capture the fantasies that figure skating represents, not just for adolescent and preadolescent girls, but for adult women who seek, consciously or not, to reenact those fantasies of performance.

The fantasies of performance are given a particularly interesting form in a film that, unlike the *Silver Blades* books, was marketed to appeal both to girls and women. In the 1979 film *Ice Castles* the rise and fall of a figure skater is quite literally charted by her relationship to the fear of falling. Lexie is from a small town in Iowa and is blessed with natural, raw talent; at a regional competition she is spotted by a prominent coach who assumes her training. Lexie is eager to follow her dreams of skating, yet she is awkward and ill at ease as an object of spectacle.

A crucial moment occurs in the film when Lexie is one of a small group of skaters profiled in a Christmas television special. One of the skaters, the French national champion, was reported to have suffered a nervous breakdown, but she is well enough to skate in the special. But when the French skater sees Lexie skate beautifully and flawlessly on a television monitor backstage, it is too much for her to bear. The French skater goes onto the ice and fails miserably, falling constantly. Lexie watches the monitor with the kind of distress that in melodrama signals much more than sympathy with the object of the look. Indeed, before too long Lexie herself will fall during an impromptu practice session following her discomfort at a party; what she suffers is not just momentary humiliation (as did the French skater) but permanent blindness.

Ice Castles is remarkably on target in the way it taps the emotion and drama of figure skating, for it is precisely the fear of falling that makes the experience of watching figure skating unique. More specifically, *Ice Castles* demonstrates the fear of falling and female spectatorship simultaneously. It is no coincidence that the two views that promote terror—terror on the part of the French skater that Lexie is too good, and terror on Lexie's part that the French skater falls so badly—are mediated by a television screen. Earlier in the film, we are told that part of Lexie's remarkable natural talent is her ability to watch skaters like Dorothy Hamill on television and imitate their moves perfectly. Lexie's dreams and fears are similarly mediated by a television screen, and in this sense she embodies not only a Cinderella story of a skater but also a fable of female spectatorship.

The emphasis in both the *Silver Blades* books and *Ice Castles* on performance and spectatorship simultaneously, and on overcoming the fear of falling, suggests that the pleasures of watching figure skating for women involve identification with and anxiety about feminine ideals simultaneously, as well as a certain satisfaction in witnessing possible spectacles of humiliation. Indeed, as much as the story of Harding and Kerrigan seemed to play on the desire to separate the bad girl and the good girl, and to see the bad girl fall and the good girl skate "flawlessly," the aftermath of the Olympic competition demonstrated how the appeal of figure skating lies in the very fluidity of the boundaries separating good girl and bad girl. For after Oksana Baiul won the gold medal, a new set of opposing pairs emerged. Baiul is an interesting study in contrasts, a young woman who skates with remarkable confidence (and with an equally remarkable persona) and who virtually always seems to be sobbing once she is off the ice. This contrast is also a variation on the fear of falling, but now in Baiul's case the question becomes when she will cry rather than when she will fall. As is well known, Nancy Kerrigan complained loudly when she mistakenly assumed that Baiul was reapplying her makeup before the Olympic presentation ceremony. Suddenly, it became common for Kerrigan to be criticized as a prima donna. During the exhibition of medal winners, Kerrigan stumbled and performed far from "flawlessly." My guess is that many female spectators were not only waiting for it to happen but were secretly enjoying the spectacle of the fall. As much as women's figure skating may embody fantasies of perfect and idealized femininity, the fear of falling makes this a spectator sport in which the fall from grace is every bit as, if not more, appealing than perfection.

Works Cited

Cahn, Susan K. 1994. *Coming on Strong: Gender and Sexuality in Twentieth-Century Women's Sport.* New York: Free Press.

Doane, Mary Ann. 1991. *Femmes Fatales: Feminism, Film Theory, Psychoanalysis.* New York: Routledge.

Feder, Abigail M. 1994. "'A Radiant Smile from the Lovely Lady': Overdetermined Femininity in 'Ladies' Figure Skating." *TDR (The Drama Review)* 38, no. 1: 62–78.

Lowell, Melissa. 1993a. *Silver Blades: Breaking the Ice.* New York: Parachute Press/Bantam Press.

———. 1993b. *Silver Blades: In the Spotlight.* New York: Parachute Press/Bantam Press.

———. 1994a. *Silver Blades: Going for the Gold.* New York: Parachute Press/Bantam Press.

———. 1994b. *Silver Blades: Skating Camp.* New York: Parachute Press/Bantam Press.

———. 1994c. *Silver Blades: The Competition.* New York: Parachute Press/Bantam Press.

———. 1994d. *Silver Blades: The Perfect Pair.* New York: Parachute Press/Bantam Press.

Modleski, Tania. 1984. *Loving with a Vengeance: Mass-Produced Fantasies for Women.* New York: Methuen.

Nelson, Mariah Burton. 1994. *The Stronger Women Get, the More Men Love Football: Sexuality and the American Culture of Sports.* New York: Harcourt Brace.

Radway, Janice. 1991. *Reading the Romance: Women, Patriarchy, and Popular Literature,* 2d ed. Chapel Hill: University of North Carolina Press.

7. Caged and Framed: The Women-in-Prison Film

There is much to love, and much to hate, about the women-in-prison film. Much to love in the sense that these films offer spectacles of female bonding, female rage, and female communities, with strong doses of camp and irony. Much to hate in the sense that scenes of rape and torture are staples of the genre, and no matter how campy the films are, they still play on the helplessness and victimization of women. Not all women-in-prison films are the same, yet however vast the range of examples of the genre, the formula is fairly simple. A young woman either participated unknowingly in a crime; or participated in a crime because she was madly in love with a man who is a murderer or a thief; or didn't really participate in a crime but just happened to be at the wrong place at the wrong time; or is framed for a crime she didn't commit. She is sent to prison. There she encounters women (often in the requisite shower scene) who challenge her, try to seduce her, and make her life miserable. They include the prison warden, who is either kind and helpful or bitter and vindictive; the guard(s), who are also either kind or bitter, depending on the character of the warden; and of course the other prisoners. Among the prisoners, certain types are almost always present: a butch lesbian, an older mother-figure, a mentally disturbed woman, several prostitutes. Divisions are sharply marked; prostitutes are considered lower on the prison hierarchy, for instance, while those convicted of armed robbery and murder have considerable prestige.

The heroine discovers that crime and corruption are going on in the prison, whether this involves a prostitution ring organized by the warden to provide women for private parties at the homes of crime lords; or a drug ring; or a crime organization that functions as a kind of sister organization to one on the outside; or straightforward mistreatment of the prisoners. By the end of the film the heroine has learned bitter lessons about life; she is no longer innocent. She leaves the prison but is destined for a life of crime (especially if she committed no crime to begin with); or is determined to get her sisters out of jail; or has learned her lesson and is determined to become a good, normal woman. Often as she leaves jail another young, innocent victim arrives.

My own introduction to the women-in-prison film began several years ago when I happened, somewhat by accident, to see *Chained Heat II* (1993) on television with a group of friends. In the movie a young American woman in Prague is framed and sent to prison, where she is subjected to the whims of lesbian dominatrix warden Brigitte Nielsen, and where she shares a cell with a transvestite who is the mascot of the other inmates. The young woman discovers a wide-ranging web of crime and corruption; there is a riot; she is set free. There was, for lack of a better word, a kind of raw energy in this film, a celebration of female revolt. Despite what I have always heard about the women-in-prison film, there was far less homophobia than what I had expected. *Chained Heat II* was a campy pleasure to watch. My interest in the genre was sparked, and I soon discovered that even if one adheres to the strictest definition of the genre, the number of women-in-prison films is truly mind-boggling. Their titles are easily confused since so many of them carry variations consisting of the following: girls, women, chains, chained, heat, bars; there are, for instance, *Caged Heat, Caged Hearts,* not to mention *Caged*; *Chained Heat I* and *II*; *Girls in Chains, Girls on a Chain Gang,* and so on.

Throughout film history, there have been periods of ebb and flow of the popularity of the women-in-prison film. The genre was popular in the 1950s and less so in the 1960s; it reemerged in the 1970s, and again in the late '80s and '90s. The women-in-prison genre extends beyond film. There was a successful soap opera about women in prison, *Prisoner Cell Block H,* from Australia, which is still shown in reruns in some markets, and which maintains a loyal fan following to this day (Zalcock and Robinson 1996). The soap-opera connection is not coincidental; the women-in-prison story is a staple on U.S. soaps, offering diva heroines like Dorian Lord (on *One Life to Live*) or Erica Kane (on *All My Children*) the chance to encounter distinctly different kinds of women, particularly prostitutes. TV shows as diverse as *Charlie's Angels* and *The Andy Griffith Show* have featured episodes about women in prison.

Particularly since the 1970s, when Roger Corman's New World production company revitalized the genre, the women-in-prison film has been defined as exploitation. The genre performs, with a vengeance, the kind of surveillance of the female body that has been central to feminist understandings of the cinema. Indeed, the women-in-prison film provides an exaggerated representation of features that are either naturalized or repressed in more so-called respectable film genres. In their introduction to an early volume of feminist film theory and criticism, *Re-Visions,* Mary Ann Doane, Patricia Mellencamp, and Linda Williams note the importance of Michel Foucault's work in the development of feminist understandings of the relationship between the gaze and power. Noting that "the historical notion of an ever-present Gaze, regulating all images and self-images, is crucial to . . . an understanding of discursive networks of power" (1984, 13), the authors cite Foucault's appropriation, in *Discipline and Punish,* of the figure of Jeremy Bentham's plan of the Panopticon, as particularly influential. The Panopticon is a model for a prison system in which the prisoners are dispersed around a central tower, from which they are always in a state of potential surveillance by the authorities located in the tower. Foucault writes that the "Panopticon is a machine for dissociating the see/being seen dyad: in the peripheric ring, one is totally seen, without ever seeing; in the central tower, one sees everything without ever being seen" (1977, 201–2). Drawing on Foucault, Doane, Mellencamp and Williams conclude:

> The dissociation of the see/being seen dyad and the sense of permanent visibility seem to perfectly describe the condition not only of the inmate in Bentham's prison but of the woman as well. For, defined in terms of visibility, she carries her own Panopticon with her wherever she goes, her self-image a function of her being for another. (14)

If woman in general "carries her own Panopticon," the women-in-prison film thematizes in a very pronounced way the capacity of the cinema not only to objectify the female body, but also to create dramas of surveillance and visibility. Arguably the spectator occupies the position of the authority figure in the central tower of the Panopticon, particularly if one assumes, as has a large body of feminist film theory, that the ideal spectator of the cinema is male. But the women-in-prison film does not just portray the "objectification" of the female body as it has been theorized in feminist film studies; the genre is also predicated on the possibility that women observe other women. To be sure, there are virtually always male figures in women-in-prison films, whether doctors or wardens, guards or prisoners, and they function, often quite stereotypically, to provide patriarchal authority. Sometimes the notion of patriarchal authority is rendered oxymoronic in the women-in-prison film, for frequently the bastions of male superiority in the films are buffoons who are unable to shoot straight, for example, and especially whose sexual desire for the inmates renders them foolish and vulnerable. Indeed, what is quite striking about the women-in-prison genre is how marginal male figures really are to so many of the plots, and how thoroughly surveillance involves women watching other women, women surveying other women, women objectifying other women. And the women-in-prison genre is one of the few established genres where lesbianism is not an afterthought or an anomaly. There is almost always a lesbian character in the women-in-prison film, and lesbian desire is represented across a wide range of activities, from longing looks between female characters, to special friendships (that provide an interesting take on romantic friendship), to sexual activity, to sexual coercion. True, many women-in-prison films verge on soft-core pornography, and there may well be an implied male spectator in these representations of lesbianism. But I want to suggest that there is more—that the women-in-prison film offers an opportunity to see beyond the strict dichotomy of the man who surveys the woman and to understand the complexities of the ways in which women, across the dividing lines of sexuality and race, see other women.

Bev Zalcock identifies 1929 as the beginning of the women-in-prison genre, when *The Godless Girl* (directed by Cecil B. DeMille) and *Prisoners* (directed by William A. Seiter) were both released (1998, 19–20). She notes that for two decades the genre went through a "period of gestation" (19) until the release of Warner Brothers' *Caged* in 1950. One can see in this period of gestation the occurrence not just of women-in-prison films per se, but women-in-prison plots that are indicative of many of the concerns that will be addressed in later films. Consider the 1931 film *Paid* (directed by Sam Wood), in which Joan Crawford plays Mary Turner, a woman wrongfully sent to prison after she is convicted of stealing from her boss. After having her photograph taken and her hair cut off, Crawford goes into the prison's communal showers. Shots of the women's legs are shown as they enter the showers, and Crawford is ordered by the guard to disrobe, with a close-up of a leering woman providing a threatening context. The women whom we see entering the showers are all white, with one exception, a prisoner played by Louise Beavers. As Crawford stares in disgust at the women's legs surrounded by water and soapsuds, a shot of the women's feet in the shower shows the arrival of Beavers's black legs. There is a brief enigmatic look exchanged between the two women, and Beavers says jokingly, "Don't worry, honey. It all goes down the same drain." Now this scene is very brief, and Beavers does not have any subsequent role to play in the film. The scene nonetheless suggests, however incoherently, a connection between the components most characteristic of the homoerotic quality of the genre—the showers, surveillance, ambiguous looks between women—and race. While Crawford's disgust precedes Beavers's entrance, the arrival of the black woman seems nonetheless to announce race rather than, or perhaps in addition to, lesbianism as the source of Crawford's disgust.

When Ruby Adams (played by Jean Harlow) in *Hold Your Man* (directed by Sam Wood, 1933) is sentenced to a women's reformatory, she shares a room with a communist and a prostitute and encounters a black woman who lives across the hall. It is as if the reformatory is significant precisely as the place where racial difference between women, otherwise absent in the film, can be staged. The 1933 film *Ladies They Talk About* (directed by Howard Bretherton and William Keighley) features a multiracial cast of women in the penitentiary to which Barbara Stanwyck, as Nan Taylor, is sentenced. Yet none of the black women is individualized; rather, they are part of the complex world of women that comprises the prison, including one stereotypically "mannish lesbian" who smokes cigars and "likes to wrestle." The world of the women's prison may well trade on limited stereotypes, but it also creates a space where a range of differences is represented, however briefly.

Genealogies of the women-in-prison film usually cite *Caged* (1950) as the prototype of the genre (Zalcock 1998, 19; Kerec 1998, 2; Morton 1986, 151). In tracing the history of the women-in-prison film, one finds an interesting tension between the respectable, social problem film and the exploitative B movie. *Caged* is a respectable, social problem film that was nominated for several Academy Awards. It may be seen as directly responsible for films like *I Want to Live!* (directed by Robert Wise, 1958), for which Susan Hayward won an Academy Award, and which is better known as a death-penalty film than a women-in-prison film, and even for *Last Dance* (directed by Bruce Beresford, 1996), Sharon Stone's film about a woman also facing the death penalty. But *Caged* also shares basic plot and character formations with those women-in-prison films that are more raw, less respectable, and frankly more explicit in their lesbianism.

Caged is worth examining in some depth, not just for what it demonstrates about the women-in-prison genre but also for how it differs from the films that came before and after it. Marie Allen, played by Eleanor Parker, is sentenced to one to fifteen years in prison. She was

Hope Emerson as Harper, Betty Garde as Kitty, and Eleanor Parker as Marie in *Caged.*

the unknowing accomplice when her husband committed armed robbery. He died in the shoot-out, and Marie is pregnant. At the beginning of the film, she is an innocent nineteen-year-old, and the film traces her transformation into a hardened, bitter woman. In prison, Marie becomes caught in the web of two sets of power struggles: first, between the kindly warden, Mrs. Benton (played by Agnes Moorehead), and the sadistic, brutal matron, Evelyn Harper (played by Hope Emerson); and second, between two prisoners who are connected to crime rings in the world outside the prison ("free side," as it is called throughout the film), Kitty, who is the organizer of a shoplifting ring, providing women prisoners with future careers, and Elvira, her arch nemesis, who enters the prison later in the film and attempts to recruit Marie for her own crime ring, presumably as a prostitute (although this is never stated explicitly). When Marie is eventually let out on parole (arranged by Elvira), she is met by a group of men who take her off to what we assume to be her life of crime. Meanwhile, the conflict between the warden and the matron has resulted in a public scandal; the matron's brutal tactics eventually lead to her death at the hand of Kitty, and the warden's hopes for reform in the prison are futile insofar as Marie's life is concerned.

The film opens with Marie's arrival at the women's prison, and the first words spoken in the film are "File out, you tramps. End of the line," the male police officer's words to the women in the police van. Marie's difference from the other women prisoners is announced immediately, for she is not only in prison for the first time (unlike the several repeat offenders with her), but she stares at her new surroundings in fear and disbelief. The theme of surveillance, both penal and sexual, is established right away, for once the vocal police officer has taken the women inside, he leers at Marie and gives her the once-over. And the act of surveillance is quickly transferred to the women who are in charge of the women prisoners. Marie is admitted to the prison by a woman official who asks for the details of the crime and who hovers over Marie as a controlling presence as Marie speaks. Marie tries to tell her story—of how she and her husband, newlyweds, were forced to live with her mother and stepfather, how her husband didn't get along with her stepfather, how her husband had difficulty finding a job. The woman official impatiently prods Marie to "get to the crime," and as Marie recounts the details, the sound of the official's typewriter almost threatens to drown out Marie's own words. The surveillance by women continues as Marie is prodded and poked by a female nurse during her physical examination (at which point her pregnancy—"Another pregnant one!"—is revealed), as she is photographed by another female official, and as she is introduced to her isolation cell by yet another female guard.

Once Marie is released from isolation, she has her first meeting with Mrs. Benton, who is comforting and kind when Marie bursts into tears. The warden's kindness serves perhaps to displace the obvious contrast between the two women. Agnes Moorehead, while a motherly warden, is also portrayed as a somewhat butch contrast to the much more feminine Marie, and the accent on the maternal serves to overshadow the accent on the butch. If the contrast between butch and femme is suggested and simultaneously displaced in the meeting between the warden and the prisoner, that contrast becomes not only exaggerated but flaunted when Marie is introduced to the matron in charge of her cell, Harper. Marie is taken to Harper's room, which is a peculiar mixture of tacky and sentimental; she has souvenir pillows, and a large needlepoint canvas on her wall with the words "For Our Matron." The actor Hope Emerson is a very large woman, and her sheer bulk seems quite out of place in her diminutive surroundings. Harper at first seems kind to Marie, inviting her to sit in a chair that is "kind of roomy." But she also gives Marie a leer when she invites her to sit. Harper provides items (candy, cosmetics) and services (visits to family members) for the inmates in exchange for favors, and while she is disappointed to learn that Marie's family is poor, the exact nature of the favors is also left open to question.

In both exchanges, with the Agnes Moorehead and Hope Emerson characters, subtle allusion is made to lesbianism. Both actresses suggest sexual ambiguity, and throughout their careers they have played the roles of "supporting characters," which, as Patricia White has argued, often exist at the margins of the heterosexual plots central to Hollywood cinema (1995). Attractions between women are part of the fabric of *Caged,* but they are subtle and mediated through various other kinds of difference. Once she becomes part of the general prison population, Marie encounters different kinds of women: CPs, or "common prostitutes" (shunned by many of the prisoners), professional criminals, and mentally ill women; old women and young women; women who wear different kinds of prison uniforms, pants, and skirts (Marie wears a skirt; only later in the film does she don pants, a signifier of her integration into the world of the prison). Until the arrival of Elvira, less emphasis is placed on attractions between the female inmates; rather, Harper is the most obvious and blatant example of a stereotypical lesbian, whose power plays in relationship to her "girls" always have a sexual edge.

Part of the maturation of Marie is the way in which she learns to negotiate not only encounters with other women but also the double entendres of the dialogue. She is immediately set up in a hostile relationship with Harper, who is actively disliked and feared by virtually all the inmates. Marie's relationship with Harper thus stands as emblematic of the relationship of all the female prisoners with the butch matron. Despite Marie's timidity, she challenges Harper when the woman orders her to scrub the floor, insisting that Mrs. Benton told her she would work in the laundry. Other prisoners get word to Mrs. Benton, and an eternally hostile relationship is forged between Marie and Harper. Harper quite literally looms over the women in prison, and her butchness is emphasized time and time again. She orders the women by barking, "File out, you tramps," thus echoing the opening words of the film spoken by the male police officer.

One of the most striking embodiments of Harper's butch identity occurs, paradoxically, when she dresses up as an ultrafeminine woman to go out for the evening. She strolls in among the inmates as they are consoling a prisoner who was turned down for parole. "Get a load of the new look," says one woman as Harper appears, outfitted in a gaudy, frilly dress with ruffles, an oversized hat, and lots of jewelry. Harper looks ridiculous, and the incongruous feminine outfit only serves to emphasize her previously established butch identity. "The guy outside likes the way I look," Harper tells the women. Close-ups of the women's faces in reaction to Harper's taunts about her boyfriend's room, his affection, and her passion display not only disgust but horror. Indeed, one suspects that there is more going on here than one heterosexual woman taunting others about their own isolation from heterosexual contact. Rather, Harper appears in a bizarre way to be flirting with "her girls," especially when she tells June, the woman who has been turned down for parole, that it is a shame she didn't get out, for they could have "double-dated." When the inmates tell Harper they are worried about June, Harper says that "all repeaters act queer when they're flopped back." Queer, indeed.

Harper is very visible during the first half of the film, but we do not see much of Mrs. Benton; rather, her presence and authority are alluded to. She does appear in the scene immediately following the scene that displays Harper's suddenly ultrafeminine identity. June has committed suicide and Marie discovers her body and as a result gives birth prematurely. The scene in the prison hospital during the birth of Marie's child shows Mrs. Benton looking quite different from the slightly butch matron to whom we were first introduced: her long hair is flowing, unencumbered, and she wears a nightgown. She paces with all the concern of a mother . . . or a husband. The two scenes that show us the two women in authority in strikingly feminine attire function to contrast inauthentic and authentic femininity in general, with Mrs. Benton's maternal concern contributing to her more authentic femininity. But there is also a parallel between the two scenes in that they reveal another, perhaps hidden side of the matron (Harper) and the warden (Benton). To be sure, the effect of Moorehead's flowing locks and nightgown is nowhere near as parodic as Harper's bizarre getup, but in both cases the sudden acquisition of feminine apparel comes as a bit of a shock. The two scenes together also function as a bridge to the following scene, in which the two butch figures finally have a showdown.

The ostensible subject of the conversation is June's suicide, for which the warden blames Harper. In the representation of the confrontation, Harper obviously takes up more space, a function not only of her considerable size but also of her bossy persona in the film. But a photograph literally mediates the threshold between the two women—of a man, presumably Mr. Benton. The looks exchanged between the two women

The portrait of the missing man in the warden's office: Agnes Moorehead as Mrs. Benton, Hope Emerson as Harper in *Caged.*

are mediated by this image of a man; Patricia White says of the portrait that, like Harper's parody of femininity, it can "easily be read as an out-and-out charade" (1995, 107). The significance of the placement is twofold: certainly, the photograph is meant to represent patriarchal authority in this potentially extremely confusing scene of two butch women, but it is also a sign that the image of the man has little authority. Put another way, the meeting of two butch women signifies both the limits and the possibilities of the women-in-prison genre—limits in that the behavior of women in a virtually women-only environment is always shadowed by figures of male authority; and possibilities in that when that figure of male authority is frozen into a portrait on a desk, relationships between women reflect but also, and especially, exceed what is possible in a male-dominated universe. As White argues, "Different tropes of lesbian seduction—nurturance and dominance—represented by different types of character actresses, Moorehead and Emerson, work in consort to keep the female community intact" (107).

When Harper leaves Mrs. Benton's office, she appears to leave triumphantly, if for no other reason than the sheer force of her size and her bulk as she negotiates the office and hallway. A well-dressed, middle-aged man crosses her path, a commissioner who has come to investigate the suicide and the medical conditions at the prison. Once he enters Mrs. Benton's office, he then occupies the place vacated by Harper, and the photograph of the man on the desk once more occupies the space between him and Mrs. Benton. This resolution of the showdown between the two women can be read two ways: the commissioner isn't nearly as big as Harper, and perhaps he functions as a pale reflection of her; he is male, yes, but not nearly as butch as Harper is. Or, perhaps patriarchal order is being restored with the advent of a "real" man to take up the place next to the purely imaginary portrait of one. Anne Morey, noting that the photograph appears in virtually every scene that takes place in the warden's office, suggests that Mrs. Benton's problem "is not that she cannot love men but simply that she is not one" (1995, 82).

After the birth of Marie's child (a boy), her mother refuses to take him (her husband, Marie's stepfather, refuses to have the child in his house). Her mother's abandonment marks the definitive moment in Marie's change from an innocent nineteen-year-old to a hardened woman of the world. She has a parole hearing, and on the same day a "vice queen," Elvira Powell, enters the prison. Elvira is a nemesis of Kitty, the queen bee of the prison population, who has offered Marie the opportunity to work in a mob-controlled shoplifting operation once she is released. At Marie's parole hearing, three men decide her fate, and the scene echoes the earlier scene when Marie was admitted to the prison. Once again, Marie's story falls on deaf ears—literally, in the case of one of the men, who has trouble adjusting his hearing aid. Her parole is denied. Marie attempts, desperately, to escape.

Elvira Powell is introduced as she strolls through the prison yard with Harper. Powell is yet another tough, butch woman. She tells Harper that she is used to comfort, and so Elvira becomes a major source of income for the matron. She is a member of the mob who has arranged to spend six months in prison in order to avoid having to testify before a grand jury investigation. Powell sees Kitty, her old rival, and tells her that she can no longer operate her shoplifting scheme as long as she, Powell, is in prison. The staging of this encounter is very striking. Harper has turned her back and looms in the background of the shot of Elvira, her large frame taking up significant space. Elvira looks down at Kitty, who is seated on the ground. Elvira's eyes then move upward as she sights Marie. She (and the spectators) now sees a new Marie, one who looks as tough as any of the inmates. "What's your name? How'd you hurt your hand?" asks Elvira (Marie's hand was hurt in her failed

Lee Patrick as Elvira Powell meets Marie (Eleanor Parker) for the first time in *Caged*.

escape attempt). After giving her the information, Marie says coolly: "If I said no to Kitty, I'm sure not going to say yes to you." Elvira laughs heartily, and in the reaction shot of her, Harper has turned around to meet Marie's gaze. "She's a cute trick," says Elvira, as she and Harper watch Marie exit. In any other film, this would be a classic setup of sexual attraction and flirtation. While the dynamics of the crime ring are the ostensible point of contact between the two women, the shades of attraction linger.

The two power struggles that shape the film come to a head when Marie finds a kitten in the prison yard and hides it in the common cell. When Harper discovers the kitten, a riot ensues; Marie's emblematic status as victim of Harper becomes the instigation of the riot. The kitten is killed. Harper claims that Marie tried to escape, and Marie is sentenced by Mrs. Benton to solitary confinement. Harper, with the assistance of another female guard, performs her most blatant act of sadistic control: she brings Marie to her room and shaves off all of her hair. This potent instance of female shame and humiliation is surely a symbolic rape. While Mrs. Benton had insisted that Marie be put in solitary as punishment for trying to escape, she is horrified by Harper's ritual humiliation of the inmate, and she asks that the matron be fired. In retaliation, Harper calls a friend with information that leads to a newspaper headline announcing "Matron Charges Prison Immorality." Kitty, who had been placed in solitary confinement because Elvira got word to the authorities about her shoplifting scheme, breaks down, and she kills Harper. Marie finally accepts Elvira's offer to find her "work." Again, the exact nature of the work is never explained, but when Marie leaves the prison, one of the men who escort her strokes her knee suggestively. The films ends as Mrs. Benton watches, powerless, as Marie leaves the prison. Mrs. Benton has survived the scandal initiated by Harper, but she can do nothing for Marie.

While men do appear in one form or another in *Caged,* this is a film—and a genre—where relationships between women are paramount. Differences between women are stressed, as if to take the place usually occupied by gender: differences between butch and femme personas, differences in age, differences between types of crime (particularly prostitution versus everything else), physical differences. Subsequent examples of the women-in-prison film accentuate various types of differences between women. Consider, for instance, *Girls in Prison* (directed by Edward L. Cahn, 1956). The film follows the formula developed in *Caged* to the extent that it begins with the arrival of a newcomer, Anne

Carson, who protests her innocence in the bank robbery for which she was convicted. Whereas *Caged* focuses on the relationships between the matron and the prisoners, far more attention in *Girls in Prison* is placed on the interactions among the women prisoners. The female warden is neither sadistic nor particularly kind. The authority figure with the most contact with the prisoners—Anne in particular—is the prison chaplain. The film focuses on Anne's cellmates—a deranged woman who killed her family, a tough career offender who befriends Anne, and a lesbian whose advances Anne rejects. Interestingly, there is a shift in roles: while Anne is hardly butch, her short dark hair and brisk manner contrast with the other prisoners. In contrast, the lesbian, Melanee, is the most feminine of all of the women in the prison. Melanee is blonde, and the film plays up the contrast between the brunette and the blonde as one more instance of differences between women.

After Anne's first introduction to her cellmates, including a come-on by Melanee, she attends an evening dance with the other prisoners. The chaplain, who believes (erroneously, it eventually turns out) in Anne's innocence, sits with her as she observes, with some disdain, the other women dancing. "You know what I'm afraid of most?" she asks the chaplain. "That I'll become like them! It's contagious!" It doesn't require too much imagination to comprehend what "it" is. One of the fears virtually always surrounding women's prisons has been the appeal of lesbianism in a secluded, all-women environment. There is an immediate cut to a shot of women dancing together, looking ecstatic. The film connects criminality and lesbianism, to the extent that the women in prison are made to seem more susceptible to lesbianism, and while Anne's story does not conclude with heterosexual marriage, she does realize, with the help of the chaplain, that a life of crime (and thus, it is implied, lesbianism) is bad.

Caged and *Girls in Prison* make the representation of lesbianism, with varying degrees of explicitness, central to the narrative of the women-in-prison film. But in both films, all of the women are white, in sharp contrast to the women-in-prison plots that we see in 1930s films such as *Paid, Hold Your Man,* and *Ladies They Talk About.* The difference in time period is of course significant, in that the three 1930s film are pre-Production Code, and the Code included representation of "sex perversion" and miscegenation as inappropriate (Maltby 1995). The lesbianism in *Caged* is mediated through ambiguity and displacement, and in both *Caged* and *Girls in Prison* lesbians die. The representation of racial difference is not so easily mediated, unless one considers the preoccupation with other forms of difference—the blonde Melanee versus the brunette Anne in *Girls in Prison,* for instance—as a displaced form of racial difference. However, race is reintroduced in *Women's Prison* (directed by Lewis Seiler, 1955), and this film is instructive for how it adapts the women-in-prison formula in an admittedly awkward attempt to represent racial diversity. Interestingly, the film also downplays the lesbianism to heterosexualize the genre. *Women's Prison* contains many of the same elements as *Caged* and *Girls in Prison*: a naive woman provides our point of entry into the world of the prison, here a middle-class woman who committed vehicular homicide, and she immediately inspires the wrath of the prison warden. Whereas *Caged* offered a power struggle between two women, in *Women's Prison* the warden, Amelia Van Zandt (played by Ida Lupino) is the sadistic figure and her main opponent is the prison doctor, played by Howard Duff (that Lupino and Duff were married at the time adds to the heterosexualization of the film). While the women's prison is obviously still a women's space, the film adds a novel element: the women's prison adjoins a men's facility, and several of the women have husbands and boyfriends living alongside of them. The authorities cannot figure out how passage is possible, but one man manages to make visits to the women's prison to see his wife, who eventually becomes pregnant. Male figures—the doctor, the male prisoner, and the warden with whom Miss Van Zandt spends quite a bit of time—are far more significant, visually and narratively, here than in *Caged.* Miss Van Zandt's mistreatment of the women prisoners eventually leads to a prison protest and a riot, during which the female warden becomes completely unhinged, her madness thus revealed. This women-in-prison film has a happy ending, for the prison doctor finally can reveal the evil that lurked behind the prison walls, and Helene, the woman whose journey into prison began the film, is released and reunited with her husband. It does not require too much imagination to see that the happier ending of *Women's Prison* is a direct result of the importance of men in the film.

Both black and white women inhabit the prison in *Women's Prison,* and while black women have little to do in the film, the way in which this supposed integration of the genre is handled is quite revealing in terms of how the women-in-prison film is preoccupied with questions of race. The black prisoners inhabit a single cell—that is, while the film is presumably integrated, the prison itself is segregated. During most of the film, black women are portrayed in stereotypical roles that are familiar from other Hollywood films seemingly far removed from this genre. Women's work in the prison takes place in the laundry, where we see black women in the background performing service work, as if the only way in which black women could really be included in the film was to draw on already establishing iconographic and narrative traditions of the black woman as maid. We also hear the black women singing at a few points in the film, again drawing on a stereotypical image.

The one black character who is somewhat individualized in the film is Polly, played by Juanita Moore, and her introduction is quite bizarre. Helene enters the prison with Brenda, another inmate, who is a repeat offender. The contrast between the two—one blonde, one brunette; one innocent, the other casual in her approach to being jailed again; one prim and respectable, the other brassy and sexually provocative in her dress and manner—suggests the virgin/whore dichotomy. The shot of the two women entering the inside of the prison shows them in the background, walking forward, and in the foreground of the image is Polly, on her knees, scrubbing the floor, singing "Swing Low, Sweet Chariot." Polly catches a glimpse of Brenda's legs and says, "I know them legs." She stands up to embrace Brenda and tells her that she is glad that Brenda has "come home." The three women are framed in conversation, with Helene looking on somewhat uncomfortably. While Polly is indeed an inmate of the prison, in her initial presentation it is not clear if she is a prisoner or a worker—or, for that matter, a slave, given the stereotypical way in which she is presented, down on her knees, singing, making a "home" for the white woman. Having supposedly integrated the women-in-prison genre, the only way the film can actually represent a black woman is to introduce her so awkwardly and self-consciously that the opposite effect is achieved—that is, the black women in the film seem to inhabit a different world, both cinematically and socially.

Like *Women's Prison, House of Women* (directed by Walter Doninger, 1962) takes the standard elements of the genre and renders them more heterosexual. The warden here is a bitter man (when he was head of a men's prison, his wife convinced him to parole a prisoner, whom she then ran off with), and he has the same sadistic relationship with the inmates that female officials do in the previous films. The film also adds a novel twist to the genre by making the women's prison a place where young children under a certain age are permitted to live with their mothers. Arguably, the presence of children diffuses the possibility of lesbian connections in the prison. Following the formula of *Caged,* a young pregnant woman, Erica Hayden (Shirley Knight), enters the prison. Her child (who has reached the age limit for children in the prison) is eventually taken away from her. *House of Women* has another twist: some of the inmates are selected to work in the male warden's house, including Erica, and he falls in love with her and eventually, out of jealousy, prevents her from gaining parole. The women in prison eventually band together in revolt, and Erica is freed and reunited with her child.

House of Women alludes only briefly to lesbianism at the beginning of the film. One of Erica's, and our, first glimpses of prison life shows a woman whose hand has been hurt from "belting a butch" in retaliation for the butch's "sideways cracks about Troy Donahue." These two women eventually engage in the first fight of the film because the butch (the only prisoner who wears pants) has defaced the picture of Troy Donahue that the other woman keeps in her cell. In response to the butch's taunt, "What's Troy Donahue got that's so special?" the other woman replies: "Honey, you're the kind that'd never know." Similarly, the film only rarely depicts black women, and usually in isolated and stereotypical ways. In the early scenes of the film, we occasionally see a black woman in the larger crowd scenes, but it is only when we move inside the warden's house for the first time that we see an individualized black woman. Once again, she is portrayed in a way that suggests confusion between the black woman as prisoner and the black woman as maid, for she wears an apron and is working in the warden's kitchen as a cook. To add to the stereotype, she is complimented by another prisoner for her biscuits. Later, when Erica begins working in the house, we once again see two black women prisoners who work in the kitchen.

The production of women-in-prison films in the 1960s and 1970s identified the genre with exploitation, primarily through the efforts of Jess Franco, based in Italy, and Roger Corman's New World Pictures (Zalcock 1998, 25–31; Corman 1990). Corman's company produced films quickly and cheaply, and his company is legendary for providing many filmmakers their first break—including a woman filmmaker, Stephanie Rothman, who also directed a women-in-prison film in 1973, *Terminal Island* (Cook 1976; 1985, 199–200).[1] In terms of Corman the popularity of the women-in-prison film tied into the emergence of a number of factors in the 1970s, including, in cinematic terms, the rise of independent production companies and the emergence of blaxploitation cinema, and in cultural and political terms, the significance and visibility of political movements such as feminism, lesbian and gay rights, black power, and third world liberation movements. Seen against the background of feminism, it may well be tempting to write off the 1970s versions of the women-in-prison film as backlash, particularly when one considers how many of the films indulge in scenes of rape and torture. But as we shall see, when one considers the ways in which lesbianism and race both diverge and intersect in these films, the entire question of "backlash" is problematized. And in any case, as Pam Cook points out, New World Pictures "has something of a reputation as a 'feminist' company because of its consistent use of the stereotype of the aggressive positive heroine obsessed with revenge" (1976, 125).

Pam Grier's film career took off with Roger Corman's first women-in-prison film, *The Big Doll House* (directed by Jack Hill, 1971). The film was an enormous popular success, particularly as a drive-in movie; according to Corman, two-thirds of the profit of the film came from drive-ins (in Maltin 1997). Shot in the Philippines, *The Big Doll House* begins the 1970s trend of women-in-prison films set in unidentified third world countries, thus creating a new kind of woman prisoner, the political revolutionary, devoted to both her man and her cause. Additionally, the setting justifies the wearing of extremely short shorts and skirts, presumably because the climate is so hot. *The Big Doll House* features Grier as Grear, a prostitute who shares a cell with several other women, all but one of them—Ferina, of unidentified ethnicity—white. (Grear is the only black inmate; there are numerous Asian prisoners, but virtually all of them are part of the background of the film.) The film draws from the women-in-prison tradition by depicting the female wardens and guards as sick and depraved. Initially, the film seems to re-create the power struggle we saw in *Caged,* here between the warden, Miss Dietrich (who is indeed German and seems to be inspired by Marlene Dietrich), and Lucian, a guard. Miss Dietrich seems initially quite caring, while Lucian is depicted throughout as a lunatic. Torture is routine at the prison, and a man is seen observing virtually every torture scene, but always wearing a mask. Later in the film, the "man" is revealed to be none other than Miss Dietrich.

The heterosexual identity of several of the prisoners is made explicit, from the political revolutionary who is devoted to Raphael, her comrade in arms, to the woman who seduces a deliveryman because she desperately is in need of heterosexual sex. Grier's character is a lesbian, and this is an important shift from earlier versions of the women-in-prison film, first because the lesbianism is made explicit, and second, because the lesbian is a major character (in previous films the latter is only the case in *Caged,* with Harper). Grear immediately recruits a new arrival as her girlfriend. Later in the film we discover that Grear has been passing secrets on to Lucian in order to procure drugs for another girlfriend, an addict. Grear's lesbianism is approached casually, but at the same time the film plays it cagily insofar as just how lesbian Grear "really" is. She also procures items from one of the deliverymen through erotic favors, mostly by letting him touch her breasts, but when she is desperate for heroin for her girlfriend, she promises to exchange sexual intercourse for the drugs. When he tells her, "I know you dig girls," Grear replies that the prison environment has turned her gay. "Strange desires creep up on you like a disease," she says and tells him that her lesbianism is curable with a "real" man—like him. One assumes that this is a performance, and it is certainly in keeping with the overall campy tone of the film. The promised sexual encounter never happens, for Grear is killed by her drug addict girlfriend before she can attempt to escape. While the film thus offers the sacrifice of the lesbian character, the population most consistently mocked in the film isn't women—gay or straight—but, rather, heterosexual men. The two deliverymen who help the women escape (unsuccessfully, for they are all either killed or captured) are forced to parade around in their underwear, while the women observe them with ill-concealed mockery and little interest.

Corman's New World Pictures also produced *Women in Cages* (directed by Jerry De Leon, 1971), which is similar in many ways to *The Big Doll House* and features several of the same actresses. Grier plays Alabama, the lesbian warden of a women's prison in yet another unidentified third world country. As in the earlier film, Alabama is virtually the only African American woman in the film; the key prisoners are all white, with one exception, Theresa. Alabama is a sadistic warden who brings women to the "playpen," a torture chamber, where she delights in their pain and suffering. A group of women plan to escape, and they take Alabama along as their hostage. Alabama is killed, and most of the women make it to freedom. The film makes an explicit connection between Alabama's lesbianism and her race, to the extent that her job as warden gives her the opportunity to demand sexual favors of some women and to torment others. When one of the women prisoners asks Alabama "what kind of hell" she crawled out of, the warden replies: "It was called Harlem, baby." And when taunted with death by one of the women prisoners, she says, "A white man raped me, a white bitch can kill me."

In *Black Mama, White Mama* (directed by Eddie Romero, 1973), Grier plays the role of Lee, a prostitute jailed in yet another unnamed

Pam Grier as Lee and Margaret Markov as Karen in *Black Mama, White Mama.*

third world country, and one of her fellow prisoners is Karen, a revolutionary from Philadelphia with blonde hair to her waist. The two principal female guards in this female prison are a lesbian couple, one of whom is a voyeur and a sadist. She watches through a special keyhole while the women take showers, and she offers favors to women prisoners who accept her sexual advances. Lee refuses but Karen accepts, yet eventually the two women end up together in the "hot box," the isolation cell. When the two women are later transported by bus to another spot for questioning, a guerilla attack by Karen's comrades offers them the opportunity to kill their guards and escape, although they must—in an homage to *The Defiant Ones* (the film in which Sidney Poitier and Tony Curtis play prisoners who escape)—remain handcuffed for most of the film.

The two women thoroughly despise each other, but in the course of the film they become devoted friends. They even discover that despite their differences—and the difference between a "political prisoner" and a prostitute is one of the characteristic divisions of the 1970s version of the genre—they have something in common. As Lee finally says to

Karen near the end of the film, "I've been a revolutionary since I was thirteen, when I was first paid to do it." Karen is killed at the end of the film while Lee sails off to freedom, and the conclusion is not that unlike many a romance. But of course there is a radical difference. These are two women, and they are not lovers; there may be moments between them that are charged with erotic connection, but the prison scenes earlier in the film, featuring the lesbian guards, mean that lesbianism is left behind just as surely as the prison itself is. In other words, the condition of the connection between the two women is the marginalizing of lesbianism. Their relationship has racist implications as well, in terms of the mind/body distinction; the black woman is put in the stereotypical position of "body," while the white woman is defined by her "mind," that is, by her political affiliations.

In *Black Mama, White Mama* the interracial friendship occurs at the price of expunging the lesbianism, of setting up the two pairs of women—Lee and Karen on the one hand, the two prison guards on the other—in strict opposition. One could say that two of the preoccupations of the genre—multiracial communities of women and lesbianism—here work at cross-purposes. They inflect each other in the sense that, in order to make possible the connection between white and black women, the distinction must be made between them and the lesbian prison guards. In the process, the heterosexuality of the two heroines is assured, somewhat blithely, by alluding to Karen's romance with the guerilla leader. (When Lee suggests that Karen bring "Romeo," as she calls him, back to Philadelphia, Karen informs her primly that that would not be revolutionary.)

Caged Heat (1974) offers another way of understanding the relationship between race and lesbianism. Produced by Roger Corman, and written and directed by Jonathan Demme (his first film), the film deserves a place alongside *Caged* as one of the most interesting and provocative of the genre.[2] In this film, a woman is sent to jail after a crime spree she and her boyfriend were involved in went bad, and the prison is seen from her perspective as she enters as a "fish," or a newcomer. *Caged Heat* includes standard women-in-prison elements: a disturbed warden, here confined to a wheelchair, and played by B-movie queen Barbara Steele; prison corruption; a hierarchy among prisoners; an eventual breakout. In *Caged Heat* the prison physician is in cahoots with the warden, McQueen (Steele), and he provides electroshock therapy to prisoners who misbehave. He also takes sexual advantage of his power. Several prisoners arrange an escape, but when they discover that a prisoner who remained on the inside is about to have a lobotomy

Advertisement for *Black Mama, White Mama.*

performed by the doctor, they return to the prison to stage a second escape. The film ends triumphantly, with the women successfully riding off into the sunset and the villains dead. However one feels about describing films from popular genres as "feminist," this is surely a conclusion that celebrates female solidarity. Does this mean that *Caged Heat* is not an exploitation film? No. But it is precisely the coexistence of exploitation with feminism—sisterhood with attitude—that makes this film, like many in the genre, so interesting. For the film appears to act out in a popular form a kind of feminist rebellion against patriarchy and in the process holds a mirror up to 1970s feminism insofar as "sisterhood" is concerned—between black and white women, between lesbians and straight women, between women who have committed different kinds of crime against patriarchy.

Caged Heat is very casual about lesbianism. The main characters of the film are Belle (played by Roberta Collins), a white woman, and Pandora (played by Ella Reid), a black woman. Belle and Pandora are a lesbian couple. While some of the women prisoners in lesbian relationships speak about their heterosexual lives on the outside, they do so in very vague terms. And in any case, the film is no great advertisement for heterosexuality. *Caged Heat* is also more explicitly interracial than other examples of the genre, even other Corman productions, in which Pam Grier tends to be the only black woman. Belle and Pandora have a joking, friendly relationship, but they are also quite devoted to each other (Belle is

Advertisement for *Caged Heat.*

scheduled for her lobotomy after it is discovered that she has been smuggling food to Pandora while she is in the hole). One of the most interesting scenes in *Caged Heat* occurs when Belle and Pandora put on a show. In this play within the film, sex and gender are theatricalized, and sexuality is discussed, presented, and performed. Pandora and Belle dress up in drag as George and Bill, respectively, and they play a vaudevillian pair who exchange one-liners about sex. In one of their routines, Pandora (George) asks Belle (Bill), "What's a good gift for a girl who has everything?" "Everything?" replies Belle, in a feminine voice, so that she is a woman imitating a man imitating a woman. "Everything!" replies Pandora in a deep butch voice, but with her eyelids fluttering somewhat incongruously. "Say, that's easy, silly," replies Belle, once more in her faux-feminine voice. "Penicillin!" The routines themselves are not particularly funny, but the performance is quite engaging, for Belle and Pandora's relationship is staged as a playful and fanciful exploration of different ways to act male and female, and lesbianism is defined less as a reversal of roles and more as an experimentation with roles. Their second routine is a class farce, with Pandora as wealthy man and Belle as his servant. The audience members—almost evenly divided between black and white—laugh uproariously. Meanwhile, the doctor and the warden respond characteristically; he is aroused, while she clenches her fists and wheels out in rage.

If *Black Mama, White Mama* offers a vision of black/white female connection sharply distinguished from the lesbianism of the prison, *Caged Heat* works in the opposite direction, for here the representation of black and white women together facilitates the suggestion of lesbianism. When we first see Pandora and Belle together in the film, it is clear they are a couple. They behave like a couple, and they embody the classic butch/femme division; Pandora may not be classically butch, but her crime was killing a man by castrating him, and in any case Belle embodies the look (long blonde hair, ultrafeminine) and the crime (theft) more associated with the femmes of the women-in-prison world. Put another way, in *Caged Heat* racial difference facilitates, and makes possible, the recognition of the lesbian couple. In both of these films there are racial plots and lesbian plots, and the connection between them is precisely one of enabling; in other words, the women-in-prison plot relies on not just the coexistence of discourses of race and discourses of lesbianism, but also on profound connections between them. In both films, the opposition of black women and white women is eroticized, albeit in different ways. The lesbian plot requires the racial plot, and the racial plot requires the lesbian plot.

Ella Reid as Pandora and Roberta Collins as Belle do their stage act in *Caged Heat.*

Much of the fascination of women in a prison setting may indeed have to do with the intermingling of race and sexuality, and again, not just in the sense of a topsy-turvy world in which black women and lesbians—and black lesbians—are so visible, but in the sense that one kind of plot depends so strongly on the other. This is not a new story. Linda Nochlin (1989) has observed how the convention in nineteenth-century Orientalist painting of representing a black woman and a white woman together was a code for lesbianism. Lynda Hart (1994) has analyzed how in the literature of sexology black women, prostitutes, lesbians, and poor white women were seen as sharing a fundamental persuasion toward *deviance,* a term coded in such a way as to suggest a wide range of possibilities, including both lesbianism and crime. Kobena Mercer (1991) and B. Ruby Rich (1993) have explored the complicated intersections between gay and lesbian sexuality and race. The women-in-prison setting thus offers a particularly intense representation, one overdetermined by the intersections of gender, sexuality, and race.

The women-in-prison film is not, by any stretch of the imagination, an accurate representation of the real situation of incarcerated women. However, the women-in-prison film shares some tropes with the literature about women in prison, and some of this literature in its turn works both as serious, investigative reporting, sometimes designed for the actual improvement of prison conditions, and as provocative and at times exploitative narratives that follow some of the same plots as the women-in-prison film. Joan Henry's 1952 first-person account of her stay in

Holloway Prison (in Great Britain) attempts to describe what the experience of prison is like, and the author does indeed address lesbianism:

> There are a great many women who are more homosexually inclined than most people would imagine, or even than they have ever imagined themselves. They are ripe for the advances of the long-term prisoner who may be determined to have some form of sexual outlet, in prison or out; and, of course, for the advances of real lesbians, of which there are bound to be a number in any large female community. (80–81)

When Henry's book was published in the United States in a paperback edition, however, the cover would have led one to believe that this was an account of prison life devoted exclusively to lesbian drama. The cover art depicts two women looking at each other in a provocative way, and it is virtually identical to the cover art of pulp lesbian fiction published in the 1950s (see Zimet 1999).

Other literature on women and prisons is preoccupied with the intersections between race and sexuality. The very title of Sara Harris's 1967 book *Hell Hole* suggests a crossover appeal, for while the book is a serious examination of the conditions of a women's prison, the title could be yet another example of exploitation literature, a companion to the pulp version of Henry's *Women in Prison.* Harris presents a series of case histories of women who had served time in the New York City Detention Center for Women; most of the histories evoke lesbianism, and several evoke race and lesbianism simultaneously. Harris tells the story of Joyce, for example, a young white woman who turns to prostitution. When she is arrested and sent to prison, she becomes involved with a black woman and when she leaves prison she finds that it is much more complex and difficult to lead an interracial life "outside" the prison as opposed to inside (67–100).

The simultaneous preoccupation with race and sexuality in women's prisons goes back at least to 1913, when an article appeared in the *Journal of Abnormal Psychology* titled "A Perversion Not Commonly Noted." The author, Margaret Otis, describes the passionate love affairs that occur in reform schools and institutions for delinquent girls between young black and white women. It will come as no surprise that the article is cautionary, warning officials to be aware of cross-racial attractions but at the same time unsure what to do about it. Otis notes that the "problem" is so serious that some institutions have resorted to segregation, but she adds that this only exacerbates the problem. The severity of the problem is suggested, according to Otis, by the fact that

THE REVEALING STORY OF THE STRANGE WARPED LIFE OF ---

25¢

WOMEN in PRISON

Joan Henry

COMPLETE AND UNABRIDGED

The U.S. paperback edition of Joan Henry's *Women in Prison*.

one inmate married a black man when she left the prison: in other words, the lesbianism in and of itself does not seem to be the worry, but when it is coupled with cross-racial desire, then a desperate fear of "pollution" sets in.

All of these texts demonstrate the extent to which the women-in-prison film, particularly those examples of the genre in which the lesbian plot and the race plot intersect and/or diverge, plays on long-standing preoccupations about how relationships between women cross boundary lines separating races and sexual identities. While there is a huge gap in time between 1913 and the heyday of the women-in-prison film, the representation of prison life for women has been relatively constant in displaying a fascination with how women desire when left to their own devices.

Like other kinds of B movies, the women-in-prison film engages, problematically but interestingly, with questions of gender in its intersections with race and sexuality. In her study of the rape-revenge film, Carol Clover (1992) notes that the two fundamental plots of films such as *Ms. 45* and *I Spit on Your Grave*—those of gender and those of class—do not simply coexist in the films. Rather, they enable each other, in some similar ways to the race and lesbian plots of the women-in-prison films. And like other kinds of exploitation films, the women-in-prison film invites a reconsideration of how such films act as a kind of id to the superego of mainstream filmmaking, or as a negotiation of something far more complex than the supposedly ideal male spectator's hatred of women. In the afterword to her book *Men, Women, and Chain Saws,* Clover describes how her lengthy exploration of slasher and rape-revenge films changed forever her view of film, and she describes *Thelma and Louise* as ultimately a very safe film—that is, as a film that borrows many conventions of the rape-revenge film but does so in a way that is far less risky than what we see in early, less polished films. I'm not ready to dismiss *Thelma and Louise,* but I have something of a similar response to Mai Zetterling's feminist revision of the women-in-prison genre, *Scrubbers* (1983). The twist to the standard "new fish" tale is interesting: a young woman deliberately commits a crime so that she can be in the same prison as her lesbian lover; and the film attempts in particular to revise the obligatory shower sequences by making one shower scene the site of a rebellion by one prisoner, and another a scene of exclusion of the main character by her lover. But ultimately one is left with a film that in its revision of the genre tends to portray women as victims.

The women-in-prison film, from *Caged* to *Caged Heat,* offers much more than the standard feminist account of women in the traditional cinema would suggest. But then the women-in-prison film is not exactly the "classical" cinema that inspired feminist accounts of the male gaze and female objectification. Carol Clover suggests, in her analysis of the presumed adolescent male spectator of slasher films, that these films do not offer an affirmation of patriarchal authority. In Clover's analysis, these films are far more preoccupied with the ambivalence of gender identification and identity than with reaffirming the power of the male gaze; they may well be addressed—in their marketing and in their exhibition in particular—to male spectators, but they do not offer that spectator simple reassurances of his power or his authority. By implication, female spectators may well find similar pleasures in the films in Clover's study, even if they are not the primary or intended audience for them.

Clover's analysis also suggests to me a different kind of female spectatorship, different, that is, from the actual watching of slasher films (or women-in-prison films) in movie theaters. Clover's study contains the occasional anecdote about renting films at a video store. All of the films that I've discussed in this chapter are films that I have seen—and collected—on video. There may be no direct link between female spectatorship and the advent of video rentals and purchases, but there is a connection, for the very notion of a film "made for the male spectator" becomes increasingly quaint as many of the factors enforcing such distinctions—particularly having to do with movie theater attendance—break down. With the advent of video rental/purchase and the attendant availability of films that might otherwise have been forbidden for a variety of reasons, the female spectator (and the male spectator, too) sees films differently and sees different films. Women may not be the "intended" spectators of the women-in-prison film, but the very notion of an intended spectator becomes increasingly difficult to maintain when so many different venues are available for the consumption of films on video. In the meantime, I welcome the opportunity to continue to discover the delights of a genre that holds such an interesting mirror up to feminism.

Notes

1. Stephanie Rothman's *Terminal Island* is not discussed here because it is far less concerned with lesbianism than other women-in-prison films of the 1970s. For a discussion of the film, see Cook 1976.

2. For a discussion of *Caged Heat* in the context of Jonathan Demme's career, see Bliss and Banks 1996, 15–23.

Works Cited

Bliss, Michael, and Christina Banks. 1996. *What Goes Around Comes Around: The Films of Jonathan Demme.* Carbondale and Edwardsville: Southern Illinois University Press.

Clover, Carol J. 1992. *Men, Women, and Chain Saws: Gender in the Modern Horror Film.* Princeton, N.J.: Princeton University Press.

Cook, Pam. 1976. "'Exploitation' Films and Feminism." *Screen* 17, no. 2: 122–27.

———. 1985. "Authorship and Cinema." In *The Cinema Book,* ed. Pam Cook. London: British Film Institute, 114–206.

Corman, Roger, and Jim Jerome. 1990. *How I Made a Hundred Movies in Hollywood and Never Lost a Dime.* New York: Random House.

Doane, Mary Ann, Patricia Mellencamp, and Linda Williams. 1984. "Introduction." In *Re-Visions: Essays in Feminist Film Criticism,* ed. Mary Ann Doane, Patricia Mellencamp, and Linda Williams. Frederick, Md.: University Publications of America.

Foucault, Michel. 1977. *Discipline and Punish: The Birth of the Prison.* Trans. Alan Sheridan. New York: Pantheon.

Harris, Sara. 1967. *Hell Hole.* New York: Dutton.

Hart, Lynda. 1994. *Fatal Women: Lesbian Sexuality and the Mark of Aggression.* Princeton, N.J.: Princeton University Press.

Henry, Joan. 1952. *Women in Prison.* Garden City, N.J.: Doubleday.

Kerec, Linda. 1998. "These Gals Don't Bake Cookies: A Look at Women in Prison Films." http://www.taponline.com/tap/life/womensroom/culture/WIP. (This Web site is no longer available; it is listed for documentation purposes only.)

Maltby, Richard. 1995. "Documents on the Genesis of the Production Code." *Quarterly Review of Film and Video* 15, no. 4: 33–63.

Maltin, Leonard. 1997. "Interview with Roger Corman." *The Big Doll House* (video).

Mercer, Kobena. 1991. "Skin Head Sex Thing: Racial Difference and the Homoerotic Imaginary." In *How Do I Look? Queer Film and Video,* ed. Bad Object Choices. Seattle: Bay Press, 169–210.

Morey, Anne. 1995. "'The Judge Called Me an Accessory': Women's Prison Films, 1950–1962." *Journal of Popular Film and Television* 23, no. 2: 80–87.

Morton, Jim. 1986. "Women in Prison Films." In *Incredibly Strange Films,* ed. Jim Morton. San Francisco: RE/Search Publications, 151–52.

Nochlin, Linda. 1989. "The Imaginary Orient." In *The Politics of Vision: Essays on Nineteenth-Century Art and Society.* New York: Harper and Row, 33–59.

Otis, Margaret. 1913. "A Perversion Not Commonly Noted." *Journal of Abnormal Psychology* 8: 113–6.

Rich, B. Ruby. 1993. "When Difference Is (More than) Skin Deep." In *Queer*

Looks: Perspectives on Lesbian and Gay Film and Video, ed. Martha Gever, John Greyson, and Pratibha Parmar. New York and London: Routledge, 318–39.

White, Patricia. 1995. "Supporting Character: The Queer Career of Agnes Moorehead." In *Out in Culture: Gay, Lesbian, and Queer Essays on Popular Culture,* ed. Corey K. Creekmur and Alexander Doty. Durham, N.C.: Duke University Press, 91–114.

Zalcock, Bev. 1998. *Renegade Sisters: Girl Gangs on Film.* London and San Francisco: Creation Books International.

Zalcock, Beverley, and Jocelyn Robinson. 1996. "Inside Cell Block H: Hard Steel and Soft Soap." *Continuum* 9, no. 1: 88–97.

Zimet, Jaye. 1999. *Strange Sisters: The Art of Lesbian Pulp Fiction 1949–1969.* New York: Viking Studio.

III
Lesbian Looks

8. A Parallax View of Lesbian Authorship

Diane Kurys's 1983 film *Coup de foudre* (English title, *Entre Nous*) has a devoted following among many lesbians, despite—or perhaps because of—the fact that the allusions to lesbianism occur from within the securely defined boundaries of female bonding and friendship. Two women, Léna (played by Isabelle Huppert), and Madeleine (played by Miou-Miou), living in post-World War II provincial France, discover an attraction for each other (an attraction that is definitely erotic though never explicitly sexual) and eventually leave their husbands to live together. As was widely publicized at the time of the film's release, the friendship of the two women has a strong autobiographical significance, for it corresponds to the experience of Kurys's own mother. At the conclusion of the film, when Léna (the fictional representation of Kurys's mother) asks Michel (Kurys's father, played by Guy Marchand) to leave, their daughter—that is, Kurys herself—is seen watching them. Over the final shot of the film, of Madeleine walking with the children on the beach, a title appears, a very literal authorial signature: "My father left at dawn. He never saw my mother again. It's now been two years since Madeleine died. I dedicate this film to the three of them."[1]

The sudden appearance of the author's signature, within the child's point of view, situates the enigma of the women's relationship in the ambiguous world of childish perception. All of Kurys's films are marked by the connection between storytelling and a female bond that wavers between the homosocial and the homoerotic. Somewhat surprisingly, perhaps, that connection is most strongly articulated in what appears to be on the surface the film that departs the most sharply from the distinctly female world central to Kurys's first three films: *Diablo Menthe*

(Peppermint Soda), Cocktail Molotov, and *Entre Nous.* In *A Man in Love* (*Un Homme amoureux,* 1987) the plot centers on a young actress, Jane (played by Greta Scacchi), whose affair with a narcissistic American movie star, Steve Elliot (played by Peter Coyote), is interwoven with her relationship with her mother (played by Claudia Cardinale), who suffers from and eventually dies of cancer.

While the film follows Jane as its central protagonist, it is not until approximately two-thirds of the way through the film that her voice emerges, quite literally, as the voice of the film, through voice-over commentary. The voice-over is the major component of the film's self-mirroring quality; in the concluding scenes, Jane begins writing a text titled "A Man in Love." The first occurrence of the voice-over is immediately after a scene in which Jane, in bed with her lover, Steve, describes—seemingly at his request—a fantasy of lesbian lovemaking. Hence, the conditions of the emergence of the female narrator's voice are bound up narratively with the lesbian fantasy, a fantasy that offers, within the logic of the film, the possibility of combining two spheres otherwise separate: heterosexual passion and the mother-daughter bond.

Some aspects of Kurys's films offer significant revisions of the components of narrative cinema, such as the rewriting of the boys' school scenario (central to two classics of French film history, Jean Vigo's *Zéro de conduite* and François Truffaut's *The 400 Blows*) in her first feature film, *Peppermint Soda,* or the exchange of looks between the two women in *Entre Nous.* The self-representation of Kurys (in *Peppermint Soda* and *Entre Nous* in particular) and the representation of female authorship are far more problematic in the present context, for they consistently evoke and dispel lesbianism simultaneously. Put another way, the lesbianism affiliated with Kurys's signature is so framed by the duality of heterosexuality on the one hand and the maternal bond on the other that female authorship is foregrounded but not significantly reframed or retheorized outside of that duality.

However, if the popular reception of Kurys's *Entre Nous* by lesbian audiences is any indication, then the film lends itself to the same kind of reading as Barbara Smith (1977) offered of Toni Morrison's novel *Sula,* a reading based, that is, on the permeable boundaries between female bonding and lesbianism. This is not to say that *Entre Nous* has been defined in any simple way as a "lesbian film." Indeed, whether Kurys's film is appropriately described as a lesbian film—permeable boundaries notwithstanding—has been a matter of some debate among lesbians. In a letter to the editors of *Gossip,* a British lesbian feminist journal, Lynette

Mitchell criticizes two essays published in the journal that represent *Entre Nous* as "an unequivocally lesbian film" (Mitchell n.d.; Grundberg n.d.; Whitelaw n.d.). Mitchell notes that in the film "the two women are shown admiring each other's bodies and at one point in the film they exchange a swift kiss, but this could just as easily be an expression of deep physical affection as erotic desire" (11–13). In any case, if *A Man in Love* offers the theory and *Entre Nous* the practice, then the lesbianism evoked in Kurys's work is not only fully compatible with but also fully dependent on heterosexual fantasy and maternal connections. In other words, lesbianism is simultaneously a limit and a horizon of female narration and authorship.

In some oddly similar ways, lesbianism is also a limit and a horizon for contemporary feminist work on the female subject. Two of the most common and persistent threads of this work have been, first, the theorizing of a double position for women, as both inside and outside of patriarchal culture, and, second, a staging of what is by now a classic fixture of feminist theory, the encounter between so-called American empiricism and French theory. While feminist theories of the subject and of subjectivity are often criticized by lesbians and women of color for being inattentive to the difference that marginalities make, it's not altogether accurate, at least not in the case of lesbianism, to describe the apparent indifference as an absence.

Consider, for example, the by-now-notorious dismissal in Toril Moi's *Sexual/Textual Politics* of American black or lesbian feminist criticism: "Some feminists might wonder why I have said nothing about black or lesbian (or black-lesbian) feminist criticism in America in this survey. The answer is simple: this book purports to deal with the theoretical aspects of feminist criticism" (1985, 86). Moi proceeds to explain that black and lesbian literary critics are as controlled by the limits of empirical criticism as their straight white sisters; while they may have *political* importance, their work is theoretically, well, theoretically retarded. Moi does note, however, that these "'marginal feminisms' ought to prevent white middle-class First-World feminists from defining their own preoccupations as *universal* female (or feminist) problems" (86). By the conclusion of her book, even this vapid concession—from which the term *heterosexual* is, in any case, conspicuously absent—is forgotten. That lesbian criticism doesn't have too much importance—political or otherwise—is demonstrated by Moi's elevation of Julia Kristeva as a model of theoretical feminism, with no mention of the extent to which Kristeva's theorizing establishes the lesbian as bad object, and with no consideration that this might be a problem for her feminist usefulness (Butler 1989; de Lauretis 1987; Grosz 1989; Silverman 1988).

This isn't to say that Moi is representative of all feminist explorations of the French-American encounter and the contradictory status of the female subject. Nancy K. Miller, for instance, has noted that Moi "manages to collapse each side of the American/French divide with an astonishing lack of concern for the bodies (and positions) under erasure" (1988, 21 n. 16). Indeed, Miller's own work is far less invested in the simple dualities of simpleminded American feminism versus smart French theory. But in Miller's book *Subject to Change* lesbianism also acquires an implicit function, one defined far more in terms of the pole of attraction (in contrast to the pole of repulsion in Moi's account). In her introduction Miller notes that "it may also be that the difference of another coming to writing requires an outside to heterosexual economies" (1988, 10). While the term *lesbian* is not used to describe the utopian female communities that figure so prominently in Miller's analyses of women's fiction, the language used is quite evocative of much lesbian writing, and Miller's own reading of Adrienne Rich with Roland Barthes can be seen as an attempt both to acknowledge lesbian writing and to redefine the intersections between homosexuality and feminism. Thus, while Miller's avoidance of the term *lesbian* has more to do with the desire to avoid a perilous opposition of "lesbian" and "heterosexual" than with the desire to dismiss lesbian possibilities, one is left with a conception of female space with distinct, yet distinctly unspecified, lesbian contours.

Moi is dismissive while Miller is more inclusive. However, if the specter of lesbianism does not necessarily haunt feminist theories of the subject, lesbianism has had a signifying function by virtue of its very status as "other"—whether untheoretical other in Moi, or utopian other in Miller. It is commonly assumed—and frequently euphemized through phrases like *radical feminism*—that a politically informed lesbian subjectivity participates in the naive affirmation of self, the unproblematic articulation of agency, and (the most common refrain of all) essentialism, taken to be characteristic of "American feminism."

Many lesbian filmmakers have engaged with the redefinition and reconceptualization of the cinema and in so doing have challenged the implicit oxymoron of "lesbian theory" that haunts so many feminist explorations of the subject. But why, one might ask, define these projects in terms of *authorship,* particularly given the suspicious reputation it has acquired—much like lesbianism itself, one might add—for harboring idealized, untheorized defenses of the fictions of identity? Furthermore, within the context of cinema studies, the very notion of authorship is far more evocative of traditional, patriarchal film criticism than even is the case in literary studies, for instance. To be sure, throughout the history of contemporary film studies, there have been calls to rethink and retheorize authorship, from Claire Johnston's insistence in 1973 that auteurism and feminism could function compatibly, to Kaja Silverman's critique of feminist film theorists whose ostensible dismissal of the film author is accompanied by the return of a desire for unproblematized agency (1988, 209). Nonetheless, the revision of the concept of authorship has not been a high priority in film studies.

The need to bring authorship into a discussion of lesbian representation is evidenced by a significant body of films in which the filmmaker writes herself into the text, although not in ways that match the common, easy equation between authorial presence and the fictions of identity. There are some lesbian films where this does occur as an affirmative and self-revelatory gesture; Barbara Hammer's celebrations of lesbian love come immediately to mind. But a far more provocative feature of contemporary lesbian filmmaking is the articulation of lesbian authorship as a critical exploration of the very components of subjectivity: self-other relations, desire, and—where lesbianism provides the most crucial challenge to theories of the subject—the relationship between the paradigms of gender and agency, for example, the presumed identity between activity and masculinity, passivity and femininity. Chantal Akerman's 1974 film *Je, tu, il, elle,* for instance, is saturated with an authorial presence that explores the possible alignments of the pronouns of its title, and Akerman attempts nothing less than rewriting the cinematic scenario that prescribes formulaic relations between those terms along the lines of heterosexual symmetry. Or, to take a related but different example, Ulrike Ottinger has written herself into her films through cameo performances. From the flashback appearance as the dead lover, Orlando, of the title character of *Madame X* to a drunken passerby in *Ticket of No Return,* these roles substantially revise the assumed equation between authorial fictions and heterosexual Oedipal narratives (see Mayne 1990, chap. 4).

Midi Onodera's *Ten Cents a Dance (Parallax)* (1985) is a short (thirty minutes) film, divided into three sections (in the catalog of *Women Make Movies,* the film is described as a kind of "*Je, tu, il, elle* in miniature"). Like other explorations of lesbian representation, *Ten Cents a Dance* is less concerned with affirmative representations of lesbian experience than with explorations of the simultaneous ambivalence and pressure of lesbianism with regard to the polarities of agency and gender. This could of course be taken to mean that the film is, because less explicitly lesbian in its focus, less lesbian, period. Indeed, the status of *Ten Cents a Dance* as a lesbian film has been crucial to its reception.

Ten Cents a Dance has had a controversial reception history. At the tenth Annual Lesbian/Gay Film Festival in San Francisco in 1986, for instance, Onodera's film was shown last on a program titled "Lesbian Shorts" with four other films. By all accounts, the film precipitated something close to a riot, with a considerable portion of the audience booing the film and demanding their money back. If the letters devoted to the screening that later appeared in *Coming Up!*—a San Francisco gay/lesbian newspaper—are representative of the controversy, then *Ten Cents a Dance* was indicative of a crisis of naming in lesbian filmmaking, to borrow a phrase from B. Ruby Rich (1980). For how could this film, two-thirds of which is devoted to the representation of gay men and heterosexuals, possibly be called a lesbian film and be advertised as such? More specific criticisms were made as well: that unsafe sex was depicted between the two men, for instance, and that the lesbian scene included a heterosexual woman. The board of directors of Frameline, the organizers of the festival, responded to the letters by explaining that *Ten Cents a Dance* "was not only by a lesbian, but was strongly pro-lesbian, despite a scene of two gay men and a straight couple having sex" (*Coming Up!* 1986, 5). The exhibition context required the charge of "not a lesbian film" to be countered with "not only a lesbian film, but a pro-lesbian film." But the reception of the film speaks to a larger issue about lesbian

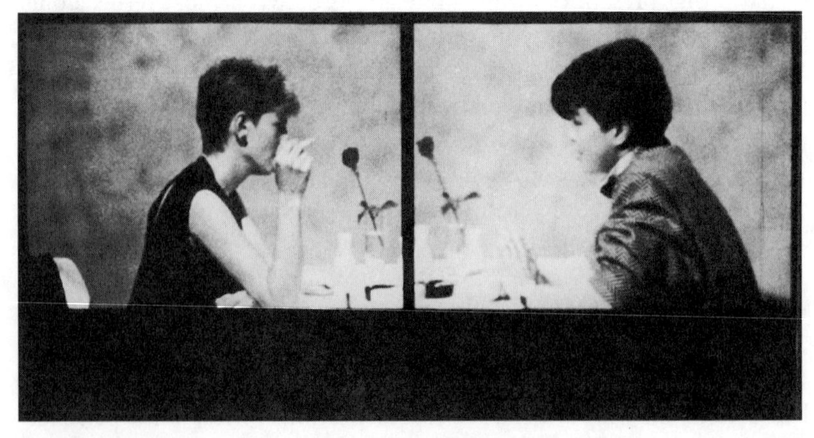

Midi Onodera's *Ten Cents a Dance (Parallax)*. Courtesy of Women Make Movies.

representation, concerning precisely the relationship between lesbianism and the contradictory subject theorized within contemporary feminist theory.

Each section of *Ten Cents a Dance* is concerned with a different configuration of sexual desire and language. A split screen is used throughout, so that the two players in every scene are divided from each other. In the first section, two women, while waiting for (or just having finished) dinner in a Japanese restaurant, discuss whether or not they will have a sexual relationship. In the second section, shot from a high angle, two men have sex with each other in a public restroom. And in the final section, a man and a woman engage in phone sex. The use of the split screen creates a wide-angle effect, since the top and bottom of the frame are masked, and the two screens appear as if projected against a black background, with a dividing line between them. Each scene in Onodera's film captures a sense of both pleasurable duration—depending, of course, on how you define *pleasure*—and uncomfortable pauses.

The title of Onodera's film cites the Rodgers and Hart song about a hostess at the Palace Ballroom who sells dances to "Fighters and sailors and bow-legged tailors . . . butchers and barbers and rats from the harbor." The song is a cynical lament, full of bitter resignation and desperation. The most obvious match to the song is the third section of the film, and it would be easy to argue that Onodera equates heterosexual sex with the pathos of sex for sale. But in this respect, *Ten Cents a Dance* has an ambiguous quality: it suggests simultaneously the difference and the analogy between different sexualities, for all of the participants in the film enact rituals of erotic connection and distance.

In any case, the title of the film also reminds us that "ten cents a dance" is not to be taken so literally: the addition of *parallax* in parentheses over the right screen can be read in relationship not only to each of the participants in the respective couples but to the distinction between straight and gay, gay and lesbian, male and female as well. If the difference between two points of view allows the "apparent displacement of an observed object" (as the dictionary says), then the *parallax* of Onodera's title refers quite obviously to the way in which lesbian and gay readings take citation and replacement as central strategies. More specifically, the parallax view of *Ten Cents a Dance* is evocative of Joan Nestle's insistence—speaking of the difference between "replication" and "resistance" in the appropriation of butch and fem styles—that lesbians "should be mistresses of discrepancies, knowing that resistance lies in the change of context" (Nestle 1984, 236).

Undoubtedly, the doubled screen is the most striking visual figure of discrepancy in *Ten Cents a Dance.* The split screen suggests a number of cinematic precedents, such as the stereoscope card, a doubled image that when viewed at the proper distance creates the illusion of depth. Other uses of the split screen come to mind as well. In *Pillow Talk* (1959), for instance, split screens are used extensively to juxtapose the telephone conversations of Doris Day and Rock Hudson, frequently with contrasting pink and blue color schemes, which Onodera adapts in her red and blue portrayal of heterosexual phone contact. If the third section of the film is the one most obviously informed by classical Hollywood conventions, all three sections play on the edges of the frame, particularly in their contrasting functions of reiterating the markers separating the two women (the rose) and rendering oblique the restroom wall and glory hole that separate and connect the two men.[2]

In all three instances, the two views are juxtaposed to disrupt the seamless fit between the participants in sexual dramas. The relationship between the two screens in each section acquires the contours of simultaneous connection and separation. The screen surfaces are figures of permeability and division at the same time. Far from serving as the unproblematized ground for the image, the screen in *Ten Cents a Dance* becomes a site of tension. This occurs by the doubling of the screens, and by the relationship between the two edges that never quite touch. In addition, the interplay of screen and frame makes the film's representation of sexuality more a question of what is *screened,* in both senses of the term, than what is unproblematically visible. In the first and last sections of the film, of course, sexual talk obscures the sexual act, but even in the second section of the film it is the threshold between the two men that is foregrounded far more than sexual acts themselves.

In her essay on lesbian representation and Sheila McLaughlin's film *She Must Be Seeing Things,* Teresa de Lauretis distinguishes films like McLaughlin's, which produce "modes of representing that effectively alter the standard frame of reference and visibility, the conditions of the visible, what *can* be seen and represented" (a description that obviously applies to *Ten Cents a Dance*), from those that provide "sympathetic accounts . . . without necessarily producing new ways of seeing or a new inscription of the social subject in representation" (de Lauretis 1989, 2). In the latter category, de Lauretis includes films like *Desert Hearts* and *Lianna.* Mandy Merck has described *Desert Hearts* as "steeped in the heterosexual tradition of the active pursuit of the reluctant woman" and goes on to cite a series of rigid dichotomies that structure the film, those of class and geography, for instance (Merck 1987, 16).

Such dichotomies have more than a passing relationship with *Ten Cents a Dance,* particularly insofar as the first section of the film is concerned. Merck notes that in *Desert Hearts* the dichotomous formula of "brunette is to blonde as active is to passive" appears as a stock feature of the genre of the lesbian romance. Dark-haired Onodera casts herself in the role of the "experienced lesbian" having relationship talks with a blonde woman whom she had considered "essentially straight" (the experienced lesbian versus the experimenting heterosexual is another typical opposition described by Merck). Yet Onodera cites the dichotomies in order to disrupt and suspend them simultaneously. For by casting herself, an Asian woman, in the role of the active pursuer, Onodera reverses one of the most common Western representations of Asians, male or female, as passive and obedient. But that such a reversal cannot function in any simple way as an alternative is made clear in the last section of the film, where the woman assumes the active role but also where her own position as sexual commodity is reinforced. More crucially, the oppositions thus cited never attain narrative or sexual resolution—or, rather, they only attain resolution by displacement and suspension.

But this displacement and suspension engage a risk, for by focusing on two women talking, *Ten Cents a Dance* could be seen as affirming the popular stereotype that lesbians talk about relationships while men have sex—whether with women or with each other. In other words, *Ten Cents a Dance* could be read as affirming lesbianism as, if not asexual, then at least presexual, or in the language of much contemporary psychoanalytic theory, as pre-Oedipal, as a re-creation of the mother-child bond. However, what seems to me most crucial in this representation of lesbian sexuality is the way it is framed, not so much in terms of the scene itself but, rather, in relationship to the sexual rituals that surround it.

In the 1989 essay mentioned above, Teresa de Lauretis is critical of the tendency, in much writing about lesbianism and feminism and the female subject, to conflate identification and desire. The so-called pre-Oedipal mother-daughter bond can be regarded as the foundation for lesbianism only if the desire *for* another woman is subsumed to the desire to be (like) a woman. As de Lauretis puts it, there is a "sweeping of lesbian sexuality and desire under the rug of sisterhood, female friendship, and the now popular theme of 'the mother-daughter bond'" (1989, 31). Implicit in such accounts is a definition of heterosexuality as mature, adult, and symbolic, whether such accounts are "straight" or symptomatic—that is, really the way things are or really the way things are under patriarchy. And heterosexual intercourse becomes the norm against which other sexualities are classified as deviant.

In Onodera's film, the possessors of the most explicit (though not completely visible) *sex* are not the heterosexuals but the gay men, and the closest thing to a sexual referent in the film is oral sex, not intercourse. Indeed, orality is one of the sexual common denominators of the film, whether through conversation, cigarette smoking, or sexual acts. Heterosexual intercourse is thus displaced from its status as the standard of sexuality against which all others are compared. The three sections of the film become, rather, sexual configurations in which orality—so long considered a major attribute of the regressive, narcissistic, homosexually inclined individual (male or female)—figures across the dividing lines of different sexualities.

As de Lauretis suggests, the conflation of desire and identification, and the attendant relegation of lesbianism to the presexual stage, serves to reinforce what are ultimately homophobic definitions. At the same time, however, the definition of lesbianism as an extension of female bonding or mother love is one to which many lesbians have been drawn. Within contemporary lesbianism, there are competing definitions of what lesbianism is, from the most intense form of female and feminist bonding (as theorized by Adrienne Rich in her controversial lesbian continuum) to a sexuality that is distinctly different from heterosexuality, whether practiced by men or women. The ironic signature that Midi Onodera brings to her performance—understood here both in terms of her role and the entire film—suggests both of these simultaneously.

In the first section of the film, Onodera is both the experienced lesbian discussing the possibility of an intimate relationship with a woman and an Asian Canadian having dinner in one of the most popularized Western clichés of Asia, a restaurant. In other words, she appears to occupy a position of some authority. But Onodera defines authorship so as to expose its fictions as well as its desires. For the position that she occupies, on the right side of the screen, is taken up by a gay man engaging in anonymous sex in the next section and a woman offering phone sex in the last part of the film. Given the extent to which anonymity and sex for sale are defined in much lesbian writing as symptomatic of either male sexuality or heterosexuality, the affiliation between Onodera's position and those of the man and the woman in the subsequent scenes brackets any simple notion of lesbian desire as isolated from other forms of sexual desire.

At the same time, of course, the lesbian scene is different from the other two, with more emphasis on conversation and the erotics of the look—the latter serving a particularly ironic function, given the extent to which the look has been defined in much feminist film theory as the province of the heterosexual male's possession of the woman. Onodera's ambiguous role in the film—as both author and actor, and both like and unlike gay men and heterosexuals—thus suggests that the lesbian author is defined as complicit in and resistant to the sexual fictions of patriarchal culture, and that lesbian irony holds competing definitions of lesbianism up to each other, while refusing to collapse one into the other.

Notes

1. "Mon père est parti au petit jour. Il n'a plus jamais revu ma mère. Madeleine est morte il y a maintenant deux ans. A eux trois, je dédie ce film."

2. A glory hole is a hole in a wall between two bathroom stalls that is used for anonymous sexual contact.

Works Cited

Butler, Judith. 1989. *Gender Trouble.* New York and London: Routledge.

Coming Up! 1986. "Lesbian (?) Short Raises Storm of Controversy at Lesbian/Gay Film Festival." *Coming Up!* 11: 4–5.

De Lauretis, Teresa. 1987. "The Female Body and Heterosexual Presumption." *Semiotica* 67, nos. 3–4: 259–79.

———. 1991. "Film and the Visible." In *How Do I Look? Queer Film and Video,* ed. Bad Object Choices. Seattle: Bay Press, 223–76.

Grosz, Elizabeth. 1989. *Sexual Subversions: Three French Feminists.* Winchester, Mass.: Unwin Hyman.

Grundberg, Sibyl. N.d. "Deserted Hearts: Lesbians Making It in the Movies." *Gossip* 4: 27–39.

Johnston, Claire. 1975. "Women's Cinema as Counter-Cinema." In *Notes on Women's Cinema,* ed. Claire Johnston. Reprinted. London: British Film Institute, 24–31. Originally published in 1973.

Mayne, Judith. 1990. *The Woman at the Keyhole: Feminism and Women's Cinema.* Bloomington: Indiana University Press.

Merck, Mandy. 1987. "Desert Hearts." *The Independent* 10, no. 6: 15–18.

Miller, Nancy K. 1988. *Subject to Change: Reading Feminist Writing.* New York: Columbia University Press, 1988.

Mitchell, Lynette. N.d. "Letter." *Gossip* 6: 11–13.

Moi, Toril. 1985. *Sexual/Textual Politics.* London and New York: Methuen.

Nestle, Joan. 1984. "The Fem Question." In *Pleasure and Danger: Exploring Female Sexuality,* ed. Carole S. Vance. Boston: Routledge and Kegan Paul, 232–41.

Rich, B. Ruby. 1980. "In the Name of Feminist Film Criticism." *Heresies* 3, no. 1: 74–81.

Silverman, Kaja. 1988. *The Acoustic Mirror: The Female Voice in Psychoanalysis and Cinema.* Bloomington: Indiana University Press.

Smith, Barbara. 1977. "Toward a Black Feminist Criticism." *Conditions* 2: 25–44.

Whitelaw, Lis. N.d. "Lesbians of the Mainscreen." *Gossip* 5: 37–46.

9. Julie Zando's Primal Scenes

A number of contemporary lesbian film and video artists are challenging, in a variety of ways and from multiple perspectives, assumptions about lesbian representation. Such assumptions include, of course, the pathologizing perspective, whether deliberately homophobic (that is, right-wing pronouncements), or unconsciously so (that is, theoretical formulations that take heterosexuality as an unquestioned paradigm). But the assumptions challenged in recent lesbian work also include the celebratory ones that have characterized much lesbian representation from "within." Some of the most exciting film and video being produced by lesbians today take on the complex and difficult project of challenging, simultaneously, heterosexual presumption and the myths of lesbian representation that exist within lesbian communities.

For instance, Su Friedrich's film *First Comes Love* (1991) is a condemnation of the virtually universal prohibition against homosexual marriage. Yet that condemnation is presented in a decidedly ambivalent way. After a series of candid images of the various preparations for different church weddings, a rolling title interrupts those images to list the countries where homosexual marriage is illegal—practically every country in the world. After another series of images of newlyweds, the final title image of the film reveals the one exception: "In 1990 Denmark became the first country in the world to legalize homosexual marriage." Two modes of documentary observation are juxtaposed: the cinema verité style of capturing weddings either about to begin or just concluded, and the more detached, dry style of authoritative recitation. In the process, different assumptions that lesbians bring to the institution of marriage are juxtaposed as well—simultaneous envy and detachment, desire and repugnance. As a result, the very notion of a single, monolithic lesbian view on marriage is questioned.

Lucretia Knapp's videos perform this challenge in yet another way. In a manner reminiscent of Todd Haynes in *Superstar,* Knapp uses Barbie dolls in *Erotica* (1989) and *Sally Cheesey Raffelyell* (1992) in a parodic way. In both tapes, the dolls are lesbianized. Their short haircuts and butch clothing make evident how unrepresentable lesbian style is in popular cultural forms like Barbie dolls. And yet, at the same time, the tapes play on the opposite impulse as well, the visibility of lesbianism, whether in porn (in *Erotica*) or in talk shows (in *Sally Cheesey Raffelyell*). Like Kaucyla Brooke and Jane Cottis in *Dry Kisses Only* (1990), a hilarious lesbian rereading of supposedly heterosexual films like *All about Eve* and *The Great Lie,* Knapp reads the conventions of porn and talk shows ironically.

A question often raised among lesbians, as among members of virtually any marginalized and politically disenfranchised group, is whether it is possible to use mass cultural forms toward, if not "positive," then at the very least "productive" ends—that is, whether lesbians should even attempt to use the talk show format (or pornography, or marriage rites), if they function therein as freaks on display. Friedrich and Knapp turn the traditional formulation of this question on its head by using such institutions and making fun of them simultaneously. The very question of "using" already established forms of popular institutions and mass culture is thus playfully—and forcefully—set aside in favor of a more complex notion of lesbian use value where lesbians are understood as always both inside and outside dominant forms.

In this chapter I want to examine how in the video work of Julie Zando such challenges to both prevailing lesbophobic and ingrained lesbian assumptions are addressed. Zando's videos are stunning representations of the complexities of lesbian desire. Stylistically, her work traces an erotics of video form. Zando's videocamera moves almost constantly, and one of the most typical devices of her work is a constant framing and reframing of her subjects. As Amy Taubin puts it, "Zando's primary expressive and organizational tool is her hand-held, herky-jerky, intrusive camera, which effectively turns every factual statement into a question, marked, moreover, with subjectivity" (1990, 51). Zando uses the qualities of video to great advantage, particularly insofar as grain and resolution are concerned. When shot in extreme close-up, for instance, her subjects appear both near to and far from the viewer, distorted by the extreme angle and grain, yet caught as well in a moment of vulnerability. Indeed, Zando plays constantly with the implications of exposure to the videocamera, whether it is of her or her subjects.

Like Friedrich and Knapp, Zando challenges prevailing orthodoxies, of both dominant institutions and lesbian culture. In her case, the challenge proceeds across two registers—psychoanalysis and narrative. The failures of psychoanalysis vis-à-vis lesbians and gay men have been detailed enough that there is no need to rehearse them here. Just as important have been the efforts of theorists like Teresa de Lauretis and Judith Roof to read those failures as the limitations not of psychoanalysis itself but of particular practitioners of psychoanalysis (de Lauretis 1991b; Roof 1991). Similarly, Zando's videos are less concerned with critiquing psychoanalysis for its shortcomings than with reframing the very question of what it means to talk about psychoanalysis in lesbian terms. Zando undoes and reframes the question of lesbianism and psychoanalysis by situating psychoanalysis as a theory, less of psychic truth or verifiable experience than of narrative. Now in and of itself, this use of psychoanalysis as a theory of narrative is nothing new (Spence 1982; Brooks 1984). Rather, what is specific to the inquiries undertaken in Zando's work is the definition of psychoanalysis and narrative vis-à-vis lesbian representation.

Narrative is not defined exclusively in the psychoanalytic terms of, say, transference and countertransference, or imaginary and symbolic, in Zando's work. For her video narratives have a very specific resonance vis-à-vis lesbian representation. One of the most persistent myths of lesbian identities is the notion that one "becomes" a lesbian as a result of a very specific intersection of experiences. Hence one of the narratives most common in lesbian culture is the fixing of lesbian identity to a particular moment, a particular experience, a particular time. Coming-out stories are the most popular version of this lesbian narrative, whereby one identifies a single experience as the turning point of one's sexual life. To be sure, there are some lesbians who are convinced that one is "born" a lesbian, but this too is a version of the lesbian narrative of identity; in this case, identity is decided well ahead of any lived experience. Popular versions of the lesbian narrative of identity invariably include scenarios of childhood ("As a child I always preferred the company of girls"; "I was a tomboy") and adolescence ("I got crushes on my female teachers"; "I was more attracted to female than to male characters on television"; "I was obsessed with Doris Day/Natalie Wood/Greta Garbo . . . or James Dean"). The very notion of lesbian identity is produced, in other words, across a narrative structured by a series of revelatory, self-sufficient moments of recognition. Bonnie Zimmerman's description of the lesbian coming-out novel is relevant here: "Whether it conforms to the *bildungsroman,* the religious tale of exile, the novel of awakening, or the picaresque, the lesbian coming out novel takes its pilgrim on a progress toward wholeness" (1990, 38).

Let me take that lesbian narrative of identity back to psychoanalysis: it is as if within lesbian representation there is a preoccupation with the primal scene, with a founding moment of sexual identity. I am admittedly using the term *primal scene* in a metaphoric way, although there is a connection to be made, I think, between how fantasies of the primal scene have been theorized in psychoanalytic writing and how fantasies of lesbian identity have been narrativized in lesbian writing. In contemporary film theory, fantasy has provided the basis for an important revision of theories of the cinematic subject, which have reproduced the very traits of dominant culture—that is, a subject that is white, male, and heterosexual. An essay by Jean Laplanche and Jean-Bertrand Pontalis, "Fantasy and the Origins of Sexuality," has been extremely influential in this rethinking of the cinematic subject. Elaborating on their claim that "fantasy is the fundamental object of psychoanalysis" (1973, 317), Laplanche and Pontalis distinguish three "original" fantasies: "Like myths, they claim to provide a representation of, and a solution to, the major enigmas which confront the child. Whatever appears to the subject as something needing an explanation or theory, is dramatized as a moment of emergence, the beginning of a history." The three fantasies of origins are as follows: "The primal scene pictures the origins of the individual; fantasies of seduction, the origin and upsurge of sexuality; fantasies of castration, the origin of the difference between the sexes" (1986, 19).

Of the three primal fantasies described by Laplanche and Pontalis, the primal scene has particular relevance for sound/image forms like film and video, which rely precisely on the relationship between participant and observer and on the spectator's knowledge as a function of sound and image. Additionally, an understanding of film in relationship to fantasy challenges any monolithic definition of the cinematic subject, for Laplanche and Pontalis emphasize that fantasy scenarios offer "multiple entries" (see also Mayne 1993, 22–23). It is not coincidental, then, that fantasy has been the point of departure for challenges to film theory's own compulsory heterosexuality. In a study of Sheila McLaughlin's film *She Must Be Seeing Things,* for instance, Teresa de Lauretis argues that the film articulates a lesbian version of the primal scene, where the positions of onlooker and participant are occupied by women (1991a).

Throughout Julie Zando's work, lesbian desire inflects fantasy and rubs against the grain of dominant psychoanalytic thinking, just as fantasy inflects lesbian desire and rubs against the grain of some cherished myths of lesbian identity. In suggesting that Zando's tapes interrogate the space where these fantasies intersect, I do not want to reduce her work to an intellectual or theoretical exercise. For what is so exciting and stunning about the work is its visual density, its sonoric field, its narrative richness. As Bill Horrigan says of Zando's work, it "evidences the application of a sympathetic intelligence, *une raison ardente,* onto lived values, in the passionate interest of restoring to the subject (themselves/us: we're both of us I) the possibility of an imagined wholeness always partly lost" (1988, 38). Zando's tapes are theoretically challenging, to be sure, but this is not theory that seeks easy hierarchies or master narratives. Rather, in Zando's work, theory is an engagement in complexity, contradiction, and most of all, in lesbian pleasure, visual and otherwise. As Zando herself puts it:

> I like theory as an intellectual game but I prefer it when I can apply it to my own experiences. I don't want my tapes to act as a light where my role is to flip the switch and illuminate some theoretical concept. I'm more interested in putting the viewer's finger into the socket allowing the shock waves to carry the message in a sudden jolt of understanding. (Cited in Molesworth 1992, 6)

My discussion of Zando's work is based on five tapes: *The Bus Stops Here* (with Jo Anstey, 1990); *The A Ha! Experience* (1988); *Let's Play Prisoners* (1988); *Hey, Bud* (1987); and *I Like Girls for Friends* (1987). All of these tapes share a concern with the implications of the primal scene for psychoanalytic and lesbian storytelling, and they share stylistic features as well: the persistent framing and reframing of the subjects; complex and sometimes dissonant relationships between sound and image track; competing and often opposing narratives. Zando herself is present in her tapes, whether as a literal performer (in *The A Ha! Experience, I Like Girls for Friends,* and *Hey, Bud*) or as an off-screen, audible narrator (*Let's Play Prisoners*). Zando's visible authorship is very much a collaborative endeavor, for she appears in her tapes with Jo Anstey, whose writings are the basis of and in many cases are recited by Anstey herself in *Let's Play Prisoners, The Bus Stops Here,* and *The A Ha! Experience.*

The Bus Stops Here and *The A Ha! Experience* are the most obviously psychoanalytic of Zando's tapes. In *The Bus Stops Here,* a complicated family triangle becomes the scene for the juxtaposition of heterosexual and lesbian desire, maternal and paternal objects, and differing views of psychoanalysis as, alternately, talk therapy and drug therapy; Jacques Lacan also makes an appearance as "Jack," the father. *The A Ha! Experience* contains perhaps the most explicit representation of the primal scene, for here a daughter, returning home from an evening out with a man, imagines her mother in her bed. That Zando appears in the role of a young woman in a heterosexual relationship gives a sense of how complicated the representation of lesbianism is in her work!

Despite the apparent heterosexual intrigue of *The A Ha! Experience,* I would argue that Zando situates lesbian desire fully center stage. In this tape the young woman returns to her apartment after saying goodnight to a man. In the bathroom, she removes her jewelry and her clothing, and it is not always clear when we are seeing her or her image reflected back to her (and us) from the mirror. As she proceeds to her room, she describes her shock at seeing her mother in her bed. Zando juxtaposes two classical psychoanalytic scenes of recognition—the mirror stage and the primal scene. In both cases the identification of woman as object of desire is at stake. During the bathroom scene, Tony Conrad, from behind the camera, speaks of his own need to be logical and instructs Zando to repeat an action. Hence the moment of (illusory) self-recognition in the mirror is complicated by the control of that image by a very literal masculine presence. So too is the primal scene segment complicated by Conrad's voice once again, as well as the reappearance of the male lover.

Yet those elements of domination are countered by the woman's fantasy of her mother speaking to her from her own bed. If there is a single absent presence in the tape, it is the mother. Masculine control is exercised on Zando's body in a virtual catalog of the techniques that have been ascribed by feminist film theorists to the (male) cinematic control of the female body: close-ups of her, framing her within the frame; sexual display for the camera; in addition, her hands are bound by her male lover, and Tony Conrad not only directs her but yells at her at one point. Yet the last freeze-frame of Zando's face in the tape is accompanied by her voice-over: "Mother, you are my camera."

The A Ha! Experience opens up an encounter, in other words, between lesbian and heterosexual desire, and in other of her works Zando pursues that encounter with more and more attention to the implications of this phrase, "Mother, you are my camera." *The A Ha! Experience* also gives some sense of how much Zando stretches the very definition of "lesbian representation." Forget about so-called positive images of lesbianism; if you are even looking for actual images of lesbians, period, you will be disappointed in Zando's work. Some of her tapes represent (more explicitly so than *The A Ha! Experience*) lesbian scenarios; *Hey, Bud* and *I Like Girls for Friends,* for instance, are inquiries into televisual images, taking lesbian relationships as their point of departure and conclusion; and *The Bus Stops Here* has a lesbian character. In *Let's Play Prisoners,* which seems to me Zando's most sustained and complex inquiry into the relationships among lesbianism, desire, and narrative, there is little that can be described as a precise, specific lesbian image, but there very definitely is a lesbian narrative. That seeming paradox—a lesbian narrative without the specific lesbian image—constitutes one of the most challenging aspects of Zando's work.

In *The Bus Stops Here* lesbian desire is by and large spoken by others. Judith (the clinically depressed lesbian sister of Ana, the novelist who is having an affair with Judith's therapist) rarely speaks, and more frequently her desire and her story are spoken by others: the therapist, a psychiatrist who prescribes different drugs for her, or the male voice-over (Zando describes him as the metanarrator), who gives her history. In another way, lesbian desire itself is appropriated by her sister, whose novel-in-progress, read aloud in the tape, is about lesbian attraction and seduction. If Judith's story (and by extension her lesbianism) is largely told, narrated, and appropriated by others, this is part of a larger pattern in the tape whereby women rarely narrate their own stories; rather, they are "told" by male figures of authority—psychoanalytic and psychiatric authority, specifically.

Yet throughout the tape, lesbian narration threatens to upset the fit between male domination of women and heterosexual control of lesbian desire. Each of the three principals in the tape—Ana, the therapist, and Judith—tells of a disturbing encounter in a public place. In Ana's case a man exposed himself and masturbated on a bus, and the therapist, also while on a bus, saw a well-dressed woman sucking her thumb. For both Ana and the therapist, the scenes provoke masturbatory fantasies, and the recounting of the tales is strongly evocative of primal scene fantasies, with their emphasis on staging and the unacknowledged presence of the observer. In addition, the sexual fantasies that result from the encounters in public places occasion the multiple identifications typical of fantasies. Ana, attending a class (during which feminist film theorist Kaja Silverman's voice is heard describing the components of fantasy), imagines a man describing masturbating on the bus, and shots of her on the bus are intercut, thus identifying her as occupying, simultaneously, the position of male masturbator and female onlooker. When the therapist fantasizes about the woman he has seen on the bus, his voice is heard reading aloud the fantasy of lesbian seduction from Ana's novel.

Finally, Judith too has an encounter in a public place that she describes, but once again the psychiatrist introduces the story, so that when Judith faces the camera and speaks, she is speaking through the psychiatrist. Judith describes seeing a woman eating a bagel while her eyes are bulging out, and she describes her discomfort. "You know, eating like that is such a very private time, you never expect to see anyone watching you," she says. "I had turned away, embarrassed that I had seen her so vulnerable." As Judith tells of the encounter, we see images of Ana and the therapist drawn from their bus encounters. But unlike their scenarios, Judith's story leads to no masturbatory fantasy, no movement across different positions in the fantasy. Rather, the tape concludes with a dream of hers, but told by the psychiatrist and from which she is virtually absent. Hence the problem of lesbian narration is that it exists only to be appropriated by others.

Let's Play Prisoners is divided into two sections titled "Remembrance" and "Recognition," suggesting a process of discovery not unlike that of the therapeutic situation. The psychoanalytic analogy situates childhood experiences as always the product and projection of a privileged, adult hindsight. The talking cure, with its accompanying dynamics of transference and countertransference, is the model undertaken here; virtually every aspect of the tape is concerned with conversation and the dynamics of power therein. As Zando herself puts it:

> Just as an analyst directs the therapeutic session, the camera directs perception and experience. In psychoanalytic terms the camera "normalizes" experiences in a deliberate, self-conscious way; my tapes often remind the audience of the camera's analytic privilege (its power to interpret and mediate experience). Like Bertolt Brecht, I am interested in self-conscious direction, except that I interpret the process as a kind of "counter-transference." (1991, 7)

Stories of games played by little girls are read and reread in the tape. The first words heard in the tape belong to Jo Anstey, who reads aloud from her own short story. Anstey's reading is directed by Zando off camera, with an occasional hand entering the frame to adjust Anstey's dress or even, at one point, to slap her to elicit an appropriate response. Zando instructs Anstey to repeat certain lines or to adjust her tone. The relationship between the two women changes in the course of the tape,

Julie Zando's *Let's Play Prisoners.* Courtesy of Julie Zando.

as does Anstey's appearance, particularly insofar as makeup is concerned. While at the beginning of the tape Anstey and Zando appear to be comfortable in their relationship, tension between them (whether real or performed) emerges as the tape continues. In the first section of the tape, Anstey does pretty much what Zando asks her to do, but in the second section there is more visible resistance on Anstey's part.

Anstey's reading of the story alternates with a young girl's (Zando's niece's) recitation of identical passages from the story. Just as Zando directs Anstey's reading, the girl's mother (also off screen) reads passages aloud that the girl then repeats. During the first part of the tape, the story concerns games between two young girls in which one is the prison guard and the other the prisoner, and as the story progresses to tell of other games (particularly in part two), the relationships of power become more and more clearly identified as modeled on the mother-child relationship. It is not only the story, as recited by Anstey and the girl, that makes the imprint of the mother-child relationship more and more foregrounded, but also the editing of the tape. For home movie–type images of mothers with their children, or babies "posing"—however unconsciously, however awkwardly—for the camera, are gradually intercut into the alternation between the two storytellers, Anstey and the young girl. For instance, Anstey says of her friend: "She gave me piggybacks, but I wanted to show her I could pick her up, too." At that moment, we are confronted with a visual match, but now of a mother picking up her child. When the girl storyteller is shown lying on the ground and speaking the words "'You tie me up,' she said," an image of a baby lying in a similar position is intercut, suggesting of course their common status as "tied up" by the mother and the camera.

To my mind the most striking and haunting images of *Let's Play Prisoners* are those that begin the tape and are repeated at key moments throughout: extremely fluid and fragmented close-up shots of two female bodies accompanied by the eerie musical score of the film (written by Paul Dickinson), and over which we hear the first words of the film, recited by Anstey: "She said, 'Let's play prisoners. Pretend you've just tried to escape.'" Even though Zando uses the grain of video to great advantage, an effect heightened by the use of black and white, these particular images have the additional texture produced by the videocamera used, a Fisher Price camera marketed for children. Like Sadie Benning, who also uses the distorted effects of this toy camera to great advantage, Zando uses a toy to ironic effect in a tape so concerned with putting into question the sanctity of childhood memories. These images suggest at once the relationship of infant to the mother's body and the relationship of lover to lover. As Cynthia Chris puts it, "As the desired object of either infant or lover, Zando portrays the body as a contested arena on which the other will experience victory or defeat, as a stage on which something will be made to happen, as the setting for a story about to be told" (1989, 21).

Jo Anstey appears on camera after this prologue, along with the title "1) Remembrance." While the alternation between Jo, directed by Julie, and the girl, directed by her mother, would suggest a parallel between Jo and the girl (both directed by the women off camera), an additional factor somewhat complicates this parallel. For during the first few alternations from Jo's story to the girl's story, Zando's camera centers not on the little girl but on one of her girlfriends, who walks back and forth in the background during the entire tape. The friend functions as a witness in the video, a bystander seemingly both engaged and perplexed by the spectacle she is witnessing. The friend has no specified position or place within the proceedings; she never speaks, has no narrational role comparable to speaker (Jo, the girl) or director (Zando, the girl's mother). Despite—or rather because of—this lack of specified position vis-à-vis the narrative, Zando's camera tracks this little girl's movements frequently. Indeed, during the girl's recitation of the story, the camera moves in more sweeping, distracted movements, as if the witness pulls the story off balance somewhat, disturbs any possible equilibrium in the movement back and forth from Jo to the girl.

If I am tempted to see the girlfriend as the tape's spectator, it is (I hope) not because of some compulsive need to assign her a fixed position but, rather, to describe her as something more than a purely disruptive, marginal presence. For her relationship to the entire proceedings, as both participant (she "enacts" one of the games described by Jo) and observer, as within and without, seems to me to embody how Zando's video challenges the spectator to read through her own memories of childhood without becoming immersed in nostalgia or sentiment.

The "Remembrance" section of the tape concludes with a series of disruptions. Voice-over narrators speak of the mother's power over the child, unconditional love, the power implicit in the other's affirmation of her love, and the loss of power. None of these voices is synchronized with the image track. The naked female bodies appear again to mark the transition to the second part of the tape, "Recognition." The recognition here is the increasingly clear link between the girls' games as narrated in Jo's story and the relationship between mother and child; thus, what was presented as something of an interruption or, rather, an eruption in the first part of the video, here becomes an integral part of the narration itself. Put another way, the way the home movie–like images of mothers and children appear during "Remembrance" suggests symptoms not yet understood, and the style of "Recognition" suggests, rather, a more complex interweaving of the different levels of "Remembrance."

The primary game recounted in "Remembrance" is the prisoner game of the tape's title, and it culminates in a fusion of past and present when Julie hits Jo on the head to get the desired reading of the story. The two games recounted in "Recognition" are more clearly defined as to how girls' games are modeled on the mother-child relationship. The first, "floppy doll," has the one girl becoming totally passive as the other grabs hold of her, lets her hang, and then drops her. In "Remembrance," a vivid match between the game and the tape's present tense occurs when Julie, acting like the dominant girl in the story, slaps Jo; a somewhat different match occurs in the second part, when the girlfriend in the background holds the girl in the way described in the floppy doll game.

The second story in "Recognition" tells of how the two girls refused to go to the bathroom all day and made signs at each other during school, the combination of pleasure and pain (or at least discomfort) creating a secret bond between them. The game changes when the more controlling of the two girls insists that they wet their pants "like little kids." In both games, then, the common denominator is the passivity of the one and the power of the other, and the passivity mimics the dependence of the child's basic needs—whether moving around or getting its diapers changed—on its mother.

As in part one of the tape, the second section is interrupted by a series of voice-over narrators: "Your source of power is an illness. . . . I want to sever the ties between us, between mothers and children." The tape concludes with the voice-over narration now taken up by Jo and the mother, so that techniques that previously marked difference and separation are collapsed. The toy videocamera images of the female bodies return, while Jo tells the story (in voice-over) of the two girls not going to the bathroom all day. Something changes in the images of the bodies, for the toy camera continues—seemingly seamlessly—to record a bathroom (but, as with the bodies, the images are fragmented) as Jo continues the story of how Jill, the dominant friend, insisted that she wet her pants. Jo's story concludes with her inability to go to the bathroom, and her attempt to make amends to her friend. Her last line is "I couldn't do anything without her."

The mother's voice tells more or less the same story (with some variations), and the image track consists of the by-now-familiar images of the girl (and her girlfriend in the background). However, the images are distorted, not enough to be unreadable but enough to suggest a parallel with the toy camera images of the female bodies (and the attendant imprint of the little girls on the grown women, and vice versa). In addition, there is in this conclusion rapid cutting within the scene, whereas before the only cutting that took place was to introduce the home movie–like images of mothers and children. Hence, the various aesthetic devices that had previously signified different material and different registers are here combined, so that it is no longer possible to easily separate one from the other—just, one might add, as it is impossible to separate adult fantasies of childhood from the supposedly "real" experiences of childhood. "Recognition" is a more complex narrational and visual process of association.

Whereas Jo's version of the bathroom story ends with the girl begging her friend to forgive her for not being able to go through with wetting her pants, the mother's version stops at an earlier point, when the girl is inside the toilet stall. "I couldn't go, and I couldn't go out without going," she says. And with those words—a loop back from the previously uttered end to the story—the tape concludes. The paradox at the heart of *Let's Play Prisoners* is precisely there, the paralysis of refusing to submit to the power of the other and refusing simultaneously not to submit.

Let's Play Prisoners is obviously preoccupied with power as it is manifested both in the mother-child relationship and in all subsequent relations between women. However, I think it is a mistake to read the tape too literally in terms of a particular parallel between mother/child and woman/woman. To be sure, Zando's tape challenges a tendency in feminist theorizing to idealize the mother-child bond as pure fusion, and she challenges as well the idealized notion of lesbianism as the re-creation of that fusion. In this sense, Zando's tape is evocative of the critical difference that Judith Roof has elaborated between heterosexual and lesbian narratives of the mother. Taking the writings of Nancy Chodorow and Julia Kristeva as symptomatic of a heterosexual tendency to idealize the mother-child bond, Roof says:

> If we see the relationship to the mother as one of lack instead of a nostalgia for plenitude suggested by Kristeva and Chodorow, if these lesbian stories privilege the moment of separation from the mother rather than the time of unity with her, we can see the genesis of an ironically heterogeneous desire as opposed to the nostalgic desire that characterizes heterosexual accounts of mothering. (1991, 114)

In Zando's tape, a lesbian remembrance allows the recognition of the complexity of the power relationship in both childhood games and mother-child relations. Put another way, *Let's Play Prisoners* is less an indictment of the power struggles that characterize relationships between women (although it may well be that on a secondary level) and more an exploration of the ways remembrance and recognition are always a function of one another.

While the mother-child relationship is certainly important in its own right in Zando's work, it also functions as a paradigmatic dualistic framework, that is, a model for the either/or of autonomy and dependence. As Christine Tamblyn puts it, "Female dyads enacting dominance/submission rituals are obsessively constructed and reconstructed in *Let's Play Prisoners*" (1990, 12). As I've suggested, *Let's Play Prisoners* works through, in narrational and visual terms, the implications of binary frameworks. The relatively strict two-termed oppositions and parallelisms of the first half of the video (Jo's reading/the child's recitation;

the relatively straightforward imagery of Jo's and the girl's narration/the more fragmented and distorted imagery of the female bodies) are transformed in the second half, so that the division between recognition and remembrance is, paradoxically, a putting into question of any such easy division.

Hey, Bud also relies for its initial structure on a two-termed opposition—here, in a much bolder way. The tape opens with images of women—their faces for the most part invisible—in colorful vintage gowns. The use of a wind machine and the sound of camera shutters clicking suggest a photo shoot and, by extension, the conventional definition of woman as object of the look. Sandra Haar suggests that *Hey, Bud* is edited "to suggest, at once, ritual and fashion photography" (1990, 45–46). During the opening minutes of the tape, these images alternate with a close-up of a woman cutting her toenails and a female voice-over reflecting on the significance of Bud Dwyer, the Pennsylvania official who committed suicide in front of television cameras during a news conference. The woman's voice describes Dwyer as a pornographer for killing himself publicly: "Hey, Bud," she says, "you dramatized a private act in a public forum."

In *Hey, Bud* Zando's own video style works through and against that of televised news, and one of the characteristics of her work is an engagement on many levels with the institutions of television. Indeed, *Hey, Bud* cites television advertising, journalism, and MTV and reworks their apparent differences in a meditation on the video form as one that flattens the distinction between voyeurism and exhibitionism. Similarly, in *I Like Girls for Friends* a woman leans on her elbow and faces the camera in a style reminiscent of the Calvin Klein jeans advertisements of some years back, where female models (like Brooke Shields) spoke in a confessional mode to the camera. In Zando's tape, the young woman's image and voice do not match—the female voice-over is unsynchronized for the most part to the image. Accompanied by generic pop music, the woman's voice starts out talking about lesbianism in some of the clichéd terms that have characterized the mythology of lesbianism: "I like girls for friends better than boys"; "I'd rather be with girls," and so on. But the story the woman tells is one that moves far beyond both the confessional mode of advertising and the mythology of lesbianism as female bonding intensified. For she tells a tale of abuse by her female lover. In so doing, parenthetically, she alludes to many of the figures that appear throughout Zando's work: she refers to herself as treated like a floppy doll by her girlfriend, and footage of Zando and Anstey from *Hey, Bud* appears here briefly.

Hey, Bud takes further this principle of juxtaposition. From its initial visual and sonoric opposition between what also might be called public and private views of the female body, the tape alternates between repeated images of two of the women (Zando and Anstey), still dressed in their vintage gowns, as they enter a room, primp, and eventually kiss and embrace, and the televised footage of Dwyer committing suicide. As in *Let's Play Prisoners,* although in a more exaggerated way, given how disparate the two tracks seem initially to be, binary oppositions are broken down. The tape combines in different ways the supposedly public act of Dwyer's suicide and the supposedly private seduction of two women in a room, all the while undoing any such easy opposition between private and public, subject and object of the look, or voyeurism and exhibitionism.

The conclusion of the tape plays on the notion of "climax." To the accompaniment of a woman's heavy breathing on the sound track, rapid alternation occurs between the black-and-white, grainy footage of Dwyer preparing to kill himself and the lush, color images of one of the women (Anstey) combing her hair as the other (Zando) watches and moves to embrace her. During the most rapid montage of these image tracks, Anstey's hands, combing her hair, seem to be superimposed on those of Dwyer preparing to kill himself. If Dwyer's suicide was, as the female narrator claims early on, an act of pornography, it has no money shot, so to speak. The first time I saw the tape, I cringed in expectation of the man's head being blown to bits before the camera. Zando (like most newscasters) stops short of showing the actual moment of suicide. Zando's climax is, rather, the juxtaposition of the seemingly disparate images of man and woman with the positioning of a lesbian narrative as inescapably connected to public theater.

I noted previously that in *Let's Play Prisoners* there is a lesbian narrative with no specific lesbian image. If *Hey, Bud* seems initially to contradict that separation of image and narrative, it is only to challenge from another direction the relationship between image and narrative. For the image of the two women embracing remains difficult to "see," obscured and overpowered by the spectacular display on television. It is just that difficulty that constitutes the power and beauty of Zando's work.

In conclusion, I would like to return to the question of how her work may be seen in the context of contemporary lesbian representation. I have characterized Julie Zando's videos as engaging critically with myths of lesbianism that exist both in dominant culture and lesbian culture. Zando's engagement with lesbian culture from within means that her work exists against the backdrop of a number of assumptions. For instance, her work is never identifiable as "lesbian" in the sense of celebratory, positive representations of lesbian life, from *Desert Hearts* to *Claire of the Moon,* from uplifting documentaries to Naiad romances. Throughout this essay I have been arguing that Zando's work, in relationship to more popular (among lesbians, at least) forms of lesbian representation, offers a more intense theorization of the very stakes of lesbianism and representation. But in some ways this argument for the particular quality of her work could be seen as an easy way out, and one that affirms a problematic dualism between "popular" and "avant-garde" art forms.

Laura Mulvey, in her classic 1975 article "Visual Pleasure and Narrative Cinema," speaks of the "passionate detachment" that will allow audiences to view the conventions of mainstream cinema critically (15). If Mulvey herself has seemed more inclined toward the "detachment" side of the formulation, its "passionate" quality is always there, too, a love of the very forms that rely so extensively on woman as object. While Mulvey's work has been subjected to extensive commentary, revision, and argument, the concept of passionate detachment remains nonetheless one of the most provocative and most undertheorized aspects of her approach to cinema. Zando's work, it seems to me, is characterized by such a passionate detachment, directed both at dominant representational forms and at lesbian mythologies.

Now by situating Zando's work in this way—that is, in relationship to the founding text of feminist film theory—one might think that I am appropriating Zando to the feminist cinematic canon. But what I want to suggest instead is that Zando's work exemplifies a process that I see in other works of lesbian representation as well: an embodiment of passionate detachment that challenges feminist theories of representation, not just for their homophobia but for their simplistic either/or's, their easy moralizing about dualisms, their insistence on making clear and absolute distinctions between what is patriarchal and what is not. Hence Zando's work—like that of Su Friedrich, Lucretia Knapp, Sadie Benning, Midi Onodera, and Cheryl Dunye (to name but a few)—suggests that the complexities and contradictions of lesbian representation may well define a new, more theoretically challenging "scene" of feminist alternative representation.

Perhaps the stakes of passionate detachment in Zando's work are best exemplified in how one of the most divisive and controversial of lesbian issues is addressed—lesbian sadomasochism. There is much in Zando's work to suggest the shadow of sadomasochism, from her investigation of power to her explorations of how violence intersects with sexuality. But these are not tapes that take up any identifiable position—that is, nowhere does Zando's work proselytize either for or against lesbian sadomasochism. Rather, her videos open up a space within contemporary debates about lesbian sexuality. And in this sense Zando's work shares an important preoccupation with other contemporary lesbian works similarly concerned to explore and redefine our very definition of lesbian representation. Lynne Fernie, codirector (with Aerlyn Weissman) of the remarkable feature *Forbidden Love,* an exploration of lesbian culture of the 1950s and 60s, from oral histories of lesbians to a reenactment of the appeal of lesbian pulp novels, has said: "It's really the s&m controversy that made this film possible" (quoted in Rich 1993, 58). I take Fernie's comment to mean that whatever else one might say about debates concerning lesbian sexuality, the controversy has introduced the kind of active, engaged debate necessary for any representation to thrive. Now in many ways Zando's work would seem to be quite different from *Forbidden Love,* but what they share is that sense of passionate detachment that encourages viewers to rethink their own assumptions about what it means to talk about lesbianism and representation in the first place. In the process, some of the problematic dualisms that have characterized debates and discussions about lesbian representation may well become obsolete.

Works Cited

Brooks, Peter. 1984. *Reading for the Plot: Design and Intention in Narrative.* New York: Random House.

Chris, Cynthia. 1989. "Girlfriends." *Afterimage* April: 21.

De Lauretis, Teresa. 1991a. "Film and the Visible." In *How Do I Look? Queer Film and Video,* ed. Bad Objects Choice Collective. Seattle: Bay Press, 223–76.

———. 1991b. "Perverse Desire: The Lure of the Mannish Lesbian." *Australian Feminist Studies* 13: 15–26.

Haar, Sandra. 1990. "Self-Lessness." *Fuse* June-July: 45–46.

Horrigan, Bill. 1988. "Essay: Question." *Frame/work: A Journal of Images and Culture* 2, no. 3: 36–38.

Laplanche, Jean, and Jean-Bertrand Pontalis. 1973. *The Language of Psychoanalysis.* Trans. D. Nicholson-Smith. London: Hogarth.

———. 1986. "Fantasy and the Origins of Sexuality." In *Formations of Fantasy,* ed. Victor Burgin, James Donald, and Cora Kaplan. London and New York: Methuen, 5–34.

Mayne, Judith. 1993. *Cinema and Spectatorship.* London and New York: Routledge.
Molesworth, Helen. 1992. "Interview with Jo Anstey and Julie Zando." Unpublished manuscript.
Mulvey, Laura. 1975. "Visual Pleasure and Narrative Cinema." *Screen* 16, no. 3: 6–18.
Rich, B. Ruby. 1993. "Making *Love.*" *The Village Voice,* 17 August, 58.
Roof, Judith. 1991. *A Lure of Knowledge: Lesbian Sexuality and Theory.* New York: Columbia University Press.
Spence, Donald P. 1982. *Narrative Truth and Historical Truth: Meaning and Interpretation in Psychoanalysis.* New York: Norton.
Tamblyn, Christine. 1990. "The River of Swill: Feminist Art, Sexual Codes, and Censorship." *Afterimage* October: 10–13.
Taubin, Amy. 1990. "The Deep: Lures and No Exits." *The Village Voice,* 13 November, 51.
Zando, Julie. 1991. "Symptoms and Stories: The Narrative Cure." In *Breakthroughs: Avant-Garde Artists in Europe and America, 1950–1990.* Columbus, Ohio: Wexner Center for the Arts, 6–9.
Zimmerman, Bonnie. 1900. *The Safe Sea of Women: Lesbian Fiction 1969–1989.* Boston: Beacon.

10. Girl Talk

Chantal Akerman's 1994 film *Portrait d'une jeune fille de la fin des années 60 à Bruxelles* (Portrait of a Young Girl at the End of the 1960s in Brussels) is a beautiful and haunting evocation of female adolescence and its discontents: desire, loss, and the complicated, ambiguous transitions between girlhood and womanhood. Central to the film are the dynamics of a love that doesn't exactly dare *not* speak its name (according to Oscar Wilde's famous definition of homosexuality) but, rather, that doesn't quite know *how* to speak its name. *Portrait of a Young Girl* is in many ways a coming-out story, for the love of one girl for another moves the film forward and structures its narrative development. Amy Taubin describes the film as a "lesbian coming-of-age story, probably the most evocative ever made" (1995, 65).

It will come as no surprise to those familiar with Akerman's work that this is no transparent coming-out tale and that the film resists any of the simple oppositions—between inside and outside, past and present, before and after—suggested by the very term *coming out.*[1] Rather, this film explores how lesbian desire is both shaped and repressed by the codes and conventions of heterosexual romance. On the surface, the film could be described as a somewhat conventional girl-meets-boy tale. But what shapes the girl-meets-boy story is the simultaneous desire, for the girl, to connect to another girl and to tell stories. In other words, this is a lesbian narrative with a difference; girl still meets boy, but that classical and timeworn plot is the pretext for the connection between two girls.

Portrait of a Young Girl was commissioned by the French television station ARTE for a series titled *All the Boys and Girls of Their Age (Tous les garçons et les filles de leur âge).* Nine filmmakers participated in the series, and the films (most of them, like Akerman's, an hour long or less) tell varied stories of adolescence, often focusing (unsurprisingly) on love and sexuality. In addition to the focus on adolescence, filmmakers were required to include a party scene in their films, as well as songs of the era. The series was designed to reflect, especially through music, the feel and sensibility of an era, and to offer filmmakers the opportunity to create unique portraits of the past. Other films in the series included *U.S. Go Home* by Claire Denis (best known in the United States for her autobiographical film *Chocolat*) and *Travolta and Me* by Patricia Mazuy.

The opening titles of Akerman's film inform us that the action takes place in April 1968, just a month before the famous worker-student demonstrations and strikes that immobilized France and Western Europe, and that have provided a mythical point of reference for virtually every political movement in Europe in the past three decades. Akerman's film follows Michèle, portrayed with luminous intensity by the marvelous actress Circe, on the day that she has decided not to return to school. The film begins with the sounds of a ticking clock and then shows us Michèle at home, going through a wallet, presumably her father's, for cash. It is early in the morning, and Michèle's father drops her off at the station where she is to catch her bus for school. The first words spoken in the film are Michèle's words of departure to her father: "Au revoir, Papa." These words prove to be prophetic in more ways than one in the course of the film.

Michèle's newfound liberty takes expression in a variety of forms. She goes to a café where she writes out a variety of excuses for school, beginning with "Please excuse Michèle. She had the flu," passing through a series of imaginary funerals she had to attend (her grandmother's, her uncle's, her aunt's, who died after the death of the uncle, her father's), and concluding with her own death, announced with flat finality: "She died."[2] The fantasy of her own death is also a fantasy of rebirth, of shedding the various institutional identities she possesses, those associated with the family and school. As if to celebrate this rebirth, Michèle leaves the café, tears up a school folder, and exuberantly throws the pieces in the air.

Michèle goes to her school but lurks outside, next to the bars that surround the grounds. First, she encounters one friend, Mireille, and announces that she won't return to school. Michèle then meets her best friend, Danielle, and they go to a café where they sit with two young men and proceed to kiss them. At one point Michèle pauses, turns away from the young man she is kissing, and observes Danielle as she continues to kiss the other boy. At this early point in the film, it is impossible to read Michèle's act of observation with any certainty. She looks at her friend but also looks at her friend as she is kissing another boy. In other words, the look could well be one of longing directed at Danielle, or it could be a look seeking encouragement and approval. It soon becomes clear that Michèle takes as much if not more pleasure in talking with Danielle about the boys they encounter as in actually experiencing those encounters. Indeed, when Danielle and Michèle leave the café, they talk about how disappointing the kissing was, and their conversation occupies more screen time than the actual kissing did.

After Danielle returns to school, Michèle goes to the cinema, where she sits next to a young man, Paul. He begins to touch her knee, and Michèle tells him that he can kiss her. This encounter begins an apparently conventional girl-boy romance, but it is a romance from which Danielle is never absent. Indeed, Michèle immediately informs Paul that he can't go any further than a kiss because she has to meet her friend at school. Michèle describes Danielle and says that he would probably like her. When they leave the movie theater, she tells Paul that she let him kiss her not just because she wanted to but "also to make someone else suffer . . . and it was to be able to talk about it, too."[3] Paul and Michèle discuss how Michèle will tell the story of her encounter at the movie theater. This girl-meets-boy story, then, is from the outset a girl/girl-meets-boy story.

At one point in their wanderings Michèle leaves Paul abruptly, announcing that it is four o'clock. She runs to meet Danielle and proceeds to tell her, in terms that she had rehearsed earlier with Paul, about going to the movies. Paul seems to be hovering off-screen; as Michèle performs for Danielle her version of going to the movies, Paul is located, figuratively and literally, in the reverse field of Michèle's sight line. Whether the story provokes any suffering on Danielle's part is debatable; she asks Michèle what's wrong with her and tells her that she appears to be in a rather odd mood. Michèle and Danielle confirm their plans to attend a party that evening.

Danielle goes home, while Michèle and Paul continue to wander around the city together, and it is revealed that Paul has deserted the army. He and Michèle thus share a common, if tentative, status as dropouts and wanderers with no particular place to go. Since Paul has no place to stay, Michèle takes him to her cousin's apartment, and we see the two in bed together and we are led to assume (although this is never explicitly shown) that they make love. On the sound track during their encounter in the apartment we hear Leonard Cohen's song "Suzanne" (Michèle shoplifted the album from a music store earlier during their wanderings), the lyrics of which form a poignant counterpoint to the encounter shown and implied on screen: "Suzanne takes you down / to a place by the river / You can see the boats go by / You could spend the night forever." This is Michèle's first sexual encounter, but given the importance accorded to Danielle and Michèle's connection, it is tempting to hear Cohen's song as the reminder of the presence of yet another woman in the room.

Michèle invites Paul to the party, but he says he doesn't like parties; he plans instead to meet Michèle afterward. Michèle and Danielle meet and wait for the bus together; as in their previous encounter, Danielle tells Michèle that she seems to be in an odd mood ("T'as un drôle d'air"). Soon, the girls begin to laugh as they observe others in the bus who are going to the party, in particular a young man with dark hair.

At the party, the young people dance in a circle, their arms around each others' shoulders. At the center of the circle is a constantly changing couple, as one person chooses another, who then chooses another, and so on. We see the young man with dark hair from the bus dance with Danielle, and then Danielle chooses Michèle. They dance, giggling, and then when it is Michèle's turn to choose a partner, she looks around the circle and again chooses Danielle. During this part of the dance, Trini Lopez's version of the song "La Bamba" is playing. An abrupt change of mood occurs when James Brown's "It's a Man's World" begins to play, signaling a shift from group dancing to close couples dancing. Danielle again dances with the young man from the bus, and Michèle stands, alone, in the middle of the group of dancing couples. In the earlier scene at the café, we saw Michèle watch Danielle as she kissed a boy, but that look was brief, and Michèle too was a participant in the kissing. Here, however, something has changed. Michèle is alone; her gaze lingers, as does the camera's gaze on her. This extended shot of Michèle simultaneously conveys passionate observation and sadness. If Leonard Cohen's "Suzanne" provided a poignant counterpoint in the earlier scene with Michèle and Paul in the apartment, here the James Brown song marks the obvious exclusion of Michèle.

Michèle leaves the party, and Danielle catches up with her. Danielle proceeds to tell her friend that she doesn't like the boy she was dancing with, and they discuss the possibility of another boy, a blond. But again, it is clear that something has changed, for Michèle acknowledges that hearing about the boys Danielle flirts and dances with makes her suffer.

Circe as Michèle, at the party in Chantal Akerman's *Portrait of a Young Girl at the End of the 1960s in Brussels.*

Paradoxically, what sustains their friendship is also what separates them. The film ends as the two young women walk, hand in hand, through a field, where Paul awaits. Michèle is crying. The setting of the film changes abruptly in these final moments, for the field through which they walk seems rural and almost idyllic. Virtually everything else in the film has taken place in a decidedly urban setting. But here, the isolated field and the sudden vast expanse of nature make the words and movements of the two girls seem even more removed from the world of the city, the dance, the heterosexual couple.

At the conclusion of the film, Michèle tells Danielle that Paul is waiting for her, and Michèle walks away as Danielle exits the frame to be with Paul. The last shot of the film shows Michèle, alone, as she walks through the field, away from the camera. Throughout the final images of the film, Paul is there but not there—visually absent yet present as the object given by Michèle to Danielle. But as Michèle turns her back and walks away, the possibility of storytelling among the two girls appears to be lost forever.

Portrait of a Young Girl thus remembers the late 1960s as both opening up and closing down possibilities of connection. True to the spirit of the series for which it was commissioned, Akerman's portrait of a young girl captures the era through music, words, and the interactions of its characters. Michèle discusses Sartre and Kierkegaard; she describes participating in a demonstration against the war in Vietnam. She and Paul share utopian dreams of a future in which there is no poverty, no war. But the film is also willfully anachronistic; there is no attempt to re-create a

Brussels of 1968, no period costumes. Paul and Michèle even browse in a store that sells compact discs! The remembrance of the 1960s is precisely that—a remembrance filtered through the present.

One sees in *Portrait of a Young Girl* many quintessential preoccupations of Akerman's work, from the patient observation of the passage of time and the everyday, to the centrality of female subjectivity. Much of her work has explored the difference that lesbianism makes vis-à-vis notions of cinematic pleasure and desire, but this film is perhaps Akerman's most sustained and provocative work to date on the topic. Several of her films have suggested how lesbianism upsets any fixed notions of subject-object relationships, while simultaneously suggesting that lesbianism is both inside and outside of dominant practices of sexuality. *Portrait of a Young Girl* continues in these directions as well but does something more at the same time; it evokes with great beauty and sadness the complex ways in which a girl's love for another girl inspires narrative and visual form.

Portrait of a Young Girl bears particularly obvious connections with two of Akerman's earlier works, *Je, tu, il, elle* (1974) and *Rendez-vous d'Anna* (Meetings with Anna, 1978). In *Je, tu, il, elle* lesbian desire problematizes any neat symmetry of the pronouns of the film's title. The protagonist of the film, Julie, is portrayed by Akerman herself, and she engages in a series of self-representing acts, including making love with another woman. But lesbian authorship in the film is no simple "alternative" to heterosexuality but, rather, a complex configuration of desire (Mayne 1990, 127–35). In *Meetings with Anna* the series of heterosexual encounters undertaken by the title character are undercut by the shadowy presence of the woman in Italy, who is marked only by a voice in the film. As a voice, as a figure who is both present and absent, the woman in Italy is a force of desire that keeps the film moving. Lesbian representation in both of these films concerns cinematic address and the undoing of dualistic structures of communication. In both films, lesbian desire is not only present and absent at the same time (as is the case with *Portrait of a Young Girl*); it is also seen as central to the very acts of self-representation. *Je, tu, il, elle* and *Meetings with Anna* are both portraits of the artist, and in a different but related way *Portrait of a Young Girl* (as of course its title suggests) is as well. In the latter film, Michèle expresses a desire to write, and the entire movement of the narrative follows the very process of learning how to see one's own desires.

In addition to its connections with these two other films, *Portrait of a Young Girl* builds on many of the themes present in *J'ai faim, j'ai froid*

(*I'm Hungry, I'm Cold,* 1984), Akerman's contribution to the omnibus film *Paris vu par, 20 ans après* (Paris Seen by, Twenty Years Later), a remake of the 1963 film in which six filmmakers contributed short films that depict different aspects of life in the city. The remake was marketed as a showcase for the contemporary filmmakers who are heirs to the directors included in the earlier film, including Jean-Luc Godard, Eric Rohmer, and Claude Chabrol. Akerman's contribution is a twelve-minute, black-and-white film about two teenage girls who have just run away from Brussels to Paris. While their movements are frenzied and always on the verge of the comic, they are nonetheless quite evocative of Michèle.

Like her, they wander the city; like her, they occupy a transitional place; and like Michèle, they have a complex relationship to heterosexuality. They say they want to fall in love, but they slap the faces of the first men who appear. The film offers another version of their budding desire; the two girls kiss each other in order to demonstrate their previous experiences with young men. In the conclusion of the film, the two girls go to the apartment of a man they met in a restaurant and go to bed. One of the girls—who is perpetually hungry—-gets up to make something to eat, while the man comes to bed with the other. The camera shows us the girl in the kitchen as the other girl has sex for the first time, punctuated by her scream. The two girls leave and walk away from the camera.

I'm Hungry, I'm Cold also might be described as a coming-of-age film. The process of coming of age involves a complicated relationship to heterosexual initiation, where the rituals shared by the two girls are as important as anything that occurs between a man and a woman. The very process of maturation has a homoerotic component, where the demonstration of how a boy kisses becomes the pretext for a shared kiss. The point here is not so much whether the girls are or aren't heterosexual but, rather, that desire is mediated in a variety of ways—through each other as much as through men. In the process, the kisses are shown on screen, and the sexual initiation isn't; instead, it is shown only through the displaced view of the girl in the kitchen eating.

Like the two girls in *I'm Hungry, I'm Cold,* Michèle participates in a heterosexual world, but she does so obliquely. Michèle narrates that world, while Danielle, at least from Michèle's point of view, becomes increasingly a part of that world. In order to narrate that world, some kind of distance is required. In *Portrait of a Young Girl* both Danielle and Michèle take pleasure in dissecting romance, in talking after the fact, in connecting with each other. They both delight in girl talk, but Michèle's stakes in that talk are ultimately quite different from her friend's. For Michèle, virtually every scene of apparent heterosexual desire is presented as quite literally that—a scene to be memorized, embellished perhaps, practiced, and then retold to Danielle.

The relationship between Danielle and Michèle is sustained and nurtured, at the same time that it is compromised and fractured, by its triangular quality. If Danielle and Michèle are adolescent girls who are being acculturated into the conventions and codes of heterosexuality, then the very process of acculturation provides the ironic basis for their own connection, their own erotic bond, their own possibilities for detachment from the presumed expectations of the world around them. Lesbian culture and literature are full of testimonies to and anecdotes about how the conventions of heterosexuality and femininity misfire in one way or another, and an important direction in lesbian filmmaking has explored how the most heterosexual conventions of film can be quite readily inverted to lesbian ends. But Akerman's film is less preoccupied with how such inversions occur and more preoccupied with the very dynamics of triangular desire.

In this context it is useful to examine the issues and debates that have surrounded the discussion of how heterosexual bonds are crossed, compromised, and often superseded by homosocial bonds. Eve Sedgwick's study of male homosociality in English literature, *Between Men,* has been enormously influential in defining the broad and far-ranging scope of homosocial desire (1985). But Sedgwick's analysis is built on what many have criticized as a most problematic assumption about women and homosociality. In order to define the range of male homosocial desire, she makes what has become a controversial distinction between women and men. For women, according to Sedgwick, the connection between homosociality and homosexuality is largely unproblematic, while for men, it is conflicted in such ways that promote and provoke intense narrative conflict and desires for resolution. Sedgwick writes that

> the diacritical opposition between the "homosocial" and the "homosexual" seems to be much less thorough and dichotomous for women, in our society, than for men. At this particular historical moment, an intelligible continuum of aims, emotions, and valuations links lesbianism with the other forms of women's attention to women: the bond of mother and daughter, for instance, the bond of sister and sister, women's friendship, "networking," and the active struggles of feminism. (2)

It is not only the "lesbian continuum" (to use Adrienne Rich's term [1980]) that differentiates women and men in Sedgwick's analysis, but also the fact that the very nature of patriarchal power requires simultaneously the defense against male homosexuality and the maintenance of homosociality as the premier form of patriarchal relationship.

Terry Castle proposes the obvious female counterpart to Sedgwick's erotic triangle: two women and a man, with the woman's romantic connection to the man displaced by the relationship between the woman and the "other" woman (1993). Castle notes that this triangle does not work in the body of literature to which Sedgwick's analysis is devoted (canonical British and American literature of the eighteenth and nineteenth centuries), but she suggests that in twentieth-century lesbian writing, a pattern exists that both confirms and challenges Sedgwick's account of the male erotic triangle. Using Sylvia Townsend Warner's 1936 novel *Summer Will Show* as her example, Castle sets out to demonstrate not only that the novel interferes with the male-female-male erotic triangle, but also that "this kind of subverted triangulation, or erotic 'counterplotting,' . . . is in fact characteristic of lesbian novels in general" (74).

Blakey Vermeule offers another reading of Sedgwick's analysis vis-à-vis lesbians, one that focuses on the problematic status of the lesbian continuum (1991). Noting the difficulty of any simple inversion of the erotic triangle (a man in a patriarchal society cannot simply be assigned the place of a woman), Vermeule stresses a kind of symptomatic reading of the lesbian continuum: "The lesbian continuum goes deep—it goes, in fact, to the heart of what makes lesbian representation problematic. Far from erasing lesbians, the female homosocial-homosexual continuum puts us at the very center of female affective bonds" (57). Vermeule's test case is a classical Hollywood film in which the boundary lines between rivalry and erotic connection are indeed blurred—*All about Eve* (1950). The film stages, as Vermeule demonstrates, "the displacement of lesbian desire as a function of growing up straight" (57).

Akerman's film does not make for a neat fit with either of the examples cited here: a twentieth-century lesbian novel or a classical Hollywood film. But both Castle's and Vermeule's rereadings of Sedgwick's definition of the erotic triangle are relevant to Akerman's film. There may be no easy way to substitute a female-male-female erotic triangle for the male-female-male one that Sedgwick describes. But it is precisely the desire for such an alternative form of triangulation that sustains Akerman's film. Her portrait of Michèle thus offers a significant twist on the desire to desire that characterizes, in Mary Ann Doane's important contribution to feminist film theory, the woman's simultaneous exclusion from yet desire to participate in the narrative and scopic regimes of the classical Hollywood cinema (1987).

It is important in this context to remember the specific frame of the film—a reflection on adolescence. There may be much to criticize about the model of the lesbian continuum for any understanding of the specificity of lesbianism. But insofar as female adolescence is concerned, the lesbian continuum, proposing as it does a fluid movement between friendship and erotic connection, has historical resonance. This is not to say that this continuum can be read as relevant to any time or to any place but, rather, that it provides the possibility to understand how, in a period like the late 1960s, female homosociality both facilitated and impeded a young girl's entry into the realm of heterosexual adulthood.

Why a particular relevance to the late 1960s? The film's signaling of the events of May 1968 indicates that new forms of political revolt and representation were on the horizon, and the film juxtaposes the promise of freedom with Michèle's disgust with school, conformity, and the routines of everyday life. Interestingly, the school in question is represented in a very displaced way. The girls' school is a classic site for representations of the lesbian continuum, a site where, according to Castle, "plots of lesbian desire are most likely to flourish" (1993, 85). The film takes place on the day Michèle has decided to leave school, and she is portrayed as an outsider when she approaches the school grounds. When we see Danielle and Michèle together, it is always in public spaces, whether outside of school, in a café, at a bus stop, or at a party. To be sure, the two girls are portrayed so as to suggest their closeness and the special quality of their bond, but this bond exists fully in the same public sphere as Michèle's encounter with Paul. The continuum cannot be maintained, and Michèle's positions as confidante to Danielle and as mediator between Danielle and Paul are precarious. The continuous exchange of dancing partners doesn't last, and Michèle's position becomes, finally, that of a spectator.

The particular relevance of the late 1960s for the lesbian continuum is also shaped by the cinematic history to which *Portrait of a Young Girl* alludes. I would like to suggest that there is here a kind of "subverted triangulation" similar, although not identical, to what Castle describes. Situated in April 1968, *Portrait of a Young Girl* takes place in an imaginary landscape of the New Wave of French cinema, a cinemascape revisioned, adapted, and paid homage to throughout the film. At various times during her journey, Michèle embodies a range of figures from French films of the 1960s. Michèle wanders through Brussels, not Paris, but her journey evokes nonetheless that of many New Wave films of this era. Indeed, one of the privileged narrative forms of these French films was that of wandering through the city, with the attendant preoccupation with the everyday, the commercial, and the patterns of both boredom and interruption. To be sure, Brussels has none of the mythic proportions of Paris, but it is an urban space that becomes both invisible backdrop and spectacle in its own right for Michèle. Like Nana in Jean-Luc Godard's *Vivre sa vie* (*My Life to Live,* 1962) or Juliette in Godard's *Deux ou trois choses que je sais d'elle* (*Two or Three Things I Know about Her,* 1967), Michèle's itinerary follows the rhythms of city life.

And just as many films of the 1960s staged self-reflexive scenes at the movies, so too does *Portrait of a Young Girl* initiate the encounter between Michèle and Paul in a movie theater, thus echoing scenes in a wide range of films, particularly those by Godard, such as *Masculin-Féminin* (Masculine-Feminine, 1966), in which film spectatorship provides both the acting out of fantasy and a moment of quiet contemplation for character and viewer alike. Finally, while most of the directors associated with the development of New Wave cinema were men, their films showcased (problematically perhaps, but showcased nonetheless) the journeys of female characters as embodiments of the desires of the directors. Godard once again serves as a primary example here, and while Akerman's character of Michèle is surely different from Nana in *My Life to Live* (played by Anna Karina, Godard's wife at the time), or Juliette in *Two or Three Things,* the journey of this female protagonist is nonetheless quite evocative of the filmmaker's own.

As is well known, Akerman is a great admirer of Godard, and she has said that seeing Godard's *Pierrot le fou* convinced her to become a filmmaker. But there are also traces of François Truffaut in Akerman's film, particularly *The 400 Blows* (1959). The first Antoine Doinel film, starring Jean-Pierre Léaud in the role that made him famous, tells the story of a lonely boy, something of a rebel, who plays hooky from school one day with a friend and sees his mother on the street kissing another man. Antoine borrows an excuse from his friend but never finishes copying it. Instead, when his teacher asks him the next day where he was, Antoine replies that his mother died. Antoine's deception is discovered immediately, and he runs away from home. In a general way, even though Antoine is younger than Michèle, their journeys are quite evocative one of the other. Like Léaud, Circe has a remarkable intensity and peacefulness at the same time, and the characters created by these two actors convey the pain of childhood and adolescence, and the simultaneity of rebellion and a desire to belong. More precisely, the scene where Michèle writes out a series of excuses for school, on the morning she has decided to run away, is a direct citation of Truffaut's film. Whereas Antoine doesn't finish copying the note (he stumbles over the name René, the name of his friend who gave him the note and unwittingly copies the name instead of substituting his own), it is only when confronted by his teacher that Antoine says that his mother died. But Michèle not only accomplishes the symbolic death of a variety of relatives (not including her mother), she concludes with her own death.

Each time I have watched *Portrait of a Young Girl,* I have been struck by several moments where the piano music that accompanies the wanderings of Michèle through the city sounds much like one of the musical themes of Agnès Varda's 1962 film *Cléo de cinq à sept* (*Cléo from Five to Seven*). For an equally brief moment, Michèle seems to retrace Cléo's steps, now in Brussels, not in Paris, and in a time several years later than the setting of Varda's film. As I've suggested, *Portrait of a Young Girl* can be read as an extended meditation on many themes associated with French cinema of the 1960s. But the brief echo of Varda's film seems particularly noteworthy in a film so preoccupied not only with an era that was so shaped by new directions in French filmmaking, but also with how, in a film directed by a woman, another young woman learns about love, desire, and longing. For the heroine of Varda's film sees the city of Paris anew as she wanders, awaiting the results of a medical examination to see if she has cancer. The waiting provides the occasion for a stripping down of the spoiled, childish Cléo, first literally—she removes her wig and her jewelry—and then more profoundly. Within this extended moment of transition in her life, she has a series of encounters that prove to be catalysts of change, most notably with a soldier, Antoine, on brief leave from the war in Algeria. While their encounter is not exactly the stuff of traditional Hollywood romance, it provides the resolution to the film.

There are aesthetic parallels between *Cléo from Five to Seven* and Akerman's film, particularly insofar as the passage of time is concerned. *Cléo* is perhaps best known as an experiment in real time: while there are indeed ellipses in the film, there is nonetheless an attempt to preserve the sense of the passage of time. But the more haunting parallel between the two films concerns the narrative infrastructure. However unalike they might be in other ways, Akerman's Michèle, like Cléo, occupies a kind of transitional space as she wanders through Brussels, and she too has a decisive encounter with a soldier, in this case (the difference between 1962 and 1968 is strikingly embodied here) a young French soldier who has deserted the army. The budding relationship between Cléo and Antoine is meant to be seen as something of an alternative, if not to the heterosexual makeup of classical cinematic resolutions, then at least to the notion of "happily ever after." For Cléo does indeed have cancer, and Antoine must leave to return to Algeria, but they still walk away together at the film's conclusion.

In order to get to Antoine, Cléo must leave her old self behind, and that old self is most definitely shaped by a female world of superstition (the first encounter staged in the film is with a female fortune teller who functions as a narrator; she summarizes the entire film), exaggerated domesticity, and companionship with Angèle, Cléo's assistant. Cléo's apartment, over which Angèle presides, is a self-contained fantasy world, an idealized private space that provides shelter from the city. Virtually everything associated with commodified femininity is dispensed with in the film, except of course for the relationship with the man.

Some of the parallels between Akerman's film and Varda's are obvious: a journey, an encounter with a man who in both cases is a soldier, and a movement into some kind of self-awareness. How, then, does Castle's notion of "subverted triangulation" come into play? If indeed *Cléo from Five to Seven* provides a point of reference for Akerman's film, there is an obvious revision one would expect, particularly given my focus on lesbian narrative: get rid of the man, and substitute a woman. That, of course, is not what happens in Akerman's film. The man is still there. But what is subverted is the need in Varda's film to get rid of the world of women. *Portrait of a Young Girl* imagines and revisions a historical and cinematic past in which the desire of one girl for another can sustain an entire narrative, even if that narrative is one that in the end traces its own dissolution.

Notes

1. Bonnie Zimmerman defines the coming-out story as "a process that includes an awareness of sexual feelings for another woman, a realization that society condemns lesbian love, and an acceptance of lesbian identity through either sexual initiation or self-naming." Zimmerman also notes that in feminist coming-out novels, there is "an affirmation of one's lesbianism to the outside world and a journey toward freedom" (1990, 35).

2. "Veuillez excuser ma fille Michèle, elle a eu la grippe. Veuillez excuser ma fille

Michèle, elle a du se rendre à un enterrement, sa grandmère est morte. . . . Son oncle est mort. . . . Sa tante est morte à la suite de la mort de son oncle. Son père est mort. Elle est morte."

3. "C'était aussi pour faire souffrir quelqu'un. C'est pour le raconter aussi."

Works Cited

Castle, Terry. 1993. *The Apparitional Lesbian: Female Homosexuality and Modern Culture.* New York: Columbia University Press.

Doane, Mary Ann. 1987. *The Desire to Desire.* Bloomington: Indiana University Press.

Mayne, Judith. 1990. *The Woman at the Keyhole: Feminism and Women's Cinema.* Bloomington: Indiana University Press.

Rich, Adrienne. 1980. "Compulsory Heterosexuality and Lesbian Existence." *Signs: Journal of Women in Culture and Society* 5, no. 4: 631–60.

Sedgwick, Eve Kosofsky. 1985. *Between Men: English Literature and Male Homosocial Desire.* New York: Columbia University Press.

Taubin, Amy. 1995. "The Nouvelles Femmes." *The Village Voice,* 7 March, 65.

Vermeule, Blakey. 1991. "Is There a Sedgwick School for Girls?" *Qui Parle?* 5, no. 1: 53–72.

Zimmerman, Bonnie. 1990. *The Safe Sea of Women: Lesbian Fiction 1969–1989.* Boston: Beacon Press.

11. Su Friedrich's Swimming Lessons

Su Friedrich's films are beautiful and moving evocations of the complexities of lesbian desire and lesbian representation. They are not necessarily, however, "lesbian" in any straightforward or obvious way. *First Comes Love* (1991) shows a variety of traditional weddings as if seen by a spy in the house of heterosexual love. But despite the titles that inform us which countries allow homosexual marriage (hardly any in the world), this is not a film that makes fun of marriage, nor is it a film that argues resolutely for gay and lesbian marriage. Rather, the film explores lesbian and gay ambivalence toward marriage, the ambivalence of both wanting the ritual of marriage and wanting to distance oneself from it. Friedrich's most recent film, *Hide and Seek* (1996), tells a story of female adolescence set in the 1960s, in which twelve-year-old Lou seems to be on the verge of understanding her own attractions to other girls; her best friend is becoming interested in boys, and Lou (played wonderfully by Chels Holland) tries to make sense of her own feelings. Juxtaposed with Lou's story are interviews with adult lesbians about their own adolescent experiences, as well as documentary and archival footage that demonstrates how "sex education" was addressed in the 1960s. *Hide and Seek* offers a tale of growing up that is "not necessarily" lesbian, but by situating that tale within the narratives of lesbian identity told by lesbians, the film traces a narrative of lesbian desire.

In this chapter I look specifically at that narrative of lesbian desire in three of Friedrich's films: *Gently down the Stream* (1983), *Damned If You Don't* (1987), and *Sink or Swim* (1990), with particular attention to *Sink or Swim.* While much of Friedrich's work is taken up directly with lesbian subject matter, her films are also explorations of ambiguity and ambivalence. A challenging question for explorations of lesbianism in the cinema is how to address those questions of ambiguity, particularly when there are plenty of reasons—political as well as cultural and artistic—to avoid ambiguity altogether, to relegate it to the days of the closet, of lesbian invisibility. Friedrich's work simultaneously offers a sustained exploration of lesbian desire and ambivalence, and her films explore the varied and complex ways that the cinema can be understood in lesbian terms.[1]

Gently down the Stream is a complex and haunting meditation on desire and its manifestations in image and text. Poems written by Friedrich, and based on a collection of her own dreams, are handwritten on the film celluloid, appearing as scratchy and mobile texts. The poems take on a variety of relationships to the images of the film, which range from religious icons, to water, to women shown engaged in a variety of solitary activities, especially rowing (on a machine) and swimming (in a pool). At times, the poems appear to illustrate the images of the film. Given that this a silent film, the poems could seem to be titles, announcing the action of the film; but these poems do not offer the direct explanation that one expects from titles in a film from the silent era. The poems could also be read as subtitles, and although this is not a film in need of translation, as would be the case with a foreign film, one could argue that given Friedrich's relationship to the development of a film language adequate to the complexities of lesbian desire and representation, she is indeed exploring another language.

Sometimes the poems have a direct relationship to the images on screen, and sometimes they are removed from them, suggesting a contrapuntal relationship between image and text. Friedrich's poems, appearing on screen one word at a time, and with their constantly wiggling letters, are difficult to read in any kind of fluid way and thus are in sharp contrast to many of the images of the film that depict water, whether in a swimming pool or in the ocean. In a more general way, most of the images depict fluid motion—a woman swimming in the pool, another woman working out on a rowing machine. The poems describe dreams of confrontation, of desire, of sexual contact, while the images, when they do show women, show them engaged in solitary activities, autonomous and seemingly unaware of being observed.

The written text and the image track are manipulated in a variety of ways. Sometimes images fill the screen, with the text intercut with them, or with the text written over the images. Sometimes the images are framed, as if they are projected in a film within the film, with a rectangle of white appearing in the background of the image, with the words of the poem appearing in the foreground of the image. In her analysis of the film, Chris Holmlund points out that while some of the poems do indeed speak of lesbian desire, this is not a film that one can describe easily or automatically as a "lesbian film" (1994). Holmlund sees Friedrich's film—and her film work more generally—as challenging the ways in which a given text can be seen and understood as "lesbian." For Holmlund, what is most interesting and challenging about Friedrich's work are not the moments of explicit lesbianism but, rather, the ways in which lesbian representation folds into questions of spectatorship and authorship, form and address. As Holmlund points out quite forcefully, studies of lesbianism in film need to be concerned with more than lesbian visibility, and Friedrich's work is a stunning demonstration of the various indirect and complicated ways in which lesbianism can be understood in relationship to film (1994, 38).

Thus Holmlund's reading of *Gently down the Stream* focuses not only on those poems, for instance, that write explicitly of lesbian desire, but of how the film as a whole frames and reframes lesbian desire: "Although the poems frequently allude to lesbian sexuality, and although the various reframing strategies Friedrich employs change how women in general are viewed, nothing in the images per se suggests the women we see are or might be lesbians" (1994, 23). Holmlund notes that the first poem that one can call explicitly lesbian is the fourth (of fourteen that appear in the film):

> A woman sits on a stage
> hunched over in the corner
> She calls up a friend from
>
> the audience
> asking her Come and make love to me
>
> She does
> I can't watch
>
> She mutters I CAN'T
> can't hold you
> the last time was too
> tense so many
> memories
> (cited in 1994, 20)

The images that accompany this poem show a woman on a rowing machine and a woman's feet stepping into a swimming pool, and both sets of images are repeated throughout the film.

I'd like to suggest that one of the most striking aspects of Su Friedrich's film work is the way in which, not lesbianism per se, but what one might call the prelesbian, or the possibly lesbian, or the potentially lesbian, takes visual and narrative form. Hence, I am struck in *Gently down the Stream* by the moments that precede the appearance of the poem cited above. After images of the woman at her rowing machine, the following poem appears:

> In the water near a raft
> I see a woman
> swimming and diving
> in a wet suit
>
> see her pubic hair (Friedrich 1983, 42)

The first three lines of the poem appear on a darkened screen with a white screen within the frame in the top right of the image. The image creates the effect that a film is about to begin on the white screen, with the scratched words of the poem suggesting an introduction of sorts. On the second appearance of the word *see* (in the fifth line of the poem), the white screen disappears, and the entire screen is dark. After the word *hair* appears, the screen fades to a lighter shade of dark, images of the woman on the rowing machine fill the space where the white screen had been, and the poem discussed by Holmlund (cited earlier) appears. These brief moments—a poem about seeing a woman swimming and diving, seeing her pubic hair (as if seeing through the wet suit), and images of a white, luminous screen—literally introduce us to the poem of lesbian desire, and to the image of, if not a lesbian, then a woman coded according to many iconic representations of lesbianism (short-haired, athletic, somewhat butch looking). Holmlund is right; the poem I have just cited is not explicitly lesbian. But the scene opens up the possibilities of lesbian representation—a woman seeing another woman, and then seeing something forbidden. The white screen within the frame suggests a dream space, in keeping with the source of the poems written into the film, but also a screen of possibility, a screen on which the various associations of the poems can be read and imagined in different ways.

In my book *The Woman at the Keyhole: Feminism and Women's Cinema* (1990), I examine a group of films, both classical Hollywood films and al-

Su Friedrich's *Gently down the Stream.* Courtesy of Su Friedrich.

ternative films by women directors, in which the figure of the screen functions both as a thematic and visual device within the films, and as a powerful figure of ambivalence, that is, as a surface that suggests simultaneous passage and obstacle. The figure of the screen complicates what has been the major paradigm in feminist understandings of the cinema, the gaze with its attendant division of the world between the man who looks and the woman who is looked at. For the screen surface embodies contradictory impulses: it is both present and invisible; it positions a fixed scene yet can interfere with the facility of that positioning. I suggest that in films such as *The All-Round Reduced Personality (Redupers)* (directed by Helke Sander, 1977), *Illusions* (directed by Julie Dash, 1982), *I've Heard the Mermaids Singing* (directed by Patricia Rozema, 1987), and *The Man Who Envied Women* (directed by Yvonne Rainer, 1986), the figure of the screen stands as a complex inquiry into the nature of cinematic spectacle, understood not only in terms of the ubiquitous (male) gaze, but also and especially the simultaneity of mastery and the breakdown of oppositions on which mastery is based. Looking at how films position and work with screen surfaces, I suggest, offers the possibility of understanding the dynamics of cinema as more than the interplay of the gaze.

The white screen in *Gently down the Stream* also suggests what I have called "screen tests," that is, meditations on the ways in which the film screen is both a projection of desires and a containment of them. The screen within the film contains a variety of images—mainly of women and of water—while the written text encourages a variety of possible configurations of those images, both in relationship to the text and to each other. When the white screen appears, coupled with the poem about seeing, the possibilities of the cinema as a source of both directed seeing and unbounded dreaming are juxtaposed. And more specifically, it is as if the lesbian possibilities of the cinema are articulated in their most specific and their most general meanings—specific in the sense of the sexual desire of one woman for another, and general in the sense of a woman looking at another woman. While I am not completely comfortable with a term like *prelesbian,* I do think that Friedrich's film work challenges the entire question of lesbian representation, for at stake is the possibility of understanding ambivalence and ambiguity in relationship to lesbian desire insofar as the founding myths of cinematic representation are concerned: seeing and being seen, watching and looking, merging and separating.

Gently down the Stream is obsessed with water, from the title of the film to the repeated images of women swimming, or stepping into a pool, to the poems themselves. As Holmlund points out, the "images stream past, just as the nursery rhyme title promised they would" (1994, 22). But as Holmlund also notes, Friedrich manipulates both the implications of the title and any conventional notion of water as uninterrupted flow: "The first woman we see 'row, row, rowing her boat' is doing so on a machine, not on a river or a stream. Friedrich plays with screen direction, too, confounding any sense of 'down' by, for example, showing the woman first swimming left to right, then reversing the image so she appears to be swimming right to left" (22). Lindley Hanlon has noted that "this is *not* a gentle movie. . . . The brash, fragmented, scratched-in text bursts out at us in a rhythmic fury" (1983, 84). Holmlund also describes the scratching of the film and the appearance of a variety of ruptures in the film: "Any notion of 'gently' is completely jettisoned" (22).

While Friedrich's use of water imagery calls up the mythic associations of women with water, she also uses that imagery in complex and sometimes surprising ways. This is perhaps all the more important given that in lesbian representation water has particularly intense associations; the title of Bonnie Zimmerman's study of contemporary lesbian fiction, for instance, is *The Safe Sea of Women* (1990). While water appears in a variety of forms in Friedrich's films, a particularly insistent image is the woman swimmer. In *Gently down the Stream* shots of a woman swimming alone in a pool are repeated, and while the image certainly suggests the flow of desire, it suggests something more—a woman going against the flow, both autonomous and connected to the rhythms of another force. The woman swimmer, then, is a narrative motif in Friedrich's work that embodies many of the same principles as the screen-within-the-film, and the two figures become central in Friedrich's visual and narrative explorations of cinema and lesbian representation.

It is thus striking that one of the images repeated in Friedrich's most unexplicitly lesbian film, *The Ties That Bind* (1984), is a woman swimmer—the filmmaker's mother. *The Ties That Bind* is an experimental documentary in which Friedrich interviews her mother about her life in Germany during Nazism and after the war during the American occupation. The film combines documentary footage with images of Friedrich's mother, and the daughter's questions are not spoken but scratched on the film in a way reminiscent of *Gently down the Stream.* Friedrich's mother describes her position as an anti-Nazi woman whose family suffered during the war and who herself was imprisoned. While the film creates a sympathetic portrait of the mother, there are moments in the film—particularly when the mother insists that everyday Germans did not know about the systematic killing of Jews—that the daughter's questions become pointed, disbelieving, and challenging. Sometimes the mother is depicted in her living room, and sometimes at work, suggesting an attempt to capture the rhythms of everyday life and the ways in which the past lives with an individual in the most banal routines. The mother is also shown swimming in a lake, and while swimming could be read as yet another of those banal routines, it suggests something more, a complex symbol of both peace and struggle, as well as a figure for the daughter's admiration for the mother—her athletic body, her autonomy, her own desire to swim against the current of Nazi Germany.

If *Gently down the Stream* is ambiguously lesbian, some of the same formal dynamics appear in Friedrich's most explicitly lesbian film, *Damned If You Don't* (1987). Taking the lesbian possibilities of nuns as its point of departure, the film provides a highly condensed rereading of Michael Powell and Emeric Pressburger's 1947 film *Black Narcissus,* narrated by a woman's voice and reedited to focus on the sexual tension between women (and men) in the film. Other stories of nuns are recounted in the film: the story of Sister Benedetta as recounted in Judith Brown's book *Immodest Acts* (1986) and narrated by another woman's voice, and commentaries by women on their own Catholic education and their crushes on nuns. All of these stories surround the depiction of a romantic and eventual sexual encounter between a woman, who at the beginning of the film is watching *Black Narcissus,* and a nun. Their paths eventually intertwine, and the film concludes with their lovemaking.

At one point in the film, the nun is seen visiting the Coney Island amusement park. We see her purchase a ticket and enter a building, and given the focus in the film on the ways in which cinema, by way of *Black Narcissus,* has represented nuns, one might think that she is entering a movie theater. We find the nun, instead, at an aquarium where she stands entranced before the lush, sensual movements of whales. The aquarium may not be a movie theater, but the nun watches the spectacle of the whales with all of the fascination of a film spectator before a movie screen. The scene is shot in high contrast so that the "screen" of the whales appears white and luminous, with the nun's darkened silhouette in the foreground. Friedrich depicts the water, separated from the nun by the glass of the aquarium, as both invitingly sensual and suggestive of a dangerous eroticism. While we—and the nun—see whales rather than women, their movements are sleek, powerful, and beautifully instinctive and are quite reminiscent of the women whose movements are repeated again and again in *Gently down the Stream.*

There are two whales, and the implications of their sensual dance are unmistakable, their sheer joy in their movements and bodies a visual reminder to the nun of her own desires. We are made to understand that what was designed perhaps as a moment of escape for the nun from her lesbian attraction becomes instead a scene of identification and pleasure. When the nun first watches the whales, she is in the company of others, parents with their children for the most part. But they leave, and we see the nun alone as she gazes at the screen of the aquarium; first one whale is visible, and then it leaves the frame, and for a brief moment we see the nun as she looks at the water and then walks off screen.

This is certainly not the most "obvious" lesbian moment in the film. The scene is enormously sensual, and it picks up on other depictions of water in the film—most particularly in the images of a swan and a water snake, both swimming through the water, and as Holmlund argues, each representative of the two principal women in the film, the nun (the swan) and the woman to whom she is attracted (the snake) (1994, 26–27). The scene of the nun, entranced before the screen-like image of the whales in their beauty, is a prelude to the actual lesbian drama of the film, and in this sense it is quite similar to the scene I have discussed in

Gently down the Stream where we see a white, luminous screen and a not-explicitly but potentially lesbian poem.

The formal device of a screen surface, the narrative and visual motif of bodies swimming, and the evocation of possible lesbian desire can be seen in relationship to another preoccupation of Friedrich's films. Much of Friedrich's work is autobiographical, with particular attention to her own childhood and adolescence. Friedrich also extends considerably the range of the autobiographical to reflect on how the lives of girls and teenagers affect who they become and how. If the screen and its accompanying text (in *Gently down the Stream*) or spectator (in *Damned If You Don't*), and its images of bodies and water suggest literally and figuratively moments of lesbian possibility, then the recollection of childhood and adolescence also opens up ways of understanding how the various components of the past make possible the emergence of lesbian identities. To be sure, this aspect of Friedrich's work is potentially more complicated than the visual device of the screen with its accompanying elements of swimming, water, and lesbian desire. For in exploring the ways in which experiences of the past can be read in relationship to lesbianism, the danger is that one downplays the overwhelming effects of gender and sexual socialization. Holmlund suggests that a particularly important aspect of Friedrich's films is the focus on kinship, on how lesbian identities are shaped by the forces of family, and how lesbians seek new definitions of relationships, often mapping the patterns of family life onto new forms that both resemble and depart from their more conventional structures (1994, 18). Indeed, Friedrich's work is quite remarkable in its ability to explore both the horrific ways in which the institutions of the family, of gender, of heterosexuality work to perpetuate themselves, and the ways in which they fail to do so.

I turn now to *Sink or Swim* (1990), which is an exploration of Friedrich's relationship to her father as well as a meditation on the ways in which identities are formed by the effects of childhood and adolescence. From both her own personal standpoint and that of a more general cultural history, Friedrich explores the ways in which we map, from the vantage point of the present, our own histories and our own ways of imagining the world. Like *Gently down the Stream, Sink or Swim* is not explicitly lesbian, but the imprint of lesbian desire is unmistakable. Whereas *Gently down the Stream* and *Damned If You Don't* contain figures of screens in order to hypothesize moments of possibility and to embody ambivalence, *Sink or Swim* in its entirety functions as a meditation on ambivalence—specifically the ambivalence of the daughter's relationship to the father, and more generally on the ambiguity of the image as a screen for contemplation. As in the other films, water figures prominently here as a source of strength and fear, and the female swimmer returns throughout the film.

Sink or Swim consists of twenty-six episodes, structured by the alphabet in reverse. The alphabetic structure of the film serves a double purpose. Friedrich's father is a linguist and anthropologist, so the alphabet makes sense as both a structural device and a reference to his occupation. In addition, the alphabet is evocative of a child's ordering of experience, particularly in terms of the recitation of the letters of the alphabet in a rhyme (which is heard in the epilogue to the film). Friedrich's father left her family when she was young, and so the narration deals with memories of childhood and adolescence filtered through the experience of abandonment. Most of the stories told about the father in the film suggest a controlling presence whose behavior was often cruel. The title of the film comes from the way he taught his daughter to swim (recounted in "Realism"). He explained the principles of swimming to her and then tossed her into the deep end of a swimming pool after telling her that she would have to manage on her own. He taught his daughter how to play chess (recounted in "Pedagogy"), but once she beat him at the game, he refused ever to play with her again. When the daughter and her sister were being bad, he punished them by forcing their heads under water in the bathtub until they felt they would explode ("Loss"). He tells his daughter that there are deadly snakes in a lake, whereas she finds out later that they are not indigenous to the region ("Realism"). Perhaps most cruelly, when he takes her on a trip to Mexico, he becomes enraged when she is late for meals with him (because of a flirtation with a boy), and he sends her on a plane back home ("Flesh").

The daughter's sense of rage, confusion, and pain is palpable in the film's narration. In "Envy," for instance, which immediately follows the description of the trip to Mexico, the daughter finds a poem that the father wrote about the experience in which he refers to her as a "child orphaned by divorce." The narration continues:

> The girl had waited so long to get some kind of apology from him, but this wasn't the one she imagined. He still didn't realize that he had been acting like a scorned and vengeful lover, and that hers had not been the tears of an orphaned child, but those of a frustrated teenage girl who had had to pay for a crime she didn't commit. (Friedrich 1991, 127)

Despite the painful memories told in the film, there is distance in the narration, for the girl's experiences are told in the third person. And even though a cruel father emerges, there is such a strong attempt to understand him that he does not come across as an archetypal villain. He is the one who introduced his daughter to the myths that will enable her to see possibilities of female strength. And he too suffered loss. In "Memory" (Part One), the death of his sister is described, and the father's own complicated relationship to female children and to water becomes somewhat more comprehensible. As a child, the father and his sister used to swim at a neighbor's pool, and one day, instead of waiting for him, she went swimming without him and died instantly of a heart attack. The home movies shown during this section of the film are of the father, as a boy, and his sister (shortly before she died) swimming in a pool. Friedrich obviously shares much with her father, for she too is an anthropologist of sorts, her camera observing and recording the rituals of father-daughter relationships.

The film begins with "Z" ("Zygote") and ends with "A" ("Athena, Atalanta, Aphrodite"), with the film's narration spoken by a girl in voice-over. In a sense the film imagines the birth, from the zygote at the film's beginning, of the three mythical women whose names give the title to the last letter of the film: Athena, the goddess of war and justice, who sprang fully formed from the head of Zeus; Atalanta, abandoned in the woods by her father at birth because he wanted a son and who was welcomed back into her father's home after she proved herself as an athlete and hunter; and Aphrodite, the goddess of love. All three of these women figure prominently in the film's narration, and they all have a strong link with the daughter and her father. In "Zygote" the story of Athena is told, and in "Temptation" the narration tells of how the father gave the daughter a book about Greek mythology, which she read voraciously. When her father found her reading the book after she had been sent to bed, he asked her which myth she liked the best, and she told the story of Atalanta.

Most of the visual episodes comment on the voice-over narration. Only rarely, however, is there a one-to-one relationship between image and narration. This illustrative effect occurs in "Pedagogy" (where the chess story is recounted and we see a chess game being played) and "Ghosts" (in which there is no spoken narration but, rather, a close-up, negative image of a typewriter as invisible hands type out the letter that forms the story, in which the daughter describes how her mother listened to Schubert lieder, and how one in particular, which we have heard in a previous section, "Kinship," made her cry the most—"Gretchen at the Spinning Wheel"). Most often the visual episodes provide associative material. In "Utopia," for instance, the girl's voice describes how she and her sister were forbidden to eat sugar and did not have a television set. One night a week, however, they visited an elderly neighbor who made them ice cream sundaes and with whom they watched *Don Ameche's Flying Circus* on television. The images show circus performers on horseback, trapeze acts, and acrobatic stunts. In "Homework," the narration describes how, as soon as the father left, a television set entered the house. Clips of various vintage television advertisements and situation comedies fill the screen, including—ironically—*Make Room for Daddy, The Donna Reed Show,* and *Father Knows Best.* The sequence concludes with a close-up of Robert Young as Jim Anderson in *Father Knows Best* in an intimate moment with his daughter Kitten.

Cross-references are made between different sections of the film. The final images from *Father Knows Best* in "Homework" echo the concluding images of an earlier section, "Virgin." In "Virgin," the narration describes how the girl imagined that water in the gutter was the Nile River, that her house was a harem, and that her father was the handsomest man she ever met. Images show footage of a parade and a creek, and finally, at the end of the episode, while the girl describes her father as the handsomest man, we see a father and daughter at the parade, in close-up. Throughout the film Friedrich's camera observes fathers and daughters—ice skating, playing, eating. This visual echo between "Virgin" and "Homework" is particularly interesting given how it introduces the sense of a gap between the idealized images of sitcoms and the painful separation from the father. "Virgin" is also interesting for the multiple levels of both image and voice. One could easily consider this one of the ambiguously lesbian sections of the film, for the girl's fantasies of harems and mermaids could be read as a girl's identification with same-sex desire. Similarly, the "Competition" section includes erotic images, both heterosexual and lesbian. Lesbian desires coexist with total adoration of the father, and *Sink or Swim* insists throughout on the complicated narratives that inform the development of sexual identities and the bond between father and daughter.

The title of the film comes from "Realism." When she tells her father that she wants to learn how to swim, he takes her to the university pool and offers the following lesson: "He took her to the deep end, explained the principles of kicking and breathing, said she'd have to get back all by herself and then tossed her in" (Friedrich 1991, 119). The narration continues: "She panicked and thrashed around for a while, but finally managed to keep her head above water. From that day on, she was a devoted swimmer" (119). Unlike other episodes described in the film's narration about the father's somewhat abusive ways of teaching, this one suggests a mastery on the part of the daughter, particularly in her devotion to swimming. But the narration continues to describe how the following summer on a family vacation, where the girl spent most of her time at a lake, the father told her that poisonous snakes inhabited the lake and attacked swimmers. Only later did the girl discover from her mother that the snakes did not inhabit the region. Much like the defeated chess player in "Pedagogy," the father emerges as jealous of his daughter's pleasure and desperate to maintain his own authority.

The images that accompany the narration in "Realism" show one girl riding her bike around the rooftop of an apartment building; a girl swimming in a pool; and a girl and her father leaning against a building, eating. When juxtaposed with the spoken narration of the film, these visual episodes encourage different views of learning, of apprenticeship. Obviously, the closest connection is between the girl swimming in a pool and the story told, but when the swimming images appear, the narration has moved from the swimming pool to the lake. The girl who rides her bicycle does so alone. And the girl and her father who lean against a building have little to do with swimming, but much to suggest in relationship to the father-daughter bond. When intercut with each other, these images suggest both intimacy between father and daughter and autonomy on the part of the girl. It is possible to read the images as a kind of utopian view of the girls portrayed and their relationships to fathers, whether visible or absent (again echoing an earlier section of the film), but the narration also encourages us to see what might be missing from the everyday images of girls' activities: family dramas of power and control, the desires of girls either encouraged or squelched by the authority figures in their lives.

"From that day on, she was a devoted swimmer": one may well question the father's particular ways of relating to his daughter, but *Sink or Swim* also celebrates what the father gave to his daughter and, more specifically, how she is her father's daughter and an autonomous observer and participant. Throughout the film, images of women and water are suggestive of the father's power and the daughter's strength. In "Kinship" there is no spoken narration but, rather, a recording of the German song "Gretchen at the Spinning Wheel," which (as noted above) we later discover was a favorite song of the daughter's mother. The images in this section are far ranging, showing two women in a shower, the desert, a car window, and a train. The most striking juxtaposition is between water and the desert. The lesbian significance is explicit in the sense that we see, in a very grainy film, two women in a shower together, yet these explicit images remain ambiguous in the sense that they are not anchored in a specific lesbian narrative. They could be seen in contrast to the images of a woman—Friedrich herself—walking alone in the desert (thus juxtaposing a woman alone and two women together), and they could be read as providing a visual counterpoint to the song, which is about a woman's longing for her absent male lover.

The last section of the film, "Athena, Atalanta, Aphrodite," returns us to the lake referred to in earlier sections of the film. The narration tells of the woman's desire to swim across the lake, as her father had done so many times. She is haunted, always, by the thought of the water moccasins, and by the presence of her father as both an inspiration and a source of fear. The water may be frightening, but it too is a source of strength, and the woman renounces her desire to imitate her father, accepting, instead, her own relationship to the water and to the world. The final lines of the narration speak of loss but ultimately reconciliation and the desire to swim freely:

> She stopped swimming and began to float under the bright sky. The sun warmed her face, and the water surrounded her like a lover's arms. She thought of her friends lying on the sandy beach and realized how tired she had become. It was time to start the long swim back to the shore.
>
> On the way, she only stopped once, to turn around and watch her father, as he beat a slow and steady path away from her through the dark orange water. (Friedrich 1991, 129)

The images that accompany this final section of the film suggest both opposition and continuity. We see two women on a beach with a young girl who plays in the sand. These could be the friends alluded to in the narration, or they could be the figures who enable the woman to watch her father depart, that is, another configuration of kinship. Alternating with the images of the two women and the girl is a shot of a lake, possibly the same setting as the accompanying images, and possibly not. Gradually, the camera zooms forward as if tracing the swimmer's movements across the lake, and removing her—and us—from the people on the beach to frame the water and the trees on the lake as a surface from which to read both the narration and the complex associations of images and text that have characterized the film.

If this last section of the film suggests a possible lesbian resolution, the "Epilogue" returns us to a scene of ambivalence. The "ABCs" song is sung by the filmmaker herself, and we see home movies of Friedrich as a

From the "Athena, Atalanta, Aphrodite" section of Su Friedrich's *Sink or Swim.* Courtesy of Su Friedrich.

girl in a bathing suit. The song is sung in a round, six times, and the final words are: "Now I've said my ABCs, tell me what you think of me." Given the complex associations that are made in the course of the film, it is too simple to see this epilogue as the girl's—and filmmaker's—return to a desire for acceptance by the distant father. Certainly, the final words and images speak to the audience as well, asking us to reflect on our own family histories. Yet the continuing desire for the father's presence, even as he swam into the distance in the final section of the film, is unmistakable. He may well have beaten a "slow and steady path away from her," but he remains a part of her. And she makes the choice, again and again, to swim rather than to sink, that is, to live with his complex legacy.

Lesbian images are present in *Sink or Swim,* but they do not offer comforting resolutions or linear narratives. Catherine Russell has described the various slippages in the film as offering a meditation on the impossibility of any certainty or any fixed identity: "The difficulty of self-representation becomes that of cinematic representation. 'Identity' becomes dispersed across a cultural spectrum of 'positions' and discourses" (1998, 365). Following Russell, one could also say that the difficulty of lesbian representation becomes that of cinematic representation. In other words, lesbian representation in Friedrich's work is a function of the cinema itself as simultaneously offering directed vision and unlimited fantasy.

As I've attempted to demonstrate in this essay, lesbian representation in Friedrich's work is tied to a preoccupation with ambivalence, and the figures that recur in her films—the swimmer, the screen, the disjunction between written text and image track—open up spaces for contemplation, for reflection on both the specificity of lesbian desire and the impossibility of fixing that desire to one specific image or narrative. In this sense, even though I too for the sake of convenience distinguished between the explicitly lesbian *(Damned If You Don't)* and the unexplicitly lesbian *(Gently down the Stream, Sink or Swim)* films, that distinction is itself undone in Friedrich's work. Even though her work is concerned with the specifics of cinematic representation, I think it is useful in this context to read her films in relationship to a novel that is also taken up with similar ambiguities of what it means to speak of lesbian representation. Carol Anshaw's novel *Aquamarine* (1992) begins with a brief and powerful narrative that becomes a kind of primal scene for the events that follow. It is October 1968 at the Olympic Games in Mexico City, and Jesse is competing in the race of her life, the 100-meter freestyle. As she gets ready to dive into the water, her eyes catch a glimpse of Marty Finch, the swimmer to beat in the race. Marty looks back, and Jesse "can't read her face. She is still trying to decipher it, to pull some important message off it, still trying to link today with last night, to figure out the connection between those events and this one" (5). In these opening pages of the novel, we do not know what "those events" are; we know only that the glance at Marty causes Jesse to enter the water one-tenth of a second late. And that time costs her the race; Marty wins the gold medal and Jesse the silver.

The novel then proceeds to July 1990, and in three different sections (each of which occurs in the same time frame) Jesse's life is imagined in three different ways. In the first, she is married and expecting a child and lives in her hometown of New Jerusalem, Missouri, where she and her husband manage a local tourist attraction, a cave. Jesse has a flirtation with the local UPS deliveryman. In the second, Jesse is a college English professor who lives in New York City with her female lover, Kit, a soap opera actress. The two visit New Jerusalem to attend Jesse's mother's retirement party. In the third, Jesse lives in Florida, where she runs a somewhat rundown swimming school; her husband has left her, and she lives with her daughter, while her son lives in town. Jesse is having an affair with a black man, Oscar. Through the three possibilities of Jesse's life, we learn that Jesse has carried with her the painful memory of that

October Olympics throughout her life. She and Marty were lovers and made love the night before the fateful race. Jesse wrote to Marty, as the two promised they would, but her letters went unanswered. A nagging fear in her remembering of the past is betrayal, that Marty manipulated Jesse in order to control the competition. The fear of betrayal is perhaps most explicitly drawn in the second possibility for Jesse's life, where she has had a number of short-lived affairs with women, and where she constantly fears that Kit, with whom she is deeply in love, will leave her. Only in the second possibility, however, is Jesse willing to take the risk of love, as she did in 1968; only in assuming the lesbian desire that was a source of passion, of conflict, and of betrayal for her in Mexico City is she able to live a life different from, yet connected to, the past.

But the lesbian Jesse is no more or less affected by the past than the other two Jesses, who also live out their own dramas of betrayal, of intimacy, of making sense of the past. In all three sections of the novel, Jesse's godmother, Hattie, is a constant source of love and strength. Jesse's close relationship with her mentally retarded brother, Willie, also takes on different forms in the three lives. Both Hattie and Willie were present in Mexico City, and they appear in Jesse's lives as privileged observers. The lesbian Jesse may be radically different from the two other Jesses, but she shares a life with them as well.

The aquamarine of the novel's title evokes both Jesse's love of the water and the ever-present, unresolved drama of the past. The first Jesse has, in the caves, a reminder of the shimmering beauty of the water and the pain of the past. The second Jesse has distanced herself from the water, as if by being a lesbian she has incorporated the past into her life. The third Jesse lives what appears to be the most continuous relationship to her past, given that she is around water all the time and continues to live her identity as a swimmer. But in all three lives, the water is mysterious, it is tantalizing, and it is a shimmering surface through which each Jesse tries to see what the past meant, what its hold on her continues to be. In the final section of the novel, Jesse makes a visit to Australia to confront Marty Finch once and for all. But the moment of reckoning is filled with ambiguity. We do not know which Jesse has made the journey—perhaps all three, perhaps none. When she finally sees Marty, she "doesn't give off so much as a blink of wondering who Jesse is, or trying to put her into this context, or wondering why she is here—none of the things that happen when you're not expecting someone" (197). What Jesse sees, at the novel's end, is neither a satisfying resolution nor a comforting explanation of the past. As Marty once again meets Jesse's gaze, "it appears she has been expecting Jesse all along, as she leans forward against the railing and moves straight into a smile of pure pleasure, her eyes filled with lies" (197). Jesse is suspended in time and desire: "Jesse waits to, wants to, hear them" (197).

Anshaw's novel and Friedrich's films share a preoccupation with water and swimming, on the one hand, and with lesbian representation that opens up hypotheses and spaces for contemplation of women looking at other women, desiring other women, loving other women, on the other. Water is a place of reverie, a place that holds memories and possibilities. When the second Jesse visits her high school swimming pool, she stands on a starting block, ready to enter the water. She "bears down, to somewhere beneath reverie, where, if all the circumstances are right, she can—for an instant—feel it all over again" (Anshaw 1992, 132). What Jesse and the daughter in *Sink or Swim* "feel all over again" is different but related, for in both cases it is the drama of fear and possibility. The second Jesse "doesn't want to spend the rest of her life racing against a someone she needs not to be anymore" (133). Neither does the daughter in Friedrich's film, and part of what she imagines herself to be is passionately detached from the world her father represents. Lesbian desire is one such passionate detachment.

There may well be an enormous difference between the significance of a traumatic event from the past, in *Aquamarine,* and the particular way in which swimming, for Friedrich, is associated both with the father's power and the daughter's complicated relationship to it. But in both cases, swimming embodies the strength to move against the current as well as the possibility of falling into the abyss, of sinking. In both Anshaw's novel and Friedrich's films, lesbian narratives do not triumphantly affirm lesbian identity but affirm, rather, lesbian possibilities. They are possibilities as rich with complexities as the color aquamarine, as Athena and Atalanta, as a swimmer moving downstream.

Note

1. For relevant discussions of Friedrich's films, see Gever 1988; Holmlund 1997, 1998; Kotz 1993; MacDonald 1992, 283–318; Weiss 1992, 155–61.

Works Cited

Anshaw, Carol. 1992. *Aquamarine.* Boston: Houghton Mifflin.
Brown, Judith C. 1986. *Immodest Acts : The Life of a Lesbian Nun in Renaissance Italy.* New York: Oxford University Press.

Friedrich, Su. 1983. "*Gently Down the Stream.*" *Heresies* 4, no. 4: 42–45.
———. 1991. *"Sink or Swim." Cinematograph* 4 (spring): 116–29.
Gever, Martha. 1988. "Girl Crazy: Lesbian Narratives in *She Must Be Seeing Things* and *Damned If You Don't.*" *The Independent* July: 14–18.
Hanlon, Lindley. 1983. "Female Rage: The Films of Su Friedrich." *Millennium Film Journal* 12 (spring): 78–86.
Holmlund, Chris. 1994. "Fractured Fairytales and Experimental Identities: Looking for Lesbians in and around the Films of Su Friedrich." *Discourse* 17, no. 1: 16–46.
———. 1997. "When Autobiography Meets Ethnography and Girl Meets Girl: The 'Dyke Docs' of Sadie Benning and Su Friedrich." In *Between the Sheets, in the Streets: Queer, Lesbian, Gay Documentary,* ed. Chris Holmlund and Cynthia Fuchs. Minneapolis: University of Minnesota Press, 127–43.
———. 1998. "Feminist Makeovers: The Celluloid Surgery of Valie Export and Su Friedrich." In *Play It Again, Sam: Retakes on Remakes,* ed. Andrew Horton and Stuart Y. McDougal. Berkeley and Los Angeles: University of California Press, 217–37.
Kotz, Liz. 1993. "An Unrequited Desire for the Sublime: Looking at Lesbian Representation across the Works of Abigail Child, Cecilia Dougherty, and Su Friedrich." In *Queer Looks: Perspectives on Lesbian and Gay Film and Video,* ed. Martha Gever, John Greyson, and Pratibha Parmar. New York: Routledge, 86–102.
MacDonald, Scott. 1992. *A Critical Cinema 2: Interviews with Independent Filmmakers.* Berkeley and Los Angeles: University of California Press.
Mayne, Judith. 1990. *The Woman at the Keyhole: Feminism and Women's Cinema.* Bloomington: Indiana University Press.
Russell, Catherine. 1998. "Culture as Fiction: The Ethnographic Impulse in the Films of Peggy Ahwesh, Su Friedrich, and Leslie Thornton." In *The New American Cinema,* ed. Jon Lewis. Durham, N.C.: Duke University Press, 353–78.
Weiss, Andrea. 1992. *Vampires and Violets: Lesbians in the Cinema.* London: Jonathan Cape.
Zimmerman, Bonnie. 1990. *The Safe Sea of Women: Lesbian Fiction 1969–1989.* Boston: Beacon Press.

Permissions

The University of Minnesota Press gratefully acknowledges permission to reprint the following essays.

Portions of the Introduction originally appeared as "Screening Lesbians" in *The New Lesbian Studies: Into the Twenty-First Century,* edited by Bonnie Zimmerman and Toni A. H. McNaron (New York: The Feminist Press at The City University of New York, 1996), 165–71; copyright 1996 by Judith Mayne, reprinted with permission of The Feminist Press at The City University of New York.

Chapter 1 originally appeared in *Seduction and Theory: Readings of Gender, Representation, and Rhetoric,* edited by Dianne Hunter (Urbana-Champaign: University of Illinois Press, 1989), 28–46; copyright 1989 University of Illinois Press, reprinted with permission.

Chapter 4 originally appeared in *Men in Feminism,* edited by Paul Smith and Alice Jardine (New York: Routledge, 1987); copyright 1987, reproduced by permission of Routledge, Inc.

Chapter 5 originally appeared in *Discourse* 10, no. 2 (spring–summer 1988): 30–47; copyright 1988 by Wayne State University Press.

Chapter 6 originally appeared in *Women on Ice,* edited by Cynthia Baughman (New York: Routledge, 1995); copyright 1995, reproduced by permission of the author.

Chapter 8 originally appeared as "A Parallax View of Lesbian Authorship," in *Inside/Out: Lesbian Theories, Gay Theories,* edited by Diana

Fuss (New York: Routledge, 1991); copyright 1991, reproduced by permission of Routledge, Inc.

Chapter 9 originally appeared as "Julie Zando's Primal Scenes and Lesbian Representation," *Quarterly Review of Film and Video* 15, no. 1 (1993): 15–26; copyright 1993 Gordon and Breach Publishers, reprinted by permission.

Chapter 10 originally appeared in *Identity and Memory: The Films of Chantal Akerman,* edited by Gwendolyn Audrey Foster (London: Flicks Books, 1999), 150–61.

Index

A Ha! Experience, The (1988), 165, 166–67
Ackerman, Forrest J., xix–xx. *See also* Ermayne, LauraJean
Adjani, Isabelle, 61
Adventures of King Pausole, The (1933), xix
Aileen Wuornos: The Selling of a Serial Killer (1992), 23
Akerman, Chantal: *I'm Hungry, I'm Cold* (*J'ai faim, j'ai froid,* 1984), 184–85; *Je, tu, il, elle* (1974), 153, 184; *Meetings with Anna (Rendez-vous d'Anna),* 184; *Portrait of a Young Girl at the End of the 1960s in Brussels* (*Portrait d'une jeune fille de la fin des années 60 à Bruxelles,* 1995), 179–92
Alice Doesn't: Feminism, Semiotics, Cinema, xvi
All about Eve (1950), 162, 187
All in the Family, 83
All My Children, 116
All the Boys and Girls of Their Age (Tous les garçons et les filles de leur âge), 179
Allegret, Yves, 57, 59
All-Round Reduced Personality (Redupers), The (1997), 197
Andy Griffith Show, The, 116
Anshaw, Carol: *Aquamarine* (1992), 208–10
Anstey, Jo, 165, 168–74, 175. *See also* Zando, Julie
Anti-Semite and Jew, 55
Aquamarine (1992), 208–10
ARTE (French television station), 179
Assassin habite au 21, L' (1942), 45
Athalie, 54
Audran, Stéphane, 30
Audry, Jacqueline, 60
Aurenche, Jean, 57, 59

Baiul, Oksana, 113–14
Bakhtin, Mikhail, 11, 16–17
"Bamba, La," 182
Bandéra, La (1935), xix
Barbey d'Aurevilly, Jules, 49–50
Barthes, Roland, xii, 152; and *S/Z,* xiv
Basic Instinct (1992), 23, 62
Baxter, John, 6
Baxter, Peter, 14

Beau Serge, Le (1958), 25
Beauvoir, Simone de, 33
Beavers, Louise, 118
Becker, Jacques, 57, 58
Bellour, Raymond, xii, xiv
Benning, Sadie, 170, 176
Bentham, Jeremy, 117
Between Men, 186
Biches, Les (1967), 24
Big Doll House, The (1971), 132–33
Bisset, Jacqueline, 26
Black Mama, White Mama (1973), 133–35, 138
Black Narcissus (1947), 199–200
Blaxploitation cinema, 131
Blé en herbe, Le, 59
Blonde Venus (1932), 5
Blue Angel, The (1930), 6–20; and the carnivalesque, 11, 16–18; and the Dietrich persona, 8, 17–20; and the femme fatale, 6–8, 9, 14–15, 18; and mimicry, 9, 12–17; and performance, 8, 9–14, 17–20; and spectatorship, 8, 14, 15–16
Bochco, Steven, 79, 80
Boileau, Pierre, 42–44, 47–49, 62n
Boitano, Brian, 103, 106
Bonnaire, Sandrine, 25–26, 31. *See also La Cérémonie*
Bost, Pierre, 57, 59
Bound (1996), 23
Bovenschen, Sylvia, 15, 18
Bresson, Robert, 45, 58, 59, 60
Britton, Andrew, 4
Brooke, Kaucyla: *Dry Kisses Only* (1990), 162
Brown, James: "It's a Man's World," 182
Brown, Judith: *Immodest Acts* (1986), 199
Bujold, Geneviève, 70, 72
Bus Stops Here, The (1990), 165, 166, 167–68
Butch and femme, 44, 46, 121, 122–24, 155
Butterfly Kiss (1995), 23

Caged (1950), 118, 119–27, 128, 129, 130, 132, 142
Caged Heat (1974), 135–37, 142
Cagney and Lacey, 80
Cahiers du cinéma, 57–60
Cahn, Susan: *Coming On Strong: Gender and Sexuality in Twentieth-Century Women's Sport,* 104
Cardinale, Claudia, 150
Carnivalesque, 11, 16–18
Carter, Angela, 8
Casque d'or (1951), 46
Castle, Terry, 38n, 43, 187, 188, 191
Cérémonie, La, 23–38; and the femme fatale, 25–26, 31–32; and *A Judgment in Stone* (Ruth Rendell), 27–30, 33–34; lesbianism and criminality in, 23, 24, 34, 38; and the Papin sisters, 33–37; and psychoanalysis, 28–29, 33–36
Chabrol, Claude, 23–38, 185; and adaptation, 29–31; and Hitchcock, 25; and the New Wave, 25. Films: *Le Beau Serge* (1958), 24; *Les Biches* (1967), 24; *La Cérémonie* (1995), 23–38; *Marie-Chantal contre Docteur Kha* (1966), 24; *Story of Women (Une Affaire des femmes,* 1988), 31; *Violette Nozière* (1978), 24–25
Chained Heat II (1993), 116
Chambers, Robert, 95
Charlie's Angels, 116
Chechik, Jeremiah, 61
Children of Loneliness (1937), xix
Children's Hour, The (1961), xix
Chocolat, 180

Chris, Cynthia, 170
Christie, Agatha, 19
Circe, 180, 189. *See also Portrait of a Young Girl at the End of the 1960s in Brussels*
Claire of the Moon, 176
Classical cinema, 5, 20, 25
Close, Glenn, 79
Clouzot, Henri-Georges, 41–62; and adaptation, 45, 49–50, 60; and authorship, 45, 57–60; and Hitchcock, 42; and the tradition of quality, 45. Films: *Le Corbeau,* 44; *Le Dernier des six* (1941), 45; *Les Diaboliques,* 45–62; *Les Inconnus dans la maison* (1942), 45; *Quai des orfèvres* (1949), 43, 44; *The Wages of Fear (Salaire de la peur),* 59
Clouzot, Véra, 41, 42, 57–60 *See also Les Diaboliques*
Clover, Carol, 142–43
Club des femmes (1936), xix
Cocktail Molotov, 150
Cocteau, Jean, 45, 57, 58, 60–61
Cohen, Leonard: "Suzanne," 182
Colette, 46; *Le blé en herbe,* 59
Collins, Roberta, 137
Coming On Strong: Gender and Sexuality in Twentieth-Century Women's Sport (1994), 104
Coming Up! (1986), 154
Conrad, Tony, 166
Cook, Pam, 132
Corbeau Le (1943), 44
Corman, Roger, 116, 131, 132, 135, 137
Cottis, Jane: *Dry Kisses Only* (1990), 162
Coup de Foudre (*Entre Nous,* 1983), 149, 150–51
Coyote, Peter, 150
Crawford, Joan, 118
Crying Game, The (1992), 42
Curtis, Tony, 134

Dallas, 83
Daly, Tyne, 71, 72
Damned If You Don't (1987), 199
Dash, Julie, 197
Daughters of Bilitis, xix
Day, Doris, 156
De Lauretis, Teresa: *Alice Doesn't: Feminism, Semiotics, Cinema,* xvi; on conflation of desire and identification, 157, 158; on female spectatorship, 16; on lesbianism and psychoanalysis, 163; on *She Must Be Seeing Things,* 156, 164; on "woman" versus "women," 89
Decoin, Henri, 55
Defiant Ones, The, 134
Delannoy, Jean, 57, 59
Demme, Jonathan, 135
Denis, Claire: *Chocolat,* 180; *U.S. Go Home,* 180
Dernier des six, Le (1941), 45
Desert Hearts, 156–57, 176
Destry Rides Again (1939), 6
Deux ou trois choses que je sais d'elle (*Two or Three Things I Know About Her,* 1967), 189
Diablo Menthe (Peppermint Soda), 149–50
Diabolique (1996), 61–62
Diaboliques, Les (1955), 41–62; and 1950s French cinema, 57–62; and adaptation, 42, 44; and Barbey d'Aurevilly, 49–50; and the femme fatale, 44, 46–47; and inversion, 45–47, 49–50, 56–57; and Racine, 53, 55, 56; and *Les Remparts de béguine* (1951), 56–57; and the Simone Signoret persona, 46–47; and *The Woman Who Was No More,* 42, 44, 47–49

Dial M for Murder, 74
Dickinson, Paul, 170
Dietrich, Marlene, xx, xxi, 4–20; *Blonde Venus* (1932), 5; *The Blue Angel* (1930), 6–20; *Destry Rides Again* (1939), 6; *Morocco* (1930), 4; *Stage Fright* (1950), and Josef Von Sternberg, 4–5, 6, 13–14, 18; *Witness for the Prosecution* (1958), 18–20
Dirty Harry (1971), 71, 72
Discipline and Punish, 117
Doane, Mary Ann, 15, 117, 187–88
Don Ameche's Flying Circus, 204
Donahue, Troy, 131
Donna Reed Show, The, 204
Dry Kisses Only (1990), 162
Duchesnay, Isabelle, 103
Duchesnay, Paul, 103
Duff, Howard, 129
Dunye, Cheryl, 176
Dwyer, Bud, 174, 175
Dyer, Richard, 4

Eastwood, Clint, 67–77; *Dirty Harry* (1971), 70, 71, 72; *The Enforcer* (1976), 71, 72, 73; *Magnum Force* (1973), 71, 72; *Sudden Impact* (1983), 71–72, 73; *Tightrope* (1984), 68–77
Eliacheff, Caroline, 38n
Ellen, 96
Ellis, Havelock, 45–46
Emerson, Hope, 120, 121, 122, 124
Enforcer, The (1976), 71, 72, 73
Ermayne, LauraJean, xix–xxi. *See also* Ackerman, Forrest J.
Erotica (1989), 162
Escape to Yesterday (1935), xix
Essentialism, 68, 76, 152

Fatal Attraction (1987), 79
Father Knows Best, 204
Feder, Abigail, 103
Feminist film studies: and authorship, 152–54, 158–59; and classical Hollywood cinema, xiv, 143, 187–88; and the female body, 166; and the female gaze, 50–51; and the male gaze, xi, xiv, 117; and Marxism, xi; and Oedipal desire, xi, xiv, xvii, 153; and psychoanalysis, xi, xiv–xvi; and queer theory, xvi–xvii, 96–97; and reading against the grain, 8, 92; and resistance, 5, 17, 18; and semiotics, xi; and sexual difference, xviii; and spectatorship, xiv, xvii–xxi, 117, 143, 187–88; and stars, 3–4; and visibility, xxi
Fernie, Lynne, 177
Figure skating, 103–14; and falling, 105–6, 107–9, 112–14; and femininity vs. athleticism, 106, 107, 108, 113; and spectatorship, 104–5, 108–10; and Tonya Harding–Nancy Kerrigan event, 103–5, 107–8, 109, 113–14
First Comes Love (1991), 161–62, 193
Fisher, Terry Louise, 79
Flanner, Janet, 33–34
Forbidden Love, 177
Foucault, Michel, 117
400 Blows, The, 150, 189–90
Frameline, 154
Franco, Jess, 131
Fried Green Tomatoes (1991), xvii–xviii
Friedrich, Su, 162, 163, 176, 193–211; and autobiography, 199, 201–7; and father-daughter relationship, 201–7; and figure of the screen, 196–99, 208; and figure of the woman swimmer, 198, 202, 205, 206, 208, 210. Films:

Damned If You Don't (1987), 193, 199–201, 208; *First Comes Love* (1991), 161–62, 193; *Gently Down the Stream* (1983), 193, 194–99, 200, 201, 208; *Hide and Seek* (1996), 193; *Sink or Swim* (1990), 193, 201–10; *Ties That Bind, The* (1984), 199

Gance, Abel, 58
Garbo, Greta, xx, xxi, 30
Garçonne, La, 46
Genet, Jean, 33, 34
Gently down the Stream (1983), 193, 194–99, 200, 201, 208
Gillers, Stephen, 95
Girls in Prison (1956), 127–29
GLAAD (Gay and Lesbian Alliance Against Defamation), xvii–xviii, 100
Go Fish (1994), 23
Godard, Jean-Luc, 25, 30, 185, 189
Godless Girl, The (1929), 118
Golden Girls, 79–80
Gordon, Linda, xvi, xxi
Gossip, 150–51
Great Lie, The, 162
Grier, Pam, 132–35

Haar, Sandra, 174
Hadleigh, Boze, 43
Hall, Radclyffe, 46
Hamill, Dorothy, 113
Hammer, Barbara, 153
Hanlon, Lindley, 198
Harding, Tonya, 103–5, 107–8, 109
Harlow, Jean, 119
Harris, Sara, 140
Hart, Lynda, 23, 34, 139
Haunting, The (1963), 51
Haynes, Todd: *Superstar,* 162
Hayward, Susan, 46, 119
Heath, Stephen, xii, 67, 68
Heavenly Creatures (1994), 23
Hedren, Tippi 30
Hell Hole, 140
Henry, Joan, 139–40
Hepburn, Katharine, 4
Hess, John, 59
Hey, Bud (1987), 165, 167, 174
Hide and Seek (1996), 193
Hill Street Blues, 80
Hitchcock, Alfred, 5, 25, 30, 42
Hoberman, J., 68
Hold Your Man (1933), 119
Holland, Chels, 193
Holmlund, Chris, 195, 196, 198, 200, 201
House of Women (1962), 130–31
Housekeeper, The (1987), 38n1, 38n2
Hudson, Rock, 156
Huis Clos. See No Exit
Huppert, Isabelle, 24, 31, 149. *See also La Cérémonie*

I Like Girls for Friends (1987), 165, 174–75
I Spit on Your Grave, 142
I Want to Live! (1958), 119
Ice Castles (1979), 112–13
Illusionist, The, 56–57
Illusions (1982), 197
I'm Hungry, I'm Cold (*J'ai faim, J'ai froid,* 1984), 184–85
Immodest Acts (1986), 199
Inconnus dans la maison, Les (1942), 45, 55
Incredibly True Adventures of Two Girls in Love, The (1995), 23
Inversion, 45–47, 49–50
Irigaray, Luce, 16
"It's a Man's World," 182
I've Heard the Mermaids Singing (1987), 197

Jardine, Alice, 67
Je, tu, il, elle (1974), 153, 184
Jenkins, Steve, 94
Johnston, Claire, 153
Judgment in Stone, A, 27–29, 33, 34

Kaplan, E. Ann, 21n
Karina, Anna, 30, 189
Kelly, Grace, 30, 74
Kerrigan, Nancy, 103–5, 107–8, 109
Kesselman, Wendy, 34
Knapp, Lucretia, 162, 163, 176; *Erotica* (1989), 162; *Sally Cheesey Raffelyell* (1992), 162
Knight, Shirley, 130
Kristeva, Julia, 151, 170
Kuhn, Annette, 21n
Kuntzel, Thierry, xii
Kurys, Diane, 149–51; *Cocktail Molotov,* 150; *Coup de foudre* (*Entre Nous,* 1983), 149, 150–51; *Diablo Menthe (Peppermint Soda),* 149–50; *A Man in Love* (*Un Homme amoureux,* 1987), 150, 151

L.A. Law, 79–101; and conflict between feminism and femininity, 89, 92; and gay sexuality, 84–85, 99, 100; and heterosexuality, 84, 85, 94–95, 98; and lesbianism, 85, 96–100; and race, 82–83, 88; and radical feminism, 94; and rape, 81–83, 87, 89–90
Lacan, Jacques, 33, 166; on Aimée, 36; Lacanian psychoanalysis, 28–29, 35; on the Papin sisters, 34, 35
Ladder, The, xix–xxi
Ladies They Talk About (1933), 119
Lafont, Bernadette, 24
Laplanche, Jean, 164
Last Dance (1996), 119
Laughton, Charles, 19
Lavender Screen, The, 43
Léaud, Jean-Pierre, 30
Leenhardt, Roger, 58
Légitime Défense, 44
Lesage, Julia, 21n
Lesbian continuum, 158, 187
Let's Play Prisoners (1988), 165, 167, 168–74, 175
Levin, Jennifer, 95
Lianna, 156
Locke, Sondra, 71
Lopez, Trini: "La Bamba," 182
Lowell, Melissa, 111–13
Lupino, Ida, 129

MacKinnon, Catharine A., 93
Madame X, 153
Mädchen in Uniform (1931), xix
Magnum Force (1973), 71, 72
Maids, The, 33, 34
Make Room for Daddy, 204
Mallet-Joris, Françoise, 56; *Les Remparts de béguine (The Illusionist),* 56–57
Mamoulian, Rouben, 30
Man in Love, A (*Un Homme amoureux,* 1987), 150, 151
Man Who Envied Women, The (1986), 197
Manèges (1949), 46
Marchand, Guy, 149
Margueritte, Victor, 46
Marie-Chantal contre Docteur Kha (1966), 24
Mary Tyler Moore Show, The, 80
Masculin-Féminin (1966), 189
Maslin, Janet, 61
Mazuy, Patricia: *Travolta and Me,* 180
McLaughlin, Sheila: *She Must Be Seeing Things,* 156, 164
Meckler, Nancy, 34

Meetings with Anna (Rendez-vous d'Anna), 184
Mellencamp, Patricia, 117
Men, Women, and Chainsaws, 142, 143
Mercer, Kobena, 139
Merck, Mandy, 156–57
Miller, Nancy K.: *Subject to Change,* 152
Miou-Miou, 149
Mitchell, Juliet, 17
Mitchell, Lynette, 150–51
Modern Language Association, 67
Modleski, Tania, 108, 109
Moi, Toril: *Sexual/Textual Politics,* 151
Monsieur Hire (1989), 31
Moore, Juanita, 130
Moorehead, Agnes, 120, 121, 122, 124
Morey, Anne, 125
Morocco (1930), 4
Morrison, Toni: *Sula,* 150
Mortal Thoughts (1991), 61
Ms. 45, 142
MTM Productions, 80
Mulvey, Laura: on the male gaze, xiv–xv, 3; "Visual Pleasure and Narrative Cinema," xi, xii, 176–77; on Von Sternberg, 13–14
My Sister in This House (1982), 34

Narcejac, Thomas, 42–44, 47–49, 62n
Nelson, Mariah Burton: *The Stronger Women Get, the More Men Love Football* (1994), 104
Nestle, Joan, 155
New Wave (of French cinema), 25, 30, 188–91
New World Pictures, 116, 131, 132
New York Civil Liberties Union, 95
Newell, Z., xx
Nielsen, Brigitte, 116
No Exit (1954), xix
Nochlin, Linda, 139

Olivia (1950), xix
Olympics, 103, 107
One Life to Live, 86, 116
Onodera, Midi: *Ten Cents a Dance* (*Parallax,* 1985), 153–59, 176
Open City (1946), xix
Ophüls, Max, 58
Orientalism: in painting, 139
Otis, Margaret, 140
Ottinger, Ulrike, 153

Paid (1931), 118
Panopticon, 117
Papin, Christine, 33–37
Papin, Léa, 33–37
Paris vu par (*Paris Seen By,* 1963), 185
Paris vu par, 20 ans après (*Paris Seen By, 20 Years Later,* 1984), 185
Parker, Eleanor, 119
Penley, Constance, xv, 21n
Petro, Patrice, 88
Phèdre, 56–57
Philbert, Bertrand, 43
Pierrot le fou, 189
Pillow Talk (1959), 156
Pit of Loneliness (*Olivia,* 1950), xix
Poitier, Sidney, 134
Pontalis, Jean-Bertrand, 164
Pornography, 76
Portrait of a Young Girl at the End of the 1960s in Brussels (*Portrait d'une jeune fille de la fin des années 60 à Bruxelles,* 1995), 179–92; and coming-out story, 179; and May 1968, 188–89; and music, 180, 181–82; and New Wave cinema, 188–91

Poststructuralism, xii; and psychoanalysis, xii
Powell, Michael, 199
Pre-Oedipal, 17, 157–58
Pressburger, Emeric, 199
Prisoner Cell Block H, 116
Prisoners (1929), 118
Psycho (1960), 42

Quai des Orfèvres (1947), 43, 44
Queen Christina (1933), 30
Queer theory, xvi–xvii

Racine, Jean, 54, 55, 56–57, 62
Radical feminism, 75–77
Radway, Janice, 108, 110
Rainer, Yvonne, 197
Rape-revenge film, 142
Rawi, Ousama, 38n1, 38n2
Reid, Ella, 137
Remparts de béguine, Les (The Illusionist, 1951), 56–57
Rendell, Ruth: *A Judgment in Stone,* 27–29, 33, 34.
Rendez-vous d'Anna (Meetings with Anna), 184
Renoir, Jean, 58
Re-Visions, 117
Rich, Adrienne, 152, 158, 187
Rich, B. Ruby, 23, 38, 70, 139, 154
Rivette, Jacques, 25
Rohmer, Eric, 25, 185
Romance novels, 108
Roof, Judith, 163, 170
Ropars-Wuillemier, Marie-Claire, 45
Ross, Andrew, 67, 68
Rothman, Stephanie, 131
Rozema, Patricia, 197
Russell, Catherine, 207
Russo, Mary, 14, 18

Safe Sea of Women, The, 198
Sally Cheesey Raffelyell (1992), 162
Sander, Helke, 197
Sans toit ni loi (*Vagabond,* 1985), 31
Sartre, Jean-Paul, 55
Scacchi, Greta, 150
Scrubbers (1983), 142
Sedgwick, Eve, 96; *Between Men,* 186
She Must Be Seeing Things, 156, 164
Signoret, Simone: and cross-gender identification, 46–47; and femme fatale image, 46. Films: *Casque d'or* (1951), 46; *Les Diaboliques* (1955), 41–62; *Manèges* (1949), 46; *Thérèse Raquin* (1953), 46
Silver Blades, 111–13: *Breaking the Ice* (1993), 111; *In the Spotlight* (1993), 111
Silverman, Kaja, 153, 167
Simenon, Georges, 45, 55
Sink or Swim (1990), 193, 201–10
Sister, My Sister (1994), 34
Smith, Barbara, 150
Smith, Paul, 67, 68
Soap opera, 86, 108, 110, 116
Spoto, Donald, 7
St. Elsewhere, 80
Stage Fright (1950), 5
Stanwyck, Barbara, 119
Steele, Barbara, 135
Steeman, S. A., 44, 45
Stojko, Elvis, 106
Stone, Sharon, 61–62, 119
Story of Women (*Une Affaire de femmes,* 1988), 31
Stronger Women Get, the More Men Love Football, The, 104
Studlar, Gaylyn, 21n
Sudden Impact (1983), 71–72, 73
Sula, 150
Summer Will Show, 187
Superstar, 162
"Suzanne," 182

Tati, Jacques, 45, 57, 58
Taubin, Amy, 162, 179
Ten Cents a Dance (*Parallax,* 1985), 153–59; and authorship, 153–54, 158–59; reception history of, 154–55; use of split screen, 155–56
Terminal Island (1973), 131, 143n
Textual analysis, xiii–xiv, xvi
Thelma and Louise (1991), 23, 142
Thérèse Raquin (1953), 46
Third sex, 45
Thomas, Debi, 103, 107
Ticket of No Return, 153
Ties That Bind, The (1984), 199
Tightrope (1984), 67–77; and Clint Eastwood persona, 68–70, 71–73; and heterosexuality, 70, 73, 74; and homosexuality, 72; and rape, 71–72, 75–76
Time of Desire (1957), xix
Tonya and Nancy: The Inside Story, 104–5, 109
Törst (1949), xix
Tradition of quality, 45, 57–60, 61
Travolta and Me, 180
Truffaut, François, 25, 30; "A Certain Tendency in French Cinema," 57–61; *The 400 Blows,* 150, 189–90
Tuggle, Richard, 68
Turnabout (1940), xix
Two or Three Things I Know About Her (1967), 189

U.S. Go Home, 180
Urmanov, Alexander, 106

Vagabond (1985), 31
Vanishing, The (1993), 62
Varda, Agnès, 31, 190–91; *Cléo de cinq à sept (Cleo from Five to Seven),* 190; *Sans toit ni loi* (*Vagabond,* 1985), 31
Vermeule, Blakey, 187
Vertigo (1958), 42
Vigo, Jean: *Zéro de conduite* (1933), 50, 150
Violette Nozière (1978), 24–25
Virgin/whore dichotomy, 50, 106–7, 130
Vivre sa vie (1962), 189
Von Sternberg, Josef: *Blonde Venus* (1932), 5; *The Blue Angel* (1930), 6–20; and Marlene Dietrich, 4–5, 6, 18, 30; *Morocco* (1930), 4
Voyeurism, 3, 134; and fetishism, 3

Wages of Fear, The (Salaire de la peur), 59
Walker, Alexander, 7
Warner, Sylvia Townshend: *Summer Will Show,* 187
Weinbaum, Batya, xii–xiii
Weiss, Andrea: *Vampires and Violets,* xvii
Weissmann, Aerlyn, 177
Well of Loneliness, The (1928), xix, 46
White, Patricia, 51, 122
Who's the Boss, 86
Wilder, Billy, 19
Williams, Linda, 117
Witness for the Prosecution (1958), 18–20
Witt, Katarina, 103, 107
Woman at the Keyhole, The, 196–97
Woman Who Was No More, The (Celle qui n'était plus), 42–44, 47–49
Women in Cages (1971), 133
Women in Prison (1952), 139–40
Women-in-prison film, 115–45; basic formula of, 115–16, 127–28, 130–31; butch and femme roles in, 121, 122–24,

125, 127, 128, 138; intersection of lesbianism and and race in, 118–19, 128–30, 131, 132–39, 140, 142; and literature about women in prison, 139–42; men in, 124–25, 127, 129, 133; and rape, 115, 132; and soap opera, 116; surveillance in, 117–18, 121; virgin/whore dichotomy in, 130. Films: *The Big Doll House* (1971), 132–33; *Black Mama, White Mama* (1973), 133–35, 138; *Caged* (1950), 118, 119–27, 128, 129, 130, 132, 142; *Caged Heat* (1974), 135–37, 142; *Chained Heat II* (1993), 116; *Girls in Prison* (1956), 127–29; *The Godless Girl* (1929), 118; *Hold Your Man* (1933), 119; *House of Women* (1962), 130–31; *I Want to Live!* (1958), 119; *Ladies They Talk About* (1933), 119; *Last Dance* (1996), 119; *Paid* (1931), 118; *Prisoner Cell Block H*, 116; *Prisoners* (1929), 118; *Scrubbers* (1983), 142; *Terminal Island* (1973), 131, 143n; *Women in Cages* (1971), 133; *Women's Prison* (1955), 129–30

Women's Prison (1955), 129–30

Zalcock, Bev, 118

Zando, Julie, 162–78; and authorship, 165; collaboration with Jo Anstey, 165, 168–74, 175; and lesbian sadomasochism, 176–77; and mother-child relationship, 166, 169–72, 173–76 and the primal scene, 164–65; and psychoanalysis, 163–68. Films: *The A Ha! Experience* (1988), 165, 166–67; *The Bus Stops Here* (1990), 165, 166, 167–68; *Hey, Bud* (1987), 165, 167, 174; *I Like Girls for Friends* (1987), 165, 174–75; *Let's Play Prisoners* (1988), 165, 167, 168–74, 175

Zéro de conduite (1933), 50, 150

Zetterling, Mai, 142

Zimmerman, Bonnie, 163, 191n, 198

Žižek, Slavoj, 28

Judith Mayne is professor of French and women's studies at Ohio State University, where she has taught since 1976. She is the author of several books on film studies, including *Private Novels, Public Films*; *Kino and the Woman Question: Feminism and Soviet Silent Film*; *The Woman at the Keyhole: Feminism and Women's Cinema*; *Cinema and Spectatorship*; and *Directed by Dorothy Arzner.*